The Miners' Bishop

To my mother, with gratitude

THE MINERS' BISHOP
Brooke Foss Westcott

Graham A. Patrick

EPWORTH PRESS

Copyright © Graham A. Patrick 2004

First published 2002 by OSL Publications

Second edition 2004
by Epworth Press
4 John Wesley Road
Werrington
Peterborough PE4 7ZP

British Library Cataloguing in Publication data

A catalogue record for this book is available
from the British Library

Bible extracts are from the
Authorized Version of the Bible (The King James Bible), the rights
in which are vested in the Crown, and are reproduced by permission of
the Crown's Patentee, Cambridge University Press;
and from the
Revised English Bible © Oxford University Press
and Cambridge University Press 1961, 1970.

0 7162 0578 5

Printed and bound in Great Britain by
Biddles Ltd, *www.biddles.co.uk*

CONTENTS

ABBREVIATIONS

Westcott's works

BC	*The Bible in the Church* (1864)
CAL	*Christian Aspects of Life* (1897)
CC	*Christus Consummator* (1886)
CGM	*Characteristics of the Gospel Miracles* (1859)
CLMO	*The Christian Life, Manifold and One* (1869)
EGH	*The Elements of the Gospel Harmony* (1851)
EH	*The Epistle to the Hebrews* (1889)
EHRTW	*Essays in the History of Religious Thought in the West* (1891)
EJ	*The Epistles of St John* (1883)
GJ	*The Gospel According to St John* (1882)
GL	*The Gospel of Life* (1892)
GFM	*Gifts for Ministry* (1889)
GR	*The Gospel of the Resurrection* (1866)
GSHCNT	*A General Survey of the History of the Canon of the New Testament* (1855)
HF	*The Historic Faith* (1883)
ICL	*The Incarnation and Common Life* (1893)
ISG	*An Introduction to the Study of the Gospels* (1860)
LFW	*Lessons from Work* (1901)
PS	*Peterborough Sermons* (1904)
RF	*The Revelation of the Father* (1884)
ROU	*On Some Points in the Religious Office of the Universities* (1873)
RRL	*The Revelation of the Risen Lord* (1881)
SAC	*Social Aspects of Christianity* (1887)

Abbreviations

SLRVNT	*Some Lessons of the Revised Version of the New Testament* (1897)
VC	*The Victory of the Cross* (1888)
VS	*Village Sermons* (1906)
WFH	*Words of Faith and Hope* (1902)

Other abbreviations

LL1, 2	*Life and Letters of Brooke Foss Westcott*, vols. I, II (1903)
ACER	Auckland Castle Episcopal Records, University Library, Palace Green, Durham
CUL	Cambridge University Library

INTRODUCTION

When he paid me short visits here, two or three things struck me: his love of flowers ... his knowledge of bridges as well as other ancient buildings; we have a beautiful bridge (at Kirby Lonsdale), and Westcott seemed to be sure of its date, and to be acquainted with all the bridges in the diocese ...[1]

One of the finest views in the whole of England is that of Durham from its railway station. The eyes are drawn first up to the towers of the magnificent cathedral perched on a hill above the river, and then to the medieval castle close by, and finally down the steep wooded banks to the river Wear, and to two of the numerous bridges which today span the river in its spectacular gorge.

On 20 July 1901 a small, very frail, elderly man with masses of grey hair was preaching to a large congregation in this cathedral. It was the annual Durham Miners' Gala day, and the town was packed with miners and their families. Brooke Foss Westcott, Bishop of Durham, was preaching at the annual Gala day service. He was a dying man – this was to be his last appearance in public – but only a few people present knew this. He spoke of the love of God in Christ, which kindles a responsive love in our hearts that is the motive for all Christian work and action. He quoted Robert Browning to the effect that life is for learning love, and spoke movingly of his own personal conviction that the love of Christ and obedience to his will are the two secrets of life. He mentioned his love for the county of Durham, and of his pride in its

[ix]

people and in its industrial relations. He spoke of his awareness of the unseen world which we touch at every moment, and concluded with a quotation from Tennyson about heaven being 'the ministry of soul to soul', and of his hope that this might be found on earth.[2]

Later that day he left the city for the last time, crossing one of the three bridges which in his day carried people across the Wear, on his way back to Bishop Auckland. He died seven days later, in the eleventh year of his episcopate and the seventy-sixth of his age.

There were themes in this final sermon which he had often expounded during his life. But the miners who gathered in the cathedral that day, and many of those who were in the town, would always remember him as the bishop who mediated in the Durham Miners' Strike nine years earlier, bringing employers and unions together after a bitter three-month dispute. Through this he gained the trust of working people and of employers, and his name became synonymous with the Church's concern to reach out to the poor and to remove barriers between the classes. In time he became known as 'the Miners' Bishop',[3] even though many of the miners would have called themselves Methodists! Today, he is featured in the new Millennium Window in Durham Cathedral which commemorates the history of the diocese, reaching out his right hand in friendship to a miner to symbolize his mediation in the 1892 strike.

In fact, much of his life had been devoted to the reconciling of contradictory positions, both in the world of scholarship and in the life of the Church. His celebrated mediation in the Miners' Strike was therefore an emblem of his whole life and work. In the light of this, the observation of a close friend that one of his rare leisure interests was a fascination with bridges must be regarded as a symbolic fact of great significance!

Just over a hundred years after his death there is still no overall study of his work and achievement, and this book is an attempt to fill that gap. We still await a critical biography[4] but unpublished letters and papers and a series of studies of different aspects of his work throw fresh light on his wide-ranging contribution to the life and thought of the Victorian Church. A study of his work, and indeed a biography, are all the more necessary since he and his Cambridge colleagues, J. B. Lightfoot and F. J. A. Hort, have been unjustly neglected by historians, who have given far more attention to their high-church Oxford contemporaries.

No apology is needed for a book about a Victorian churchman. Respect for and interest in the Victorian period have grown enormously in recent years. It is widely recognized now that the nineteenth century is the seed-bed of many of our contemporary problems. It was the period when Christians faced the combined challenges of historical criticism, evolution and social inequality. Many leading thinkers gave up faith and acknowledged 'God's Funeral'.[5] While many Christians retreated into a traditionalism which ignored the challenges of the time, Westcott and his colleagues tried to find a middle way between these two extremes, reinterpreting the Scriptures and theology for a new age.

In Westcott's case we shall see how issues with which he wrestled have returned to challenge us again in the twenty-first century. The rise of Christian fundamentalism has raised in a quite new way questions about his pioneering work on the text and translation of the New Testament, which eventually helped to undermine the authority of the Authorized Version. The revival of Christian Socialism in the 1990s has given a fresh relevance to the nineteenth-century roots of the movement, in which Westcott played a significant part. The relationship between Christianity and the other world faiths is a pressing concern in our multicultural society; the responsibilities of a worldwide empire and a particular interest in India meant that Westcott faced this issue 120 years ago. In his theological explorations, too, he anticipates some of the issues of our time – the difficulty of living with theological diversity, the inadequacy of language to express the deepest truths, the urgent need to 'contextualize' the gospel in the world. Our three central chapters explore this theological legacy which has never been fairly appraised.

Perhaps Westcott would have approved of a Methodist writing a study of him for he married a Wesleyan Methodist, was on friendly terms with several leading Free Churchmen of his day, and had a particular admiration for Primitive Methodists, who were numerous in the Durham diocese. A few months before he died he sent out an enquiry to his clergy asking them to gather information about the Primitive Methodists in their parishes: 'If we can ascertain the causes of their influence we may be able to learn from them valuable lessons for our own guidance.'[6] Such an eirenical spirit at a time when there were real tensions between Anglicans and Methodists is typical of the bishop who was a student of bridges.

I should like to acknowledge the help and encouragement of the following people in the preparation of this book. The Revd Professor C. K. Barrett encouraged me from the outset, as did Revd Dr Brian Powley. Revd Gerald Burt and the Revd Dr Cyril Rodd read the manuscript as it developed, making many helpful suggestions, and Dr Rodd read and commented upon the final manuscript. His advice and encouragement have been invaluable. The secretarial skills of Helen Dalgleish in the early stages, and of Susan Charlton in the later stages and in the preparation of the manuscript for publication, have been indispensable. Finally, I acknowledge the assistance given by the University of Keele and the Methodist Church in granting me sabbaticals, without which I could not have completed this in the course of a busy pastoral ministry.

1

LIFE AND CAREER

He edited the Greek New Testament: he settled the Coal Strike. Where is the scholar whose epitaph might include two such items as its most typical features?[1]

If we are to understand Westcott's contribution to the life and thought of the Victorian age, it is necessary first to grasp something of the shape of his life and work. While this is a study of his work and not a biography, it is nevertheless true that the work has to be seen in the context of his life. We begin therefore with an outline of his life and career which sets his published work and what we may term his 'practical theology' within a biographical framework.[2]

1 Early years and education (1825–48)

Brooke Foss Westcott was born on 12 January 1825 in Birmingham. His father, Frederick Westcott, was a lecturer in botany at the local Sydenham College Medical School, and his mother, Sarah Armitage, the daughter of a local businessman. Among his ancestors was a great-grandfather, Foss Westcott, who was a member of the East India Company's Madras establishment in the eighteenth century. The family link with India was to be an important factor in Westcott's later life. He was the only surviving son, and since he was twelve when his only sister was born his upbringing was practically that of an only child. His home life was simple and frugal. It does not seem to have been an especially religious home. His father's scientific interests were the dominant influence in his upbringing: among his hobbies were the collection of ferns, butterflies and moths, and the study of fossils. He also sketched and painted, and this would remain a lifelong pastime.

He would dedicate his first book[3] to his father, describing it as 'the firstfruits of those studies in which I have ever been aided, guided, and encouraged by his sympathy and love'. He may have learned from him the method of detailed scientific study which would be invaluable for his later work on the New Testament text.

One of his childhood memories was of seeing the Chartist demonstrations and riots in Birmingham in 1838–9. He would recall this frequently in later life, when his interest in social questions was rekindled. He was already a serious-minded and earnest child, and it was possible to detect that intensity which was to be one of the characteristics of the mature man.

From 1837 to 1844 he attended King Edward VI's school in the city. At the age of 14 he reached the highest form in the school, and was under the immediate care of the headmaster, James Prince Lee. Lee, who later became Bishop of Manchester, was one of the finest teachers of his time, and he inspired in Westcott a concern for accurate scholarship and the precise meaning of words, and introduced him to classical literature and theology. In him he encountered a moral and religious earnestness which was not present, it appears, in his home. He derived from Lee a love of the Greek New Testament which was to shape and influence his whole life and work. In later years Lee's picture would always be prominent in his study. Westcott became head of school, and showed great promise intellectually. Contemporaries remembered a small, shy, intense boy, who had a quick and eager walk, was devoted to work, and rarely joined in games. There were signs of a developing religious sensitivity during his last years at school.

In October 1844 he went to Trinity College, Cambridge where he read for the Classical and Mathematical Tripos. He quickly established the ascetic lifestyle for which he was later renowned, rising early, eating very little, and working till the early hours. He read widely in art, literature, architecture and history. He also kept up the childhood habit of collecting mosses and ferns, and at this period compiled an elaborate botanical catalogue. He formed lifelong friendships with men such as D. J. Vaughan, J. Llewelyn Davies and C. B. Scott; with them and others he formed an essay-reading club called the Philological Society, or 'Hermes'. Academic honours soon came his way: he won prizes, scholarships and medals in Greek and Latin. In January 1848 he gained a first class in the Mathematical Tripos, and the following month he was placed joint first class in the Classical Tripos.

This academic distinction was accompanied by a deepening religious awareness. He had by now dedicated himself to a life of earnest piety: frequent self-examination, commitment to loving his neighbour, and the eschewing of amusements or relaxation are hallmarks of his undergraduate lifestyle. Poverty and social injustice are a particular concern to him, and he teaches in a local Sunday school. He is now reading Keble, Coleridge and F. D. Maurice. He seems at this time to have discovered in Maurice a thinker with whom he felt a deep affinity, and although Westcott himself for some years deliberately refrained from reading Maurice, it is very clear that he shared some of his leading ideas. It is at this period that he is becoming aware of the divisions within the Church of England, but he resolves to learn from them all and not to become anyone's disciple. He longs for the recovery of the apostolic simplicity of the Church. There are doubts and difficulties with his faith at this stage in his life. By his third year at Cambridge, however, he is aware of a vocation to the Church, either as a clergyman or as a schoolteacher.

2 The teacher: Cambridge and Harrow (1849–69)

In 1849 he was elected to a fellowship at Trinity. He was now able to take private pupils, and soon gained a reputation as a gifted tutor who took a close personal interest in his pupils and inspired in them great affection. Among them were J. B. Lightfoot and E. W. Benson, both of whom like him had been at King Edward's School, Birmingham, and F. J. A. Hort, from Rugby School. These were all to become close and lifelong friends, and the association with Lightfoot and Hort was to affect profoundly the pattern of his whole life. In them and in Benson, later to be Archbishop of Canterbury, he had found people with whom he could share his deepest concerns and convictions. Outside his teaching he formed a society, the 'Ghostlie Guild', to investigate alleged supernatural appearances. He eventually concluded that its investigations could not be fruitful.

In 1850 he was awarded the Norrisian Prize for his essay, *On the Alleged Historical Contradictions of the Gospels*, which the following year was published as his first book, *The Elements of the Gospel Harmony*. It was an attempt to find a middle way between the sceptical German approach to the historicity of the Gospels and the uncritical view of so many English people that tried to explain away all the difficulties. It anticipated some of the issues that were to surface in the *Essays and Reviews* controversy nine years later.[4] By now he had decided to become a priest in the Church of England, and on 15 June 1851 he was ordained deacon in Prestwich parish church by his old headmaster, Prince Lee, who was now Bishop of Manchester. Six months later on 21 December Lee ordained him priest in Bolton-le-Moors church.

Westcott had now decided to leave Cambridge, having become engaged to be married some two years previously. (College Fellows were not yet allowed to marry.) He applied for the post of principal of Victoria College, Jersey, but withdrew before interviews and eventually accepted the post of Assistant Master at Harrow School in January 1852. On 23 December 1852 he married Louisa Mary Whithard, an acquaintance since childhood, in St James' Church, Bristol. She was the eldest of three sisters, and her parents were Wesleyan Methodists. There were to be ten children of the marriage, seven sons and three daughters. Family life was to be a source of great strength and happiness to Westcott, and in his later years he spoke frequently about the social and religious significance of the family in the life of the nation.

His duties at Harrow were to assist the headmaster, Dr Vaughan, with the sixth form, and to be in charge of a small boarding house initially, and later of a large one. He was not a natural schoolmaster. His own secluded and serious childhood had not prepared him for the liveliness and high spirits of the average boy, and there were problems in maintaining discipline. He also missed his Cambridge friends and college life. He felt increasingly unhappy, and was sustained largely by his sense of duty. As time went on, encouraged by Lightfoot and Hort, he looked elsewhere for fulfilment, in particular towards a return to Cambridge. His influence at Harrow was perhaps greatest on the more thoughtful boys. A sermon preached in school chapel in 1868 on 'Disciplined Life' made a lasting impression on a pupil named Charles Gore, later to be the founder of the Community of the Resurrection. In his later years at Harrow, Westcott was preoccupied with the idea of a 'coenobium', a community of families living according to common discipline and principles.

He may not have found fulfilment in the work of a schoolteacher, but his own disciplined use of time made the Harrow years with their school holidays fruitful ones for the pursuit of scholarship. In particular, he now embarked with his two friends upon a number of important projects. First, there was the joint editorship with Hort of a critical edition of the New Testament in Greek, begun in 1853. This was to occupy the two men for the next twenty-eight years! Secondly, there was the ambitious commentary scheme covering the whole of the New Testament which the publisher, Daniel Macmillan, initiated in 1860, in the wake of the *Essays and Reviews* controversy. Westcott, Lightfoot and Hort agreed to collaborate in a new kind of commentary which accepted the demands of historical criticism but also recognized the unique nature of the New Testament documents. Westcott's part in this was to be the Gospel and Epistles of John and the Epistle to the Hebrews, and his commentaries on these were published in the 1880s.

[5]

The three friends also contributed numerous articles to Dr Smith's *Dictionary of the Bible* (1863).

The New Testament was clearly becoming the focus of his scholarship, and among the books he published during this period were *A General Survey of the History of the Canon of the New Testament* (1855), a response to the historical scepticism of the Tübingen school, and *Characteristics of the Gospel Miracles* (1859). In the latter he argued that the miracles were not, as was generally taught, proofs of the truth of the gospel, but rather revelations of the divine nature and purpose. This caused some to question his orthodoxy, and this may have delayed his eventual return to Cambridge. In the *Essays and Reviews* controversy of 1860 Westcott found himself in a mediating role. He was unhappy both with the assaults of the traditionalists on the essayists' attempts to help the Church to come to terms with historical criticism, and with the essayists' own inadequate views of the inspiration and interpretation of Scripture. He wanted to show a 'true mean'[5] between the two, and urged his friends to join him in a volume of essays.

Alongside his work on the New Testament, Westcott was at this period 'discovering' the Alexandrian Fathers, Clement and Origen, who represented a different theological tradition from that of the West. He felt increasingly that they lived in an age similar to his own, where a broad, incarnation-centred theology was the brightest hope for a solution to so many pressing issues. Teaching classics at Harrow kept him in touch with Plato, Aeschylus and Euripides, and he also discovered Benjamin Whichcote, the seventeenth-century Cambridge Platonist. All these authors were crucial for the development in these years of his Christian Platonism, of which the essence was a conviction about the spiritual dimension of Christianity over and against the growing materialism of the age. He also turned to the poems of Robert Browning in his later years at Harrow, finding in him a striking contemporary witness to the incarnation as the key to all life and thought. He wrote a series of articles on all these writers in the *Contemporary Review*, which were later brought together in his *Essays in the History of*

Religious Thought in the West (1891). He was fascinated, too, by the Positivist philosophy of Auguste Comte, whose strong emphasis on the unity and solidarity of the human race was to colour Westcott's later preaching and teaching.

It was during these years, then, in isolation from the wider academic world, that Westcott was working out his very individual and distinctive theological position. His early desire to be independent of all parties in the Church was reinforced by his isolation. His first wholly theological work, *The Gospel of the Resurrection*, in which he works out a Christian apologetic for the times, was published in 1866.

3 The Fenland years: Peterborough and Cambridge (1869–83)

Recognition by the Church of his distinction as a scholar came at last when in 1868 he was invited to become examining chaplain to Dr Magee, the Bishop of Peterborough, and in the following year was offered a residential canonry. His ambition to return to Cambridge was also fulfilled when he was appointed Regius Professor of Divinity in November 1870. He was now back in what he had long believed was the centre of the nation's spiritual power, where he could contribute to the education of the clergy and the wider renewal of the Church. Cambridge became his permanent home for the next fourteen years, while he resided at Peterborough for three months during the long vacations.

In comparison with Cambridge, Peterborough was a provincial backwater. Westcott believed, however, that the canonry marked a new phase and a new opportunity in his life. He was now a public servant of the Church, and so was in a position to fulfil his mission on a much wider canvas. From the outset he addressed the question of the role of the cathedral in the contemporary world. He corresponded with his friend Benson, now Chancellor of Lincoln Cathedral, and wrote two articles on the subject in *Macmillan's Magazine* (1870) and an essay in a book on cathedrals edited by J. S. Howson.[6] He believed that they must become centres for worship and for the education of the clergy. Cathedral worship must be re-ordered. He formed a voluntary choir to sing at special services in Peterborough, and published the *Paragraph Psalter* (1879) to make the words of the psalms more comprehensible. He also held special services in the nave in Lent and Advent, and arranged devotional gatherings of clergy and church workers. Some of his sermons and addresses were later published in *The Christian Life, Manifold and One* (1869), *The Revelation of the Risen Lord* (1881) and *The Historic Faith* (1883). His aim was that the cathedral should become the centre of the religious and intellectual life of the diocese. Ordinands came to him for direction, and he frequently lectured on St John's Gospel at this period. Among his students was Henry Scott Holland, an Oxford graduate who was to become a canon of St Paul's and one of the leading churchmen of his day. His name is best known today for his reassuring 'Death is Nothing At All', an extract from one of his sermons, which is frequently read at funerals and memorial services. His life and thought were to be profoundly influenced by Westcott's teaching and example. He later recalled Westcott's physical characteristics at this time – the smallness of stature, the high thin voice – and the prayerful way in which he lectured on St John: 'He speaks of St John's Gospel with a sort of hushed awe: it is like Fra Angelico, he cannot venture to criticise a verse without a prayer.'[7]

Westcott's main work in the 1870s and 1880s, however, was to be in Cambridge, where he joined Lightfoot, the Hulsean Professor, in the Divinity School. Hort, too, returned to Cambridge in 1872 after fifteen years in a Hertfordshire parish. In 1870 the three friends embarked on another new venture when they joined the New Testament Revision Company. This was a time of transition in the life of the university. The abolition of religious tests for university entrance in 1871, which enabled nonconformists to enter Cambridge and Oxford for the first time, meant that there had to be a rethinking of the relationship between the Church of England and the university. Westcott addressed the issue in a series of sermons and papers published as *On Some Points in the Religious Office of the Universities* (1873), arguing that the university still had a central religious role in the life of the nation. This was not primarily to teach the doctrines of the Christian faith, as some argued, but to provide a broad education which embraced history and science, the old and the new knowledge, and reconciled the two.

He was also very involved in the revision of divinity studies, and was the leading figure in the establishing of a new preliminary examination for those entering the Anglican priesthood. He saw raising the standard of the education of the clergy as an important part of his life's work now. He became president of a Clergy Training School in Cambridge established in 1881, and played an active part in its work. In 1887 a house was purchased to be the home of the school; it was eventually named 'Westcott House' in 1905. He himself was a parish priest for much of this time since the Regius post carried with it the Rectorship of Somersham near Huntingdon, which included three small churches. Some of the sermons he preached in the village churches were published in his *Village Sermons* (1906).

Within the divinity school he lectured at first on church history and the creeds. After 1874 Christian doctrine was his main concern, and the substance of these lectures was published in *The Gospel of Life* (1892). This is Westcott's only attempt to set out his theology systematically, and is one of his most important books. His lectures were not very popular at this stage. After Lightfoot became Bishop of Durham in 1879 the New Testament became his central concern. Students later remembered most of all the more informal weekly lectures on the fourth Gospel and the letters of John, in which he communicated his special love of these writings. His lectures became more popular in the 1880s, when it was common for him to address 300 undergraduates. There is a pen-picture of him from this period, in a crowded lecture room

with grey tumbled hair, in silk gown and scarf . . . He is saying a prayer with intense earnestness, his face flushed and working, and he begins to lecture in a clear voice of great range and with marked and singular emphasis, his eyes downcast and occasionally uplifted, but seldom dwelling on the audience, and every now and then wreathed into a rapt smile.[8]

1881 was a significant year for him. On 12 May he and Hort published their Greek New Testament text, the 'Introduction and Appendix' following on 4 September. The English Revised Version New Testament was published on 17 May. Both were major contributions to nineteenth-century biblical scholarship, and both provoked controversy. The 'Text' and the 'Introduction' opened a new era in textual studies, basing study of the Greek New Testament for the first time on clear, scientific principles. However, its rejection of the *Textus Receptus* – the Greek textual tradition upon which the Authorized Version was based – upset conservative scholars. The Revised Version was another important event, a precursor of the many modern translations of the Bible which were to follow in the twentieth century. Westcott made a major contribution to this according to most accounts. It, too, however, provoked criticism. Neither Westcott nor Hort publicly defended their work in the immediate controversy. Westcott later spoke publicly, and wrote articles, about the Revised Version, and these were collected together in *Some Lessons of the Revised Version of the New Testament* (1897). He later worked with Hort and W. F. Moulton in jointly editing Wisdom and 2 Maccabees for a Revised Apocrypha.

Foreign missions were another of his principal concerns at Cambridge. He reflected deeply on the theology of missions, and read widely in the literature of the other great world faiths, to understand their relationship to Christianity. It was largely through his enthusiasm that the Cambridge Delhi Brotherhood was founded. This remained a cause close to his heart for the rest of his life: four of his sons would serve in the Church in India. He also founded the Eranus Club, a discussion group that brought together scholars of different disciplines to consider issues of common interest. He was a member of the Council of the University Senate during 1872–6 and 1878–82. While generally supporting university reform he was opposed to the proposals to grant degrees to women and to abolish compulsory Greek. He supported the university extension movement which planned lecture courses in industrial areas. In 1882 he was elected a fellow of King's College.

He was now a well-known figure in the academic world and in the wider Church. In 1875 he had been appointed a chaplain to the Queen. He was Select Preacher at Oxford from 1877 to 1880, and received an honorary degree from Oxford in 1881. Edinburgh and Dublin universities granted him honorary degrees in 1884 and 1888 respectively.

In 1883 his ties with Peterborough were severed abruptly when, under pressure from the bishop, he resigned from his office as examining chaplain. To his surprise he was then asked to resign his canonry. The bishop apparently believed that he had neglected his duties at Peterborough. Almost immediately, however, he was invited to become examining chaplain to his friend E. W. Benson, who had recently become Archbishop of Canterbury. Three months later the Prime Minister, Gladstone, offered him a canonry of Westminster Abbey, where he was installed on 2 February 1884.

4 A different world: Westminster and London (1884–90)

This move was a crucial one for Westcott, marking a turning-point in his life and work. He had spent most of his life so far in the relatively cloistered worlds of Cambridge, Harrow and Peterborough. He found himself now, for three months of the year – Cambridge was to remain his home for another six years – in the heart of the capital, living in a cathedral precinct surrounded by a large slum parish. He was also associated with a great church, which had a central role in the nation's life. In the 1880s, moreover, there was a growing realization of the extent of urban poverty in England. Social problems were being widely debated, and 'socialism' was very much in the air. Westcott was always very sensitive to the context in which he lived, and it seems that it was all this which rekindled his earlier interest in social questions.[9]

His central concern now, and for the rest of his life, was to apply the Christian faith more directly to the social and political issues of the day. This change of emphasis is seen very clearly in the sermons he preached at Westminster on Sunday afternoons, published as *Christus Consummator* (1886) and *Social Aspects of Christianity* (1887). The incarnation is still the focus of all his thinking, but it is the practical implications of this belief and their significance for the Church which have become his chief preoccupation. It is at this time that he rediscovers his affinity with F. D. Maurice, whose books he had refrained from reading lest he be influenced by him.

He became involved in public movements that protested against the massive expenditure of the European nations on armaments, and urged the settling of international disputes by arbitration. In 1889 he became the first President of the Christian Social Union, one of the most important of the second-generation Christian Socialist organizations. He now regarded himself as a Christian Socialist. He even considered resigning his professorship to devote himself exclusively to Westminster. Now very much a national figure within the Church, he was offered the deaneries of Lincoln in 1885 and Norwich in 1889, but he declined both. His final year at Westminster was overshadowed by the death, in December 1889, of his great friend Lightfoot. The final service he conducted in the Abbey was, appropriately, the funeral of Robert Browning.

5 Bishop and public figure: Durham (1890–1901)

His life now took a final, unexpected turn. At the age of 65 he was invited to succeed his friend in the northern see. There was some surprise at his appointment. Some – including the Prime Minister, Lord Salisbury – thought him too reclusive and not practically-minded enough for the task. It was almost three months before Queen Victoria and Archbishop Benson convinced the Prime Minister of Westcott's suitability for the position. After an initial reluctance, he himself welcomed the opportunity to follow in Lightfoot's footsteps, and to pursue the broader understanding of the Church's mission which he had worked out at Westminster. His consecration took place on 1 May 1890 in Westminster Abbey. In his sermon Hort spoke of a 'sacred friendship of forty years' with Westcott, and of the latter's concern for a 'social interpretation of the gospel'. His enthronement service was held in Durham Cathedral on 15 May. Later in 1890 Queen Victoria recommended Westcott for the vacant Archbishopric of York, but Lord Salisbury blocked her suggestion because of the 'Socialist tendencies of the speeches he has made since becoming a bishop'.[10]

Lightfoot had devoted much time and energy to diocesan reorganization, and to writing works of scholarship at Durham. Westcott's main emphasis as bishop was on the application of the Christian faith to the great social and national problems of the day, and on encouraging the clergy and lay people of the diocese to make this a priority in Christian mission. In this task he was greatly assisted by his role in the Miners' Strike of 1892. He came to the north-east at a time of deteriorating industrial relations in the coal industry, which culminated in a bitter three-month strike in the spring of 1892. He invited miners' representatives and the owners to meet at Auckland Castle on 1 May. He entertained them to lunch, addressed them persuasively, and then went to and fro between the two groups, while crowds gathered outside awaiting the outcome. Eventually, the miners agreed to return to work on the basis of a 10 per cent reduction in wages, as opposed to the 13.5 per cent which the owners has previously insisted on, and a joint promise to establish a conciliation board to settle the course of wages in the future. There was public jubilation at the outcome, and Westcott was widely praised for his intervention. A few, however, felt that he had sided too obviously with the employers; the conciliation board, too, would prove to have limited value for the miners. But the vast majority believed that he had acted from the best motives, and the whole episode undoubtedly helped to secure his acceptance by the people of Durham. Future bishops of the diocese would feel in West-cott's shadow when faced with similar situations. The year 1892 also saw the death of his friend, Hort, with whose name his would always be linked because of their joint work on the New Testament text. He attended his funeral in Cambridge, conscious that he was now the sole survivor of the triumvirate.

Throughout his episcopate he brought together employers, trade union representatives, MPs and people involved in the life of the local community for conferences at Auckland Castle, where he would chair discussions on current social and economic issues. In 1891, for instance, co-operation and national insurance were the subjects discussed. He took a close interest in workers' organizations, and was an enthusiastic champion of the theory and practice of the co-operative movement. He worked for more and better housing and for homes for aged miners. He opposed gambling and excessive drinking and even made the proposal, radical for its time, that public houses should provide food and non-alcoholic drinks.

He preached on three occasions at the service in Durham Cathedral on Durham Miners' Gala day. In 1894 he addressed 5,000 people at the Northumberland Miners' Gala day in Blyth, the first time a churchman had been invited to do so. A former student of Westcott who was present later recalled the 'slight, frail and rather weary figure, with the thick masses of hair now turned grey . . . [who] held them spell-bound', and whose speech was greeted with 'unwonted and enthusiastic cheering' by the usually silent northern men.[11] The working men of the north-east had come to believe that their bishop had a genuine concern for their welfare. Letters reveal that he also had the trust and respect of many landowners and industrialists of the region, whom he frequently tried to involve in his Auckland conferences.

Within the diocese, his relationships with his clergy were on the whole good. He was tolerant of theological diversity amongst his men, but on occasion could act firmly to enforce the Church's stand on ritualistic practices. His work with young ordinands gave him special satisfaction, and he continued Lightfoot's 'Auckland Brotherhood', a group of young clergy who came to Auckland Castle regularly for devotional and theological support. He worked hard to keep before the diocese the claims of foreign missions. In his time at Durham thirty-six men went to serve in the Church overseas. There was also a link with the diocese of Adelaide. He was convinced that lay people should have a greater voice in the councils of the Church, and he supported the Church Reform League in its aims. From the outset of his time at Durham, one of his overriding priorities was to create relationships with leading lay people in the diocese. He frequently welcomed parties of church workers and working people to Auckland Castle. He maintained good relationships with nonconformists in the north-east, and had a particular respect and admiration for the Primitive Methodists.

As a nationally known figure and a senior member of the episcopate, he was frequently invited to speak and preach at meetings and services in London, Cambridge and elsewhere. He attended the House of Lords as often as was possible. Each year he gave the address at the annual meeting of the Christian Social Union. He was still involved in the movement for international peace and arbitration. When the Boer War broke out in 1900, however, to the surprise of some people he supported the British cause because of his concern about Boer supremacy in South Africa. He had always believed that war was justified in some circumstances, but now found himself at odds with people like W. G. Kitchin, the Dean of Durham, who spoke out strongly against the continuation of the war.

In his spare time he prepared his Cambridge lectures for publication, and worked on a commentary on Ephesians, which was published posthumously in 1906. He turned often to the writings of Ruskin now; another constant companion was Thomas à Kempis's *On the Imitation of Christ*. Many of his sermons and addresses from the Durham period were brought together in three important collections: *The Incarnation and Common Life* (1893), *Christian Aspects of Life* (1897), and *Lessons from Work* (1901). These all reflect his overwhelming concern in the last decade of his life to apply his incarnational theology to the social questions of the day. Poverty, unemployment, class conflict, gambling, drink, the pressures of family life – all are considered realistically, and yet with an optimism about their solution which derives from his belief in Christ as the 'Fulfiller' of all things.

The strain of his work began to affect his health by 1897. His youngest son's death in Delhi in August 1900 was a great blow to him and his wife. She herself died on 28 May 1901 after a marriage lasting half a century. He continued with his diocesan duties with a heavy heart. A photograph taken shortly before he died shows him seated in a chair in the garden at Auckland, surrounded by almost a hundred members of the 'Auckland Brotherhood'. He looks tired and sad, and seems almost unaware of those around him.[12] His last public engagement, very appropriately, was his sermon at the Miners' Gala service in Durham Cathedral on 20 July. His strength now failed rapidly, and he died on 27 July 1901 at Auckland Castle. The funeral was held in the chapel of the castle on 2 August, and he was buried beside his wife in the chapel.

2

THE STUDY OF THE NEW
TESTAMENT

It was an awkward moment when at one of his early ordinations the candidates were sent from the writing-room 'to fetch your Greek Testament from your bedroom', and it was found that in most cases there was none to fetch. To the Bishop it seemed strange (and he told them so) that a man should leave home for more than a night without his Greek Testament.[1]

1 A true mean

The New Testament was Westcott's first love, and it always remained the fulcrum of his life and thought. His earliest ventures in scholarship were attempts to vindicate it against its critics on one hand, and those who read it uncritically on the other. The Old Testament, for him as for Lightfoot and Hort, was never to be a subject of study in itself, but only for the light that it cast on the New. This love was probably kindled in his schooldays by Prince Lee, of whom it was said that the 'study of the Greek Testament was that which he prized for them (his pupils) beyond every study and every honour'.[2]

There were, however, other reasons why Westcott's earliest studies should centre on the New Testament. There was a crisis of confidence in its authority and status in the 1850s and 1860s in England. On the one hand were the German scholars from Tübingen, who assigned the majority of the New Testament books to the second century and so raised doubts in the minds of thoughtful people about its reliability. On the other were the vast majority of Christians who clung to an inerrant Bible, and felt threatened by the increasing tendency to apply historical critical methods to its study. There seemed to be no alternative to the two approaches.

Westcott was very much aware of this dilemma. The gulf between the two extremes seemed to be even wider when in 1860 a group of seven radical clergymen of the Church of England published *Essays and Reviews*, an attempt to commend the new historical study of the Bible, and were met by a storm of criticism and condemnation. Westcott wanted Lightfoot and Hort to join with him in a series of essays which would show that there was 'a true mean'[3] between the attitudes of the essayists, who wanted the Church to embrace free enquiry, and the hysteria of their critics. The mediating essays were never written – Lightfoot withdrew from the scheme – but the questions raised by the controversy form the background to much of Westcott's early New Testament work.

His very first scholarly work was, in fact, a remarkable anticipation of the issues that would surface in the 1860 controversy. *The Elements of the Gospel Harmony* (1851) grew out of a prize essay he wrote at Cambridge in 1850. He revised and enlarged it, and it was published in 1860 – the year of *Essays and Reviews* – as *An Introduction to the Study of the Gospels*. The preface to the original book states that its aim is to show that 'there is a true mean between the idea of a formal harmonization of the Gospels and the abandonment of their absolute truth'.[4] The phrase 'true mean' was, as we have seen, precisely the one he used to characterize the proposed mediating essays. In the chapter on the difficulties of the Gospels in the later edition, Westcott stated again the inadequacies of the two extremes:

> we are not to decline with some the labour of a searching criticism, or with others, the veneration of the humblest faith; for it is only by the combination of these that the deepest meaning of Holy Scripture is laid open. Reason and Faith are not antagonistic principles, but another form of the great antithesis which lies at the basis of all our knowledge.[5]

The substance of the 1860 book is a discussion of the basic principles of the interpretation of Scripture applied to the study of the Gospels. The aim is to show that Christians have nothing to fear from a reverent use of historical criticism. Variations and even discrepancies in the Gospels matter not at all if we are convinced of the divine inspiration behind them.

Westcott prefaces all this, in fact, with a discussion of the thorny question of inspiration. Here again we find him striving to establish a 'true mean' between the Calvinistic doctrine of the inerrancy of Scripture, and the modern critical view which regarded it as merely a book of Hebrew legends. Neither was an adequate view. The divine and human elements are inextricably combined in inspiration, just as they were in the incarnation. It is impossible to separate them. Scripture is a 'message of God *through* men and *to* men'.[6]

Westcott's early New Testament work, then, shows him as a mediator, attempting to bring the light of calm reason to the polarized attitudes of the 1850s and 1860s. It was a role for which he was well fitted, and one he was to play often in his life. Owen Chadwick described him as a 'reconciler to his marrow'.[7]

He would not again give attention to the relationships between the Synoptic Gospels as he did at this period. Circumstances, and an instinctive affinity with the Johannine world, would lead him to concentrate his mind almost exclusively on the fourth Gospel. His theory, set out in these early books, of an oral tradition of the sayings of Jesus as an explanation of the common material in the Gospels would soon be set aside in favour of a theory of a literary dependence. Oxford would lead Cambridge in the development of synoptic criticism. And in the following century critics would upbraid Westcott, and his colleagues Lightfoot and Hort, for neglecting the study of the Synoptic Gospels, and of the Old Testament.[8]

Westcott's major work on the New Testament, however, was to be done not in isolation but in collaboration with others.

2 *The text of the New Testament*

The genesis of Westcott and Hort's revision of the Greek New Testament text may be found in a diary entry of Westcott's when he was a Cambridge undergraduate. He wrote on 8 February 1846: 'If I am enabled – what a glorious employment for one's leisure hours it would be to prepare a new edition of the New Testament'.[9] He bought a Greek Testament two months later. It was another five years before Hort, encouraged by Westcott, began reading the Greek Testament in earnest and discovered the problem of the unreliability of the most commonly used text of that time, the *Textus Receptus*, which was the basis for the Authorized Version.[10] The initial impetus for a revision may have come from Westcott, then, with his early devotion to the Greek New Testament inspired by Prince Lee.

The two friends began their work in 1853. Unpublished letters[11] shed light on their relationship and attitudes as the work developed. At first they thought revision would take just two or three years! It soon became clear that it was not to be so simple a task. One early discovery was that many of the texts of the Versions (the translations of the Greek into the vernacular) and the early Fathers were corrupt, and needed restoring. Hort proposed that they should embark on a massive scheme to produce new editions of these before they could properly pursue their larger work. This was typical of Hort's propensity for conceiving vast projects incapable of realization. Westcott, fortunately, was more realistic: 'However deeply I must sympathize with the work, yet I feel sure that it may not be entered on at short notice, and I hardly know how far my whole life is not already pledged to another work.'

Quite early in the project, Westcott seemed aware of the controversial nature of their work. It must be remembered that the *Textus Receptus* was held in reverence by a large number of scholars at the time. He wrote to Hort in April, 1861: 'I feel sure that our text will be called . . . an "abridged edition of the New Testament". It will be extremely unpopular, and there will be no means of convincing opponents who do not understand the force of evidence which lies in scholarship and not in numbering.' (By numbering he meant the practice of weighing manuscript evidence purely by numerical support for a reading). Three years later there was an exchange of correspondence in which Westcott suggested that even the minor changes in form they were introducing would be branded as 'heresy'. Hort seemed less concerned about the thought of heresy than his colleague, and told him that he had always felt a 'predestined heretic' in the eyes of others. It is worth remembering here that it was during the early 1860s that there were doubts about Westcott's theological orthodoxy in Cambridge, following publication of his book on the Gospel miracles in 1859. Lightfoot was acting at this time as the 'keeper of his orthodoxy', realizing that he would not get a Cambridge post if he were regarded as 'unsound'. This may be the reason for Westcott's discomfort at being involved in a controversial, even radical scheme of textual revision. In any case, he always shunned controversy.

As time went on – the project was to take twenty-eight years – it is not surprising that the work grew wearisome. It seems that it was Westcott who grew tired of the minutiae of textual work more than his friend. In May 1862 he wrote to Hort of his 'very great repugnance to the whole work of revision', and of the 'positive dislike – I want a stronger term – with which I look on all details of spelling and breathing and form'.[12] There were similar expressions of impatience in March 1865 ('What a blessing it will be when breathings are done with forever') and in October of the same year ('This is my last growl. I wish that stops and accents were a nightmare only.') Hort, who was perhaps the more natural textual critic, firmly rebuked his friend on one occasion, admitting that he himself sometimes had 'off' days, but that their work was so important that it would be 'utterly unpardonable for us to give up our task'.[13] This kind of exchange raises questions about the generally accepted view that it was Hort whose enthusiasm flagged as time went on. An obituary in *The Times*, quoted in Westcott's *Life and*

Letters, comments: 'To Westcott also must be given the merit of having by his earnest cheerfulness kept up the courage of his shy and nervous colleague.'[14] The evidence suggests that it was Westcott who needed encouragement!

His impatience is clear in an exchange of letters in June and July 1869 about the final form of the 'Introduction' and 'Appendix' to the text. One was to set out the principles of textual criticism, the other to contain notes on spelling and on suspect and rejected readings. Westcott wanted both to be brief. When Hort disagreed he was quick to suggest that his friend should be responsible for both. He himself was clearly not prepared at this stage in the scheme to give the time and effort required. He did, however, want it to be made clear that the 'Introduction', which was to become a classic statement of textual critical principles, was Hort's work,[15] and he was initially reluctant to accept a share of the profits from the 'Introduction'.

For all this, it must be remembered that the two-volume Greek Text was a joint work in every respect. Hort wrote the 'Introduction', but the principles set out there were those which the two men had worked out together over almost three decades. Anyone who doubts this should read Westcott's article on the 'New Testament' in Smith's *Dictionary of the Bible* (1863) in which he sets out in masterly, concise fashion the thirteen principles of textual criticism.[16]

How does Westcott and Hort's achievement stand today, in the light of new discoveries and advances over the past 120 years? It would be widely agreed that the publication in 1881 of their Greek New Testament text began a new era in textual studies. Building on the work of earlier scholars, they for the first time placed the study of the Greek New Testament on clear, scientific principles. This set the pattern for all future textual study of the New Testament. The 'Introduction' was the first attempt in any language to summarize the theory and science of textual criticism, and its conclusions still stand. As Stephen Neill asserts: 'No sane scholar would ever think today of tackling the work of textual criticism on any principles other than these.'[17] It has even been acknowledged that the criteria are valid for evaluating the value of historical manuscripts and other kinds of evidence.

Their application of these principles to the text of the New Testament itself has not, however, stood the test of time so well. They isolated four early types of text: the Syrian, seen in its latest form in the *Textus Receptus*, the Western, the Neutral, and the Alexandrian. The Neutral, based on the great uncial MSS, Codex Alexandrinus (ℵ) and Codex Vaticanus (B), was the most reliable of all the textual families, while the Syrian, on which the Authorized Version was based, was late, corrupt, and not to be trusted. This was a quite fresh, radical solution to the textual problem of the New Testament, and it is not surprising that some of their contemporaries were outraged by their conclusions. Textual study has, however, moved on since 1881, and led to a substantial modification of their thesis. Many new manuscripts have been discovered, some of which cannot be assigned to their four families. The central contention in most recent work is that no one manuscript or family of manuscripts has preserved the original text of the New Testament. The critic must be open to all traditions and possibilities, and not preclude one particular group of readings because of *a priori* views of their origins. This eclectic approach is very different from Westcott and Hort's predilection for one textual family.

Even so, their achievement was a massive one. The *Times* obituary mentioned earlier claimed that 'in the whole history of the New Testament since the time of Origen there has been nothing more remarkable than the quiet persistence with which these two Fellows of Trinity started . . . "in the spring of 1853" to systematise New Testament criticism . . .'. This may have been an exaggeration. What is indisputable is that their work has had a lasting effect on textual study, and on printed editions of the New Testament in the second half of the twentieth century. The New English Bible translation of 1961 and the United Bible Societies edition of the Greek text of 1966 are two examples that bear the stamp of their text.

The radical nature of their work must also be recognized. Criticism of their work was almost immediate, led by J. W. Burgon, Dean of Chichester, a traditionalist with a gift for polemic who had spent twenty years gathering evidence about the New Testament text to support his convictions about the *Textus Receptus*. He published three articles in the *Quarterly Review* between October 1881 and April 1882 attacking both their text and the Revised Version, which had been published a few days after the text.[18] He argued that Westcott and Hort had attached too much importance to two manuscripts while ignoring the vast majority of Greek witnesses and early evidence from the Fathers, and that it was unthinkable that the divine truth had been left uncertain for so long until a pair of scholars in the nineteenth century brought it to light.

Burgon was not the only critic. In 1897, nine years after his death, his 'disciple', Edward Miller, reiterated his precise views at an important debate about the textual criticism of the New Testament held in Oxford.[19] This critique has been renewed in more recent years within conservative Christian circles in the USA and Britain. The strong movement to bring back the King James Version as the only truly inspired translation of the Bible has meant that the *Textus Receptus* has received a new lease of life and a renewed reputation over the past forty or so years. A growing number of scholars have challenged the consensus that no single family of manuscripts preserves the original text of the New Testament, and have followed Burgon in defending the textual theory which Westcott and Hort rejected.[20]

The controversy which their work created, then, still rumbles on 120 years later. One criticism often made of Westcott and his colleagues is that they always arrived at conservative conclusions in their biblical work. This was emphatically not the case with *The New Testament in the Original Greek*, which may justly be described as a subversive piece of work!

For all the criticisms of their textual theory Westcott never doubted that it would stand the test of time. In the preface to the second edition of their 'Introduction and Appendix' (1896) he wrote:

No arguments have been advanced against the general principles maintained in the Introduction and illustrated in the Notes, since the publication of the first Edition, which were not fully considered by Dr Hort and myself in the long course of our work and in our judgement dealt with adequately.

Nor did he doubt the value of the long years spent on this work once it was published. He wrote to a correspondent in 1886:

I should be the last to rate highly textual criticism; but it is a little gift which from school days seemed to be committed to me. I have tried to put it to account, and certainly it has been my joy to find in almost every result . . . a new source of light. So it will be while the world lasts.[21]

3 Translating the New Testament

Westcott made a significant contribution to another major project of the late Victorian Church, the translation of the 'Revised Version of the New Testament'. Since the 1840s scholars had been aware that the King James, or Authorized, Version of the Bible was no longer a wholly reliable translation. Textual scholarship was raising questions about the underlying Greek text and there was increasing dissatisfaction with its archaic English. The Churches, however, were firmly opposed to a new translation. The King James Version was a strong bond uniting Christians of all denominations; it was also almost universally loved for the beauty and dignity of its language. When pressure for a new translation became too strong to resist, the Convocation of Canterbury voted in May 1870 to undertake a conservative revision. There was to be no alteration to the language of the King James Version except when it was thought necessary, and then such changes were to follow closely the style of the original. No changes were to be made in the underlying

[25]

Greek text unless two-thirds of those present were in favour of such a change. It was to be a cautious translation, but in the climate of opposition to revision only such a translation had any chance of being accepted.[22]

Westcott, Lightfoot and Hort were all invited to join the panel revising the New Testament. It was a work closely related to the textual revision he and Hort had been engaged on for seventeen years. Westcott, like his friends, was unhappy with the scheme proposed. He doubted whether Convocation had the authority to act in this way, and thought that the text needed to be more accurately determined before an improved translation could begin. Hort and Lightfoot both wanted a more thorough revision than that proposed. In the end Westcott agreed with them that such an opportunity should not be set aside.

The meetings were held in the Jerusalem Chamber at Westminster Abbey. Westcott wrote to Dean Stanley to suggest that a celebration of Holy Communion might be held before the first meeting. Stanley agreed on the condition that an invitation should be sent to all the members of the Revision Company. (Most were Anglicans, but there were Nonconformists and a Unitarian, Dr Vance Smith, among them.) The service was held on 22 June 1870 in the Abbey. When it became known that a Unitarian had received communion, there were protests from groups within the Church of England, and an outcry in the Church newspapers. The following February the bishops of the Upper House of Convocation voted ten votes to four that nobody denying the Trinity should be a member of the Revision. The Lower House, however, refused to endorse this, and the Company proceeded with its work. Westcott was deeply disturbed at the reaction within the Church of England to the Holy Communion. After all, it had been his suggestion. He was angry with the bishops over their 'disastrous mistake', and wanted the Company to assert its independence of Convocation. He threatened to resign if the invitation to Dr Vance Smith was retracted.[23]

The incident reveals a side of Westcott that has never been adequately appreciated. When the revision was nearing completion, he wrote to

[26]

W. F. Moulton, the Methodist scholar, with whom he had formed a close friendship during the meetings of the New Testament panel:

> From the first I felt that the Revision itself would not be the greatest result of the gathering. May our common work be fruitful for each one of us, and for the whole Church in ways which we cannot yet foresee.[24]

Perhaps this was why he suggested the inaugural communion, which he later called 'that wonderful Communion'. It was clearly a significant event for him. What we might describe as Westcott's 'ecumenical' sympathies are another example of his eirenical outlook.

Over the next ten years the work of Revision was to absorb a good deal of his time. He rarely missed the meetings, and kept careful notes of all the discussions and decisions. Early meetings were relatively harmonious, but within a year the Company divided between the conservatives, led by Dr Scrivener, and the more radical element who sided with Westcott and Hort in textual matters. The private circulation within the Company of their text of the Gospels (1870) and the Epistles (1871) inevitably polarized opinion. As early as May 1871 Westcott is writing to his wife of the 'hard fighting' within the group. Four years later the work is 'positively distressing', and there is real regret that the project is taking up so much of his life.'[25] An unpublished letter from July 1877 expresses his 'despair' at yet another victory for Scrivener.[26] He later said, in a sermon preached in Trinity College Chapel immediately after publication, that revision and using the fruits of revision, 'both bring some disappointments and, as we are inclined to think, some losses', but this was inevitable given the nature of the Bible, which always demands effort and hard work if it is to yield up its treasures.[27]

Most accounts of the Revision agree that Westcott, like Hort, played a major role in the work of the panel. One of the earliest historians of the Revised Version emphasizes the strong influence within the panel of the 'progressives', and in particular Westcott and Hort's powerful standing and determined spirit. While Hort was the 'strongest will of the whole Company', reference is also made to the 'quiet determination of Westcott, who set his face as a flint'.[28] There is an observation, however, purporting to come from the chairman of the New Testament panel, Bishop Ellicott, to the effect that his influence was less than had been thought because when it came to voting on changes to the King James Version Westcott would retreat into a corner and refuse to vote.[29] This is difficult to believe since Westcott usually played a full and active part in whatever committees he joined, and in the years after publication in 1881 he was the most doughty champion of the Revision. It is nevertheless important to remember that in textual matters Westcott and Hort's influence was relatively modest: the Company accepted their text before others in only 64 places.

When the work was finished he wrote to Hort: 'how terrible some things look now that all is unalterable. Yet I think the work is very fair, and it will do good. The work upon it has certainly been instructive in many ways.'[30] In the Trinity College sermon referred to earlier he claimed that a new page had been added to the history of the English Bible:

> It will bring home to us the conviction that the English Bible is not to be regarded essentially as a finished work of literary skill, an un-rivalled monument of the fresh vigour of our language, a precious heirloom whose very defects have gathered grace from time . . . The very idea of a revision of the Bible which extends to the ground texts, as well as to the renderings, suggests to us that the Bible is a vital record to be interpreted according to the growth of life.[31]

Given the popular affection for the traditional version, however, it was inevitable that the new translation would face criticism. The strongest and most sustained attack came, as we saw earlier, from Dean Burgon, who pinpointed the inferior English style of the translation as well as the deficiencies of the underlying Greek text. He was far from being the only critic. The greatly respected Oxford New Testament scholar, W. Sanday, who had a great admiration for the Cambridge triumvirate, criticized the literary style of the new translation. He argued that the Bible is not a book of science or philosophy, but of religion; its object is 'to touch and stir the hearts of men', and to this end 'rhythm and the choice of words are far from being unimportant'.[32]

Neither Westcott nor Hort replied to these criticisms. Westcott was strongly urged to do so by Robert Scott, Dean of Rochester, who wrote to him appealing to him to respond because of the effect Burgon's article was having on many people. When Westcott demurred, Scott wrote to him again warning him that the articles were 'doing much mischief' among the multitudes who were wondering whether to accept the new translation or not, and would do much more.[33] Westcott's silence was true to character: he did not relish controversy. It was unfortunate that Hort, too, kept silent. In retrospect, the two friends were unwise to ignore the attacks on their work. The Revised Version sold slowly, and never replaced the King James Version in popular worship and devotion. Convocation refused to authorize it to be read in churches until 1899 and then it was only the Convocation of Canterbury that did so. Its cardinal weakness was the literalness of the translation, which has made it a favourite with Bible students, but has not commended it to the wider public. One lesson learned from this whole episode was that the work of scholars in translation needs to be checked by readers who have a sense of the impression language will make on the ordinary reader.

Westcott's belief was that quiet advocacy of the new translation, and usage, would eventually prevail. In a speech to the Convocation of York in February 1892 he expressed confidence that the Revised Version New Testament was slowly and surely gaining ground, and would eventually be recognized. He was content to appeal to the next generation for a just judgement on the new translation.[34] This was typical of his optimism. In his 1897 collection of material which he had used over the years to explain and commend the new version, *Some Lessons of the Revised*

Version of the New Testament, he claimed that the revisers had not been surprised by the criticism, and defended and explained the principles used and many of the changes made. Translating the Bible is arduous work: the best translation is no more than an imperfect copy, 'an engraving, as it were, of the master's drawing'. If people used the new version, they would discover its merits for themselves, and would then learn 'to look with something more than suspicion upon the criticisms of scholars who appear to find nothing better than solemn music in the English version of the words of life and to admit no hope of riper knowledge from the discoveries of two centuries and a half'.[35]

Westcott's optimism was not justified, but he was right in seeing its publication as a landmark in the history of the Bible. In retrospect the Revised Version was an anticipation of the many modern translations that were to be made in the next century, and some of the issues raised then have recurred since. Most important of all, the resurgence of fundamentalism in the late twentieth century, with its claim that the King James translation is the only divinely inspired version of the Scriptures, has resurrected the controversies of the 1880s. In an astonishing replay of history, some American conservative scholars have outdone even Dean Burgon in their attacks on Westcott and Hort, attempting to discredit their work and influence by arguing that they were not truly Christians.[36] This both underlines the lasting significance of their textual and translation work, and gives fresh relevance to the controversies of the Victorian Church over a century later.

4 The interpretation of the New Testament

One of Westcott's Harrow pupils, Charles Gore, later recalled visiting him about ordering a commentary on Thucydides. Westcott 'almost shivered, as was his way, at the idea of a boy beginning so early the use of a commentary . . . Then he explained to me how fatal was the premature use of commentaries'.[37]

It is ironical that the man who voiced these doubts about the value of commentaries for the young should have written two or three of the finest New Testament commentaries of his age, and that his scholarly reputation should rest partly upon these. It so happened, however, that by the 1850s the time was ripe for a new type of biblical commentary, which would accept fully the demands of the new historical criticism, and at the same time recognize that the New Testament documents are written 'from faith to faith'. This was the agenda for the ambitious scheme covering the whole of the New Testament, in which Westcott joined Lightfoot and Hort in 1860. It is not an exaggeration to claim that this opened a new era for biblical exegesis in England. When the first commentary of the series was published in 1865 – Lightfoot's *Galatians* – it was immediately recognized as an 'altogether new type of commentary'.[38] Westcott's share in the scheme was the Johannine writings and the Epistle to the Hebrews. He later added Ephesians to this, although the original plan was that Lightfoot should cover the Pauline epistles. *The Gospel of St John* was published in 1880, *The Epistles of St John* in 1883, and *The Epistle to the Hebrews* in 1889. He never finished *Ephesians*, but it was published posthumously in 1906 with much editing and added introductory material. Although his early books on the miracles and the resurrection exemplify his distinctive exegesis, his reputation as a commentator rests on these four books.

The Gospel of St John is the best known of his commentaries. It has its roots in his lifelong affection for and affinity with the fourth Gospel. As early as his undergraduate days he dreamed of writing a commentary on the Greek text, and corresponded with two publishers about it before agreeing, in 1869, to write a commentary on the English text for the 'Speaker's Commentary' series. His commentary on the Greek text was published posthumously in 1908. The 1880 book is based upon his lectures on John in both Cambridge and Peterborough. It has had a lasting influence. E. C. Hoskyns (1884-1937), whose exposition of John is one of the landmarks of twentieth-century New Testament interpretation, described it as 'still the classical English commentary' on the fourth Gospel because of its distinctive theological insight.[39] It was reissued in 1958 in a new edition by James Clark with an introduction by Adam Fox.

The commentary itself is preceded by an 'Introduction' ninety-seven pages long, in which he argues forcefully for the authorship of John the Apostle, with a very full account of both the external and internal evidence for this. There are also sections on the date, object, plan, style, historical exactness, and characteristics of the Gospel. He emphasizes particularly its Jewishness, its symbolism, and its theological intensity and insight.

The Epistles of St John, like *Hebrews* and *Ephesians*, is a commentary on the Greek text. Like *St John*, this is the fulfilment of a dream of his early years, and he was working on it for over thirty years. In the 'Introduction' he argues that the letters are a later work of the Apostle John. The same fundamental ideas are present in both, but they are presented differently, reflecting the contrast between the historian and the preacher. The background to the epistles is a period when Docetism is the chief internal threat to the Christian community. To the commentary are appended three long essays: 'The Two Empires: The Church and the World', 'The Gospel of Creation', and 'The Relation of Christianity to Art'. As has often been pointed out, there is only a very tenuous relationship between these essays and the commentary proper.

Some people would say that *The Epistle to the Hebrews* is Westcott's finest commentary. He found in the author, on his own admission, a kindred spirit: 'No work in which I have ever been allowed to spend many years of continuous labour has had for me the same intense human interest as the study of the Epistle to the Hebrews.'[40] His sympathy with the Alexandrian tradition and his concern to expound a writer's theology found here a sympathetic subject. The letter had an important influence on his own theological development, for he found here too the biblical basis for his very original concept of 'Christus Consummator'. The 'Introduction' points out the similarities between the Epistle and St John, and argues that the author, who cannot have been St Paul, may have been Luke, Barnabas, or even as Luther suggested, Apollos. As in his commentary on the Johannine epistles, each chapter has significant notes appended on key words and concepts. There is a concluding essay on 'The Use of the Old Testament in the Epistle'.

St Paul's Epistle to the Ephesians was edited by J. M. Schulhof after Westcott's death from materials left by him in manuscripts. The commentary itself is substantially his work, but the introduction, appendix, and added notes have been constructed from fragmentary notes and jottings, with some material included from Lightfoot and Hort's work on the Epistle. Westcott, like Hort, had a particular affection for this letter, and worked on it in the brief intervals between official work in the Durham years. Its unfinished state, however, has meant that it has never been regarded so highly as the other three works.

These commentaries share some distinctive features. There is a strong emphasis on the need to pay attention, not only to external evidence about a book (such as authorship and date), but also to the structure and shape of the work itself. Howard Kuist makes the point well:

> He insisted, when questions of authenticity were being raised, that the plan and characteristics of each text must also be considered as essential to the total picture. The most distinctive characteristic of a 'Westcottian' Introduction is its emphasis upon Plan and Character of the Text itself.[41]

He mentions that it was this feature of Westcott's 'Introduction' to *St John* which impressed Edwyn Hoskyns, who believed that Westcott was one of the outstanding interpreters of the fourth Gospel.[42] Having established a plan he then uses this as a framework for his exposition of the text.

The exposition and exegesis are set out in a clear, well-defined pattern. The leading topic of a paragraph or chapter is stated, and the main themes within it are established; then each of these is analyzed in detail, with comments on words and syntax. Then the thought of the whole paragraph is summarized. Finally, there are additional notes on special problem words or ideas within the section.

The immense amount of detail and the closeness of the argument mean that these are very demanding commentaries, which do not yield up their fruits without a great deal of concentration and effort. There is a telling review of *The Epistle to the Hebrews* which describes it as 'emphatically a student's book . . . from one who is now perhaps our greatest scholar and greatest commentator. But it *needs* hard work to get the use of it . . . The preacher who is in a hurry need not turn to these pages.'[43] This is not something, however, for which the author would have apologized. He believed, as we shall see in a later chapter, that the essence of education was active participation not passive acceptance, and in the prefaces to two of his commentaries and in his two strictly theological books he invites the reader to join him on a journey which will not necessarily be an easy one. The words with which he introduces his *Hebrews* commentary illustrate this well:

I have endeavoured to suggest in the notes lines of thought which I have found to open light upon problems which we are required to face. In doing this it has throughout been my desire to induce my readers to become my fellow-students, and I have aimed at encouraging sustained reflection rather than at entering on the field of controversy. No conclusion is of real value to us till we have made it our own by serious work.[44]

There has long been division of opinion over whether the difficulty of these commentaries is exacerbated by that lack of clarity of expression which some have thought mars his written work as a whole. Another contemporary review of *The Epistle to the Hebrews* by Dr Alfred Plummer expresses the 'complaint which all students of Westcott's work make, that there are passages in which even those who are well acquainted with the subject find it hard to extract the precise meaning'.[45] This charge is refuted, however, by Adam Fox in the introduction to the 1958 'Re-Issue' of Westcott's *St John*:

> Westcott's style is neither ponderous nor light. It can seldom be read without a steady attention if it is to be understood, but it cannot be called obscure. The thought is sometimes too subtle and over-refined, but that does not mean that there is much doubt as to what the thought is. Westcott is a lucid writer.[46]

We shall return to the question of Westcott's alleged obscurity of expression in Chapter 4.[47]

One other general feature of Westcott's commentaries must be mentioned – their conservative scholarship. As with the other commentaries in the series by Lightfoot and Hort, Westcott invariably upholds the traditional view of authorship, date and provenance. His 'Introduction' to *The Gospel of St John*, for example, is still regarded as the classic statement of the argument that the author is John the Apostle. For some, especially continental scholars, this was a real drawback, a timid and defensive response to one of the key issues in New Testament scholarship. We must remember, however, that these commentaries were being published at a time when the British public generally was very suspicious of radical continental biblical criticism, and only work which reached traditional conclusions would be acceptable.

We turn now to look more closely at the nature of Westcott's exegesis. As early as 1860 he was clear that there were two aspects of biblical interpretation: 'Two great objects appear to be included in the work of the interpreter: the strict investigation of the simple meaning of the text, and the development of the religious teaching which lies beneath it.'[48] He writes elsewhere of a 'double sense' in scripture, the literal and the spiritual, and the one is the sound foundation for the other.[49]

The foundation for everything in his commentaries is a rigorous study of the exact words of Scripture. 'All intelligent interpretation of

Scripture must . . . be based upon a strict analysis of its idioms and words.'[50] He had learned from his old headmaster 'an intense belief in the exact force of language' and an 'absolute belief in the force of words',[51] and had found a similar concern for exactness and care and the scrupulous study of detail in the work of Origen. The introductions to his *Epistles of St John* and *Hebrews* both contain strong assertions of this fundamental conviction.[52] The long years spent first in revising the Greek text and then in translating this into English were therefore, for him, years well spent, since they were concerned with recovering and reflecting on the exact words of Scripture. As Bishop of Durham he would defend the Revisers against those who claimed that many of the changes made to the Authorized Version were trivialities. To Westcott, no change that restored the true meaning of the original text could be trivial. The aim of all their work had been to 'allow Apostles and Evangelists to speak in their own words to the last syllable and the least inflection . . . I know no way in which we can understand the meaning of a message except by the patient observance of the exact words in which it is conveyed'.[53]

One fruit of this is the number of studies of Greek words which are found in his commentaries. In his Westcott Memorial Lecture C. K. Barrett lists a number of notable examples of these, and suggests that in this respect he anticipates the work in the twentieth century of Kittel in his famous *Theologisches Wörterbuch*.[54] In every case exposition is based on the Old Testament background to the word, and often quotations from the early Fathers shed light on the meaning. His love of individual Greek words shines out from such studies. Just one example is the 'Additional Note' in his *Hebrews* on the word 'perfection' ($\tau\epsilon\lambda\epsilon\acute{\iota}\omega\sigma\iota\varsigma$) deriving from the phrase in 2.10, 'made perfect through suffering'. There are exhaustive surveys of the use and meaning of the word in the LXX, the New Testament books, and the early Fathers. Then a summary of the conclusions: 'He who is $\tau\acute{\epsilon}\lambda\epsilon\iota\sigma\varsigma$ has reached the end which is in each case set before him, maturity of growth, complete development of powers, full enjoyment of privileges, perfect possession of knowledge.'

This is then applied to the context in Hebrews. This is followed by another 'Additional Note' on the perfection of Christ in Hebrews, which concludes with a summary of the theological implications of this.[55] There is an immense amount of material for the teacher and preacher in such studies. Even though papyrus finds in the twentieth century have transformed our conception of the language of the New Testament word studies like this have an enduring value.

It has to be said, however, that sometimes Westcott is over-subtle in his exegesis. In his famous 'Essay on the Interpretation of Scripture' in *Essays and Reviews*, Benjamin Jowett had criticized this kind of approach:

> There is a danger of making words mean too much; refinements of signification are drawn out of them, perhaps contained in their etymology, which are lost in common use and parlance. There is the danger of interpreting every particle, as though it were a link in the argument, instead of being . . . an excrescence of style.[56]

This undoubtedly touched a raw nerve in Westcott, totally opposed as it was to his most fundamental convictions, and there are several places in his work where he refutes such criticism. It is precisely this kind of over-subtlety which some people have felt detracts sometimes from the positive qualities of Westcott's commentaries. Stephen Neill's comment sums it up well: 'He could be tiresomely detailed in elucidating shades of meaning which did not really exist.'[57] Arthur Benson believed that it was Prince Lee who was responsible for passing on to his pupils this over-emphasis on the nuances of words, and that it affected not only Westcott's exegesis but also his style of writing.[58] Whether this be true or not it is one of the criticisms of Westcott as commentator which has been repeated over the years.

In fairness to him it must be said that he and his contemporaries were not aware that New Testament Greek was a less exact language than Classical Greek. So in his exposition of the dialogue between Jesus and Peter by the lakeside in John 21.15ff. he insists on the exact distinction between the two Greek words for 'love', φιλέω and ἀγαπάω ('do you love me?'), whereas modern commentators generally do not press the distinction between these when used as verbs.[59]

The other aspect of biblical interpretation for Westcott was the spiritual. 'Faith in words is the beginning, faith in the Word is the completion of Biblical interpretation . . . the true student will find the simple text of Holy Scripture ever pregnant with lessons for the present and promises for ages to come.'[60] Here, his theological sensitivity enabled him to show continually the relevance of New Testament teaching for contemporary readers. The opening words of the 'Introduction' to his *Hebrews* express precisely what he always felt in expounding the words of the New Testament: 'Every student of the Epistle to the Hebrews must feel that it deals in a peculiar degree with the thoughts and trials of our own time.'[61] It is this quality which in Hoskyns' view made Westcott an outstanding interpreter of John's Gospel:

> When Westcott wrote his commentary the Fourth Gospel was still a great work of Christian Theology able to deliver up its secret only to those who were themselves sensitive to theological truth, prepared to assume that it is a 'good' book, and ready to listen to what it has to say without seeking to justify or defend it, or even to interpret it and explain it, save on its own terms.[62]

Two brief examples from his *St John* will illustrate this quality in his exegesis. There is, first, his comment on the phrase 'but by me' in John 14.6: 'It is only through Christ that we can, though in God . . . apprehend God as the Father, and so approach the Father . . . It does not follow that every one who is guided by Christ is directly conscious of His guidance.' In this second pregnant sentence Westcott reflects contemporary concern to relate Christianity to other world religions, and anticipates an important question that would often arise in interfaith discussion in the next century.[63] Second, there is his comment on 'that the world may believe' in John 17.21: 'The end, as here regarded, is to be brought about by the spectacle of the unity of the disciples . . . The unity of disciples, therefore, while it springs out of a direct relation to Christ, must have some external expression that it may affect those without the Church'.[64] This seemingly effortless move from exegesis to practical application of the text is one of the distinctive features of Westcott's commentaries.

Allusion has already been made to the wealth of biblical and patristic material in his work. When he discusses a word or phrase or sentence you can be sure that he has cited almost every parallel from both Old and New Testaments. His patristic knowledge is similarly encyclopaedic. He always has the appropriate quotation from classical writers, or from the Greek and Latin Fathers – and these are always presented in the original language, without translation! In his exegesis of the well known passage in 1 John 4.16ff. ('God is love . . .') he quotes from Jerome, Philo (three times), Clement of Rome, Augustine (four times), Bede, and Ambrose.[65] His comments on Hebrews 4.14–16, to give another example, include references to no less than twelve different authorities, mostly the early Fathers.[66] C. K. Barrett suggests that the presence of this kind of material is one reason why his commentaries will never become wholly out of date, even though they do not contain the important Jewish writers of the intertestamental period, the Qumran material, and the like, which have only been discovered since Westcott's time.[67]

In a review of Westcott's *Life and Letters* in 1904 the American textual critic and scholar, Caspar René Gregory, quoted a remark Westcott once made to him about the essence of biblical interpretation: 'I feel every year more and more that the real work of the commentator must lie, not in searching out the thoughts of other men about the text, but in sinking himself into the text itself.'[68] This leads us to a further point about his interpretation of Scripture. It is based on a deep conviction that God speaks to us through our immersing ourselves in the words of Scripture. Exegesis for him was not primarily a literary exercise; it was the offering of one's scholarship and gifts in order to hear God speaking, and then to communicate that to the reader. This is the conviction that undergirds all his commentary work. In studying the words of Scripture we are hearing the living word of God. In an address to the junior clergy of his diocese two years before he died, he set out what for him were the important principles of Bible study: the need to be systematic, thorough, historical, patient, reverent. His final point was that Bible study must be 'vital':

> The Bible is more than a book: it is the voice of God answering to the voice of man . . . Behind, beneath, in each act and word there is an unseen power. Virtue comes forth from the letter in answer to the touch of faith . . . The words fail in their function if they do not lead us to the Word.[69]

It is this deep reverence for the words and details of the scriptural text which gives his exegesis a particular character, and indeed gives a distinctive tone to his whole theology.[70]

His sense almost of awe in the presence of the words of Scripture, which the young Scott Holland noticed when he heard Westcott expounding St John,[71] brings us to one final point about his exegesis. Such was his respect for the words of the New Testament that he found it difficult to fully accept that there is a human element in the composition of Scripture. He conceded that there was a need to treat the Scriptures in a critical way, yet he himself found it very difficult to do this in his own exposition and exegesis. Whenever he writes about the inspiration of the Bible, he cannot help using terms like 'unerring truthfulness', 'perfect truthfulness', and 'perfect inspiration'. He often glossed over discrepancies in the Gospels, and believed that difficulties in Scripture left room for humility and faith. C. K. Barrett believes that this was the great weakness of his commentaries, that he was temperamentally unwilling to accept fully the human element in Scripture:

'Sometimes it seems that he almost thinks of a vertical descent of . . . a Westcott and Hort New Testament, with a divine significance in every mood, tense, and case.'[72]

Here we see the defects of his great virtue, that earnest, reverent approach to Scripture which still lights up the teaching of St John and the Letter to the Hebrews a century after his death.

3

THE HISTORY OF
THE CHURCH:

The Alexandrian Tradition and Christian Platonism

I never, for my part, could help the feeling that he was an Alexandrian
Father revived under modern conditions . . .Westcott, like Clement of
Alexandria, seemed to me to take his reader through a golden Platonic
mist . . .[1]

1 *Westcott as historian*

Westcott is not usually thought of as a historian. Within the
Cambridge triumvirate it is Lightfoot who is generally regarded as the
historian 'par excellence'. In a series of lectures on 'Famous
Birmingham Men' given in the city during 1908, Professor C. F. G.
Masterman included addresses on Lightfoot, Benson and Westcott. He
characterized Westcott in this way: 'His special province was the future
. . . There was something of the prophet's vision in those keen eyes of
his. In a very real sense he watched all his life long for the coming of
Christ.'[2] He then contrasted this with Lightfoot's concern for the past
and Benson's for the present.

Over half a century later Stephen Neill would see Westcott's greatest
strength elsewhere when attempting to compare the gifts of the triumvirate: 'Lightfoot was primarily the historian, Hort the philosopher,
and Westcott the exegete.'[3] Once again it is Lightfoot who is seen as the
historian.

This all goes to show that generalizations of this kind are often simplistic and highly subjective. This is true above all where Westcott is concerned, for the breadth of his interests and gifts has never been truly appreciated.

Any attempt to evaluate his work must take seriously the fact that one of his earliest and most enduring books was a massive study of the history of the New Testament canon. Further, his whole outlook and theology was deeply influenced by his knowledge of the Alexandrian Fathers and of the Christian Platonist tradition in English thought. To suggest that he was indifferent to the past or lacking in historical sensitivity is quite misleading.

It is true that we do not find in his work that continual awareness of the cloud of witnesses from past ages that permeates Lightfoot's sermons and addresses. In Westcott's Durham period, for instance, there is little of that vivid awareness of the Celtic Church that marked his predecessor's public ministry. We have only to think, however, of the masterly summary of the significance of Antony, Benedict, and Francis in the development of the monastic tradition in his famous sermon on 'Disciplined Life', or of his discussion of the Franciscans and Quakers in his 1886 Westminster sermon, to realize how deeply aware Westcott was of the Church's past.[4]

The most characteristic feature of his historical sense is the concern to apprehend the lessons of the past for the present and the future. His preoccupation with the Alexandrian Church of the second century was grounded in a deep conviction that its insights and vision had an extraordinary relevance to the Church in the second half of the nineteenth century. It was during his Durham years that he turned more and more to the reading of the signs of the times: the discernment of God's purposes in the contemporary movements of thought and action. There is an address he gave in Peterborough Cathedral in 1892, which begins with reference to the past inheritance of the Church of England and to the sense of continuity embodied in a great cathedral. He then continues: 'When it was my happy privilege to minister here, I was glad to speak once and again of our debt to the past. Now I wish to speak of our debt to the future.'[5] He goes on to speak of the prophetic task of the Church, and to analyse contemporary aspirations towards unity of various kinds.

This is typical of his outlook in these later years of his life. His move to the north-east had brought him face-to-face with the economic and social realities of life. The impact upon him of being in central London while in residence at Westminster for three months of the year has already been noted. He was now permanently resident in one of Britain's great industrial regions, and his main energies are devoted to applying the Christian faith to the many social and ethical issues raised by industrialization. His main concern is with what Masterman called 'the prophet's vision', which involved appropriating the lessons of the past for the present and future.

This was all a far cry from his earlier years when at the age of 30 he wrote a dry, lengthy academic study of an issue in the history of the Early Church.

2 The history of the New Testament canon

A General Survey of the History of the Canon of the New Testament (1855) was written while he was a schoolmaster at Harrow. It followed his early work on the Gospels, but was prompted by a particular contemporary challenge, namely, the radical biblical scholarship of F. C. Baur and the Tübingen school.

They argued that primitive Christianity consisted of a conflict between Jewish and Gentile Christianity (or Paulinism), which was resolved in the synthesis of Catholic Christianity in the second century. The New Testament documents reflect this controversy and eventual compromise. According to their theories the earlier books reflect the hostility of the parties, while anything that shows a conciliatory tendency must be late. So only four Pauline letters – Galatians, Romans, 1 and 2 Corinthians – are regarded as authentic. Most of the other letters are dated well into the second century, as are Acts, John's Gospel, and the Johannine letters, amongst others.

This was a formidable and thoroughgoing theory of the genesis of the New Testament, placing the New Testament documents within a firm historical framework: they were not timeless documents, but part of the history of the Early Church. It challenged sharply the orthodox view of the Early Church as a haven of peace and harmony. More seriously, it called into question the unity of the New Testament.

Henry Chadwick has shown that this German reconstruction of Early Church history was in no way easy to set aside: 'It might be possible to puncture it here and there by negative criticism . . . But the theory could only be effectively answered by an alternative framework which saw the evolution of the early church as a whole.'[6]

The great merit of Westcott's work is that it provides such an alternative hypothesis. He accepts that the central issue at stake is the unity of the New Testament, and shows that a quite different account of the evolution of the Early Church can be given from that offered by the German scholars. He does this by tracing methodically and in great detail the history of the acknowledgement of the authority of the New Testament literature. He works through the evidence in the Apostolic Fathers, in the Apologists, and in the Councils of the Church, concluding with a short discussion of the views of the Reformers of the sixteenth century. His conclusion is that with the possible exception of 2 Peter all the canonical books of the New Testament are genuine, that is, from the first century. He finds

> a belief in the authority of the books of the New Testament so widely spread throughout the Christian body, so deeply rooted in the inmost consciousness of the Christian Church, so perfectly accordant with all the facts which we do know, [which] can only be explained by admitting that they are genuine and Apostolic, a written Rule of Christian Faith and Life.[7]

Westcott acknowledges the merit of the Tübingen thesis in the Preface to the first edition of his book. It had pointed up the diversity of the New Testament literature, and the fact that it is a product of the pressures and movements within the Early Church. The great weakness of their reconstruction is that 'they should not have found in those writings the explanation instead of the result of the divisions which are traceable to the Apostolic times'.[8] By meticulously sifting the evidence for the authority and use of the New Testament literature in the early centuries, he is able to show that the evidence will not support the theory.

Just one example of his method is his treatment of Justin Martyr, the second century Greek Apologist who died in AD 148. In eighty closely argued pages he deals with all the relevant primary and secondary quotations, and shows quite convincingly that 'it appears to be a fact beyond doubt that Justin used the first three Gospels as we use them, as the authentic memoirs of Christ's life and work'.[9] He deals firmly but fairly with the objections of the mainly German critics who attempted to deny this. Thus, another plank is added in the cumulative argument: if Justin was acquainted with the Synoptic Gospels, whether in oral or written form, they must be from the first rather than the second century. This is his method of dealing with the German challenge, by calmly weighing the historical evidence, and constructing an overall hypothesis that comes to very different conclusions. He shows in this way that the Tübingen reconstruction is 'altogether too abstract, remote from any imaginable sequence of actual events, in short, psychologically incredible'.[10]

Later scholarship has generally confirmed the view that the bulk of the New Testament books belong to the first rather than to the second century, and in this respect Westcott has been vindicated. There was a strong contemporary attack on the book, however, in the anonymous *Supernatural Religion*, published in 1874. The author, later revealed as W. R. Cassels, criticised Westcott's 'discreet reserve', 'apologetic partiality', and 'disingenuousness'. Lightfoot came to his friend's defence in a series of articles in the *Contemporary Review* and Westcott defended himself in a long preface to the fourth edition of the book.

In his Westcott memorial lecture of 1960 Henry Chadwick expressed the view that the *History of the Canon* was the best book that Westcott wrote. He nevertheless concedes that there is, as Cassels suggested, an apologetic interest in the book. He believes that Westcott 'looked at the second century through the spectacles of Irenaeus', and was more concerned to uphold the view of the tradition than to ask what really happened.[11] In this sense, the whole work is a typical product of Westcott's essentially conservative cast of mind.

For all that, this has been the most durable of all his books, being used as a student text book almost into the last decade of the twentieth century. Its argument that the formation of the canon was among the first instinctive acts of the Christian Church, and that recognition came gradually and progressively over a long period, has been generally accepted by later scholars, who have had the benefit of new discoveries and new manuscripts.

If we compare Westcott's book with a recent survey of the subject by Bruce Metzger, the main difference is in the survey of the second century heresies like Gnosticism, where the twentieth-century discoveries of Gnostic material at Nag Hammadi and of the Gospels of Thomas and Philip have provided much material that is lacking in Westcott's survey. Metzger's overall conclusion about the canon is, however, almost as confident and optimistic as Westcott's:

> The knowledge that our New Testament contains the best sources for the history of Jesus is the most valuable knowledge that can be obtained from study of the early history of the canon ... it is certain that those who discerned the limits of the canon had a clear and balanced perception of the gospel of Jesus Christ.[12]

In the later years of the twentieth century the New Testament canon became one of the central issues in biblical scholarship. Raymond

Brown wrote in 1989: 'The issue of the canon has moved from the erudite periphery to the center of scriptural relevance.'[13] There has been much discussion of the question, raised at the Reformation, of 'a canon within a canon', and whether some books are more authoritative than others. This is clearly not without relevance to Westcott's own work. Some scholars, the foremost of whom has been B. S. Childs, have developed 'canonical criticism' which asserts the significance of the canon in a unique way. What matters most in New Testament interpretation is the final form of the text, of individual books, of the whole collection; even the order in which the books occur is significant. Implicit here is a critique of historical criticism, which wrongly isolates individual books and concentrates unduly on authorial aim and purpose.

Another recent issue is that of the 'larger audience'. With the inclusion of a book within the canon, words once addressed to a first century community are now addressed to the whole of Christendom, which changes the way in which these words are interpreted and understood. Another group of scholars has seriously challenged the validity of the New Testament canon, claiming for instance that in his letters Paul suppressed the radicalism of Jesus, or that the 'original gospel' is represented by the Magnificat and the Beatitudes in Luke's Gospel. This raises the question of whether the canon is open or closed: can it be either added to or subtracted from? There has even been a debate about the canonicity of the New Testament text. This arises, interestingly, from the theories of Westcott and Hort. Is one type of text to be regarded as the canonical text, and if so, what status is to be given to the variant readings? The consensus is that 'canonical' must be broad enough to include all variant readings. For example, the so-called 'longer ending' of Mark should be regarded as part of the canonical text, in spite of the internal and external evidence against it.[14]

All this gives fresh significance to Westcott's study of the history of the canon almost 150 years ago. The reason he addressed the issue then was the particular challenge from Germany, but it is clear that in some degree he anticipated later lines of enquiry and developments in scholarship.

Finally, it is worth noting that he wrote another book about the canon that is often overlooked. *The Bible in the Church* (1864) was written primarily to put the material in the earlier work in a simpler form for the general reader. In the event he widened its scope to include the reception of the Old Testament as well as the New in the Church. He traced the reception of the books from the Apostolic age to the sixteenth century, showing how the formation of the Christian Bible was a slow and gradual process, the result not of any formal decisions by the Church but of usage within its common life. He concludes that the history of the Bible is

> an epitome of the history of the Church. Both came to their full form slowly, silently, surely, by the combination of manifold elements . . . Both include treasures new and old, of which now this now that is needed for the instruction of men . . . The Bible, no less than the Church, is Holy, Catholic, and Apostolic.[15]

3 The Alexandrian Fathers

Westcott's work on the New Testament canon involved close examination of the evidence in the early Fathers of the Church. It was during his later years at Harrow that he became increasingly interested in the Church of Alexandria, and in particular with the work of Clement and Origen.

The Anglican tradition had always valued the contribution of the early Fathers. In the nineteenth century, however, there was a significant revival of interest in them under the impact of the Oxford movement. The very basis of the Tractarian ethos was a deep concern that the Church should be true to the tradition of the ancient and undivided Church. Liturgy, spirituality, and study of the Bible were to be nourished by a study of the Fathers; hence the importance of projects such as *The Library of the Fathers* in making editions of their work available to the English reader. With Keble the appeal to the Fathers became a reforming principle: a demand for the restoration of those beliefs and practices approved or authorized by antiquity, but wanting in the contemporary Church.[16] Newman discovered the Alexandrian Church when he was invited to write a history of the Early Church by H. J. Rose in 1831. The result was his 1833 book on the Arian controversy. The discovery was a landmark in the development of his mind and theological understanding:

> What principally attracted me in the ante-Nicene period was the great Church of Alexandria, the historical centre of teaching in those times . . . The battle of Arianism was first fought in Alexandria . . . The broad philosophy of Clement and Origen carried me away; the philosophy, not the theological doctrine . . . Some portions of their teaching, magnificent in themselves, came like music to my inward ear, as if the response to ideas, which, with little external to encourage them, I had cherished so long.[17]

Newman found in the Alexandrians the sacramental principle and the recognition of the element of mystery, which were to become central in his life and thought.

There was a similar interest in the Alexandrians at Cambridge, although here the emphasis was less devotional and more historical. For example, we find F. D. Maurice recommending to Charles Kingsley in January 1851 that the 'Christian Alexandrian School is worthy to be thoroughly restudied'.[18]

It was not surprising, then, that Westcott should turn to the early Fathers for inspiration and help when he encountered the challenge from Tübingen. His friend Lightfoot found them to be key witnesses in the reconstruction of an alternative history of the Early Church, and was to spend much of his life in producing a massive edition of *The*

Apostolic Fathers. Westcott concentrated his attention mainly on the Alexandrian Fathers. As with Newman his affection deepened into something akin to a love affair. Second century Alexandria became his ideal period in the whole history of the Church, to which he constantly looked back. He frequently expressed the view that the only solution to the crisis facing the Church of his own day was a revival of the spirit of the Alexandrian school. In an essay first published in 1883 he wrote of the crisis in which 'it is impossible not to see the highest hope for Christendom in a living appreciation of the spirit of the great Greek Fathers . . . a work remains for Greek divinity in the nineteenth century hardly less pregnant with results than that wrought by the Greek classics in the fifteenth'.[19]

Clement and Origen had an especially profound influence on his whole outlook, shaping his theology and having a crucial effect on his missiology and his attitude towards other world faiths. Much that is distinctive in Westcott has its origin in his love of the Alexandrians.

Surprisingly, he never published a book on them. His only written work in this field consists of articles he wrote for various dictionaries, and one for a periodical.[20] His article on Clement of Alexandria in the 1877 *Dictionary of Christian Biography* outlines the course of Clement's life, gives a full description of each of his main works, and then summarizes his significance and influence as a Christian teacher. He singles out two aspects of Clement's teaching as especially significant. One is the centrality of the incarnation:

This thought of the Incarnation as the crown and consummation of the whole history of the world is perhaps that which is most characteristic of Clement's office as an interpreter of the faith. It rests upon his view of human nature, of the providential government of God, of the finality of the Christian dispensation.

The other is the recognition of the work of providence in preparing the way for the gospel, both in the Jewish people and in the speculations of

Greek philosophy. Both were partial and imperfect, but each in different ways helped to point the way to the final revelation in Christ:

> Towards this great unity of all science and all life Clement himself strove; and by the influence of his writings he has kept alive the sense of the magnificent promises included in the teaching of St Paul and St John . . . He affirmed, once for all, upon the threshold of the new age, that Christianity is the heir of all past time, and the interpreter of the future. Sixteen centuries have confirmed the truth of his principle, and left its application still fruitful.[21]

Westcott's most significant contribution in this area, however, lies in his two lengthy articles on Origen. He was his great hero among the Fathers. As a student of Plato Westcott found in Origen the supreme exposition of Platonic idealism in the Early Church. If John was his favourite Gospel, Origen was his ideal in the patristic period, and his life and work profoundly influenced his own.

There are numerous interesting parallels between the two men. In his 1886 Bampton lectures, C. J. Bigg commented on Origen's versatility: 'The range of his activity is amazing. He is the first great scholar, the first great preacher, the first great devotional writer, the first great commentator, the first great dogmatist.'[22] One is reminded of Westcott's own wide interests in scholarship. Like Origen he devoted a vast amount of time to restoring the text of the New Testament and to its interpretation, and yet found time also for that wider theological work and speculation which Origen believed to be important. Origen's essential optimism about human nature, his strong emphasis on the grace and mercy of God, and his central conviction that in the incarnation we see perfect humanity and perfect divinity in one Person – all are hallmarks of Westcott's distinctive theological outlook. That he found in Origen a pattern and an ideal for his own life can be seen in the eulogistic prose with which he concludes his long article in the 1877 *Dictionary of Christian Biography*:

He lived only to work. He combined in a signal degree sympathy with zeal. As a controversialist he sought to win his adversary and not simply to silence him . . . His faith was catholic, and therefore he welcomed every kind of knowledge as tributary to its fullness. His faith was living, and therefore he was assured that no age could seal any one expression of it as complete. In virtue of this open-hearted trust, he kept unchilled to the last the passionate devotion of his youth. And therefore he was enabled to leave to the Church the conviction . . . that all things are its heritage because all things are Christ's.[23]

This dictionary article is the most comprehensive of the two pieces he wrote about Origen. It discusses his life and chronology, lists his works and the editions currently available, and outlines his view of the Christian life, his work as critic and interpreter, and his theology, before summarizing his essential characteristics. There is, significantly, little criticism of the man who was later to be condemned by the Church for his unorthodox speculations on the origins of the soul and on the resurrection. All that Westcott will venture by way of criticism is that as an interpreter of Scripture Origen was 'without true historic feeling' – a criticism that has sometimes been made of Westcott's own exegesis! – and that his gravest errors are attempts to solve the insoluble: 'Thought must break down soon in the attempt to co-ordinate the finite and the infinite.'[24]

It is generally recognized, however, that his other piece on Origen, 'Origen and the Beginnings of Christian Philosophy', has been the more influential of the two articles, perhaps because it was reprinted in one of his more popular books. This deals in its first part with Origen's early life and education, with his method of teaching, and with his condemnation by Justinian. In part two he turns to his philosophical treatise, 'On First Principles', and attempts to place this within the history of Christian thought. He claims that there are two overriding principles in Origen's teaching: '(1) that the whole world is

[53]

a manifestation of the goodness and righteousness of God in every detail; and (2) that the moral determination of each individual is a decisive element in the working out of the divine counsel'.[25] This assertion of the unity of all creation and the individuality of each human being is, he believes, of supreme importance in our understanding of Origen. It was this combination that led Westcott to describe Christianity as the 'Absolute Religion'.[26]

He then draws out the implications of these two principal ideas. One is that philosophy has a moral end: 'No teacher of the present day could insist with greater earnestness upon the importance of conduct than he does. There is absolutely nothing in which he does not see ethical influences.' Secondly, Christianity is a philosophy: 'it has for its domain every human interest and power ... it is capable of co-ordinating all thought and all experience. Faith is the foundation of knowledge.' Thirdly, reason cannot attain to knowledge of God on its own; this comes by revelation, which complements and crowns man's intellectual searching. Here, of course, Origen parted company with Plato. The stress on morality is important since it is only the 'pure in heart' who are able to receive the divine revelation. Finally, Origen was intensely aware of the reality of the spiritual world: 'He already lives and moves in it. Eternal objects, peoples, cities, are to him veils and symbols of invisible things. Phenomena are shadows, and he looks upon the substances by which they are cast.'[27] Here Origen's Platonism is strongly affirmed again.

While Westcott is expounding Origen, it is apparent that these are all deep convictions which he himself shared, and which were to become the foundation of his theological work and, indeed, of his whole life.

He then moves on, in what is perhaps the most striking passage in the essay, to point out Origen's relevance to the contemporary world:

With all his faults and shortcomings, he is the greatest representative of a type of Greek Christian thought which has not yet done its work in the West. By his sympathy with all effort, by his largeness of view, by his combination of a noble morality with a deep mysticism, he indicates, if he does not bring, the true remedy for the evils of that Africanism which has been dominant in Europe since the time of Augustine.[28]

There follows a sustained criticism of St Augustine, whose tragedy was that he had no real knowledge of Greek. Rather, he was a Latin thinker who regarded everything from the side of law, and not freedom, and who froze ideas into rigid shapes. What is more, the 'centre of his whole dogmatic theory is sin'.[29]

Westcott is sensitive to the weaknesses of Origen too, and concludes that he and Augustine were the 'representatives of two ages', responding to two very different crises, and that Augustine did in fact prepare the way for the Middle Ages. He is emphatic, however, that Augustine's heritage cannot help to solve the problems facing the Church of his day. It is rather the spirit of Origen which is needed now, who saw Christianity as 'the fulfilment of Philosophy . . . Human wisdom . . . is the school of the soul: Divine wisdom is the end. Faith, knowledge, wisdom – that, in his judgment, is the order of spiritual growth.' These are affirmations which need to be made again: 'We now seem to be entering again upon the controversy which he supported . . . And still, after sixteen hundred years, we have not yet made good the positions which he marked out as belonging to the domain of Christian philosophy.'[30]

Westcott's sympathetic account of Origen's life and thought is still regarded by patristic scholars as a valuable exposition of the mind and outlook of the great second-century scholar.

Westcott, then, found in Origen, and in the whole Alexandrian tradition, a positive attitude to knowledge and human speculation which he felt was lacking in so much of the Church of his own time. They reinforced that breadth of outlook that he had discovered in the fourth Gospel, where the divine Logos was active in all things, in the past and in the present, in the Church but also in the world. There could, therefore, be no dichotomy between theology and science, between the gospel and politics, between Christianity and other faiths. The Greek spirit would profoundly influence his theological speculation and his work as a bishop, and would inspire him in his determination to build bridges wherever people took up entrenched positions.

It is undeniable that there is an element of idealization in this love of all things Alexandrian. In this respect Westcott was very much of his age. Historians have detected in the last decades of the Victorian period, with all its rapid changes, an intensification of that nostalgia for a simpler age that was one of the characteristics of Victorian England. The interest in Alexandria that we saw in Newman in the 1830s had now become more widespread. In 1886 C. J. Bigg gave the Bampton lectures on *The Christian Platonists of Alexandria.* In a letter of 1893 William Bright, an Oxford Tractarian Professor, bemoaned the fact that 'it is the fashion . . . to exalt Alexandrianism, and depress, to the lowest depths, Augustinianism'.[31] In the twentieth century, too, there would continue to be a fascination with the northern Egyptian city, albeit from a very different perspective.[32] For Westcott it would always be 'that marvellous city . . . a meeting-place of the East and West – of old and new – the home of learning, of criticism, of syncretism . . . a unique example in the Old World of that mixture of races which forms one of the most important features of modern society'.[33]

4 *Christian Platonism*

In his 1925–6 Hulsean lectures, Dean Inge made a plea for the recognition of a third type of Christian thought and belief alongside the Catholic and Protestant, which he termed 'the religion of the Spirit'. He claimed that this strand was to be found in St Paul, St John, and in the Greek Fathers, but that it had been sadly neglected in the history of the English Church apart from in three or four periods. He characterized this form of Christianity in this way:

a spiritual religion, based on a firm belief in absolute and eternal values as the most real things in the universe – a confidence that these values are knowable by man – a belief that they can nevertheless be known only by whole-hearted consecration of the intellect, will, and affections to the great quest – an entirely open mind towards the discoveries of science – a reverent and receptive attitude to the beauty, sublimity, and wisdom of the creation . . . a complete indifference to the current valuations of the worldling.[34]

Inge had been a student of Westcott's at Cambridge, and his former teacher featured in his discussion as an exemplar of this 'third way'. Indeed, Westcott's teaching and example were clearly a major inspiration for the plea that the 'religion of the Spirit' was an idea whose time had come.

The origins of Westcott's Christian Platonism lie in his education at Birmingham and Cambridge, where the great classical authors dominated the curriculum. Looking back on his Cambridge years from Harrow, he wrote to Lightfoot that 'those hours which were spent over Plato and Aristotle have wrought that in me which I pray may never be done away'.[35] He remained in touch with this world at Harrow, where he taught classics, and it was during the Harrow years that he began the series of articles, later to be published as *Essays in the History of Religious Thought in the West*, which contain the essence of his distinctive Christian Platonist ideas.

He was already making connections between the Greek philosophers and his Christian faith as an undergraduate. He read a paper on 'The Theology of Aristotle' to the Philological Society, and wrote of wanting to 'publish something of Aristotle's'.[36] It is significant that he was an admirer of Aristotle at this time. It has been suggested that this corresponded with the period of his doubts about his faith, and that his eventual rejection of Aristotle's system of logic in favour of Plato's imaginative and poetic mythology is closely related to his rejection of the rigid dogma and systematizing of much contemporary theology.[37]

Westcott's essay on 'The Myths of Plato' shows his sympathy with the great philosopher's intuition that there are limits to what reason can apprehend, and his feeling for an unseen world behind the phenomena of the world. He found in the myths a 'devout recognition of an all-wise and all-present Providence' and an 'unfailing testimony to the religious wants of man'. In their concern with the great issues of creation, providence and immortality, they are 'an unconscious prophecy, of which the teaching of Christianity is the fulfilment'. Even the form of the myths reminds us of the historical shape of the Christian revelation. So 'Plato is an unconscious prophet of the Gospel. The Life of Christ is, in form no less than in substance, the Divine reality of which the Myths were an instructive foreshadowing . . . Plato points us to St John.'[38]

Plato was not alone in this respect. In his sympathetic essays on Aeschylus and Euripides Westcott suggests that they also had a role, admittedly a lesser one, in preparing the way for the Christian gospel. Aeschylus was the prophet who reminds us that the voice of law addresses us from Athens as well as from Jerusalem. He spoke of the reality of sin and the inevitable penalty it carries, and of the need of a divine deliverer to check and control the consequences of violated law.[39] Euripides, on the other hand, prepares the way for the coming of Christianity by his sympathy for all that is human, his recognition of the mystery of life, of suffering and of death.[40]

The connections were confirmed and reinforced by Westcott's reading in the Alexandrian Fathers. He found in Clement and Origen a firm grasp of the mutual influence of Christianity and the Neo-Platonic tradition. In his article on 'Philosophy' in Smith's 1863 *Dictionary of the Bible*, he quotes approvingly Clement's famous maxim that ancient philosophy in its purest and grandest form was 'a schoolmaster to bring men to Christ', and points out that in the porticoes of Eastern churches Pythagoras and Plato are pictured among those who prepared the way for Christianity.[41]

There were other aspects of the Platonic tradition, however, which had a profound influence on Westcott. David Newsome suggests that two of his most distinctive convictions derive from the tradition. One was his lifelong belief in the union of polarities. Truth was 'never to be found in the mean position, but always at the extremes'. The second is a consequence of this, namely, that the truth is to be found in the most improbable places, and especially in the argument of your opponent.[42] This is seen, for instance, in Westcott's interest in Positivism, which at first sight seems so opposed to all that Christianity stands for, but which he believed contained hidden truth for Christians. He once said: 'I have learnt some of my most precious lessons from those who would hold themselves to be bitter opponents.'[43] Newsome admits that these principles are remarkably similar both to Hegelianism and to F. D. Maurice's fundamental convictions, but believes that Westcott derived them from 'a recognised Platonic tradition'.[44]

Newsome also shows how Westcott's Platonism affected him in two other areas of his life. One was his Christian Socialism, where his understanding of socialism as the opposite of individualism derives from a view of society as a 'mighty organism directing or directed towards a moral end' which is 'very Platonic'. The other was through the Platonic maxim that 'a philosopher really has to be a saint', which he suggests underlies Westcott's lifelong self-denial and earnestness, which some found to be extreme.[45]

As we have seen, Westcott found the perfect marriage between the Platonic tradition and the Christian faith in the Alexandrian Fathers. There were two other periods in the history of the Church, however, from which he drew inspiration. One was the seventeenth century, and in particular the life and work of the Cambridge Platonist, Benjamin Whichcote. The Cambridge Platonists were a loose group of mostly university teachers who sought a middle way during the bitter controversies of the Restoration period when Laudians and Calvinists were involved in the theological disputes. Drawing on the Platonic tradition after centuries in which Aristotelian philosophy had been dominant, they represented Christianity as both intellectually defensible and spiritually satisfying. There was no dichotomy between faith and knowledge, reason and revelation, right doctrine and sound morals. They offered a restatement of Christian truth at a time of growing atheism and acute theological controversy.

Westcott discovered Benjamin Whichcote during the 1870s. He sent a copy of a paper on him to Lightfoot in the summer of 1877. The latter replied with obvious approval: 'It is a pleasant surprise to me ... to find that I have been a disciple of Whichcote without knowing it.'[46] It was doubtless the Cambridge connection that drew Westcott to Whichcote. He had been undergraduate, fellow and tutor at Emmanuel College, then tutor and Provost of King's College, and finally Vice-Chancellor of the University. It was, significantly, when Westcott became a fellow of King's that he delivered his paper on Whichcote at the opening of a new lecture room in the College in October 1885.

He sets Whichcote against the background of his time, when 'a larger, a more human, faith' was necessary, pointing out that he became Provost of King's in the year that Descartes published his *Principia Philosophiae* – 1644. He contrasts Whichcote's dictum, 'I act therefore I am' with the philosopher's famous maxim, 'I think therefore I am'.[47] At a time when both philosophers and theologians agreed in separating philosophy from religion, Whichcote appealed to reason, which in his most celebrated phrase was the candle of the Lord, lighted by God and lighting us to God, *res illuminata illuminans*.[48]

He highlights Whichcote's eirenical nature, and sees in him a fine embodiment of the Platonic virtue of openness to the views of your opponents. He quotes a contemporary judgement: 'Though Whichcote had a most profound and well-poised judgment yet was he of all men I ever knew the most patient to hear others differ from him, and the most easy to be convinced when good reason was offered; and ... more apt to be favourable to another man's reason than his own.'[49] This was all the more admirable since Whichcote came under increasing criticism from Puritans at Cambridge, and eventually was removed from his office as Provost at the Restoration and was forced to return to parish life.

He sees the foundation of Whichcote's teaching in the belief that 'man was made by God to know Him, and to become like Him'.[50] Man's ability to know God has not been obliterated by the Fall. Sin is unnatural, and in Christ God re-establishes his loving purpose. There is no sharp division between reason and revelation. In the life of faith, our reason is not to be laid aside, but rather is awakened and stimulated. Reason and faith are not to be separated.[51] The other pole of his teaching is the supremacy of the moral element: religion affects the whole person, and involves right relationships and the shaping of character. It is fulfilled in 'homely duties'.[52] Organized religion must be subservient to moral ends. True teachers 'are not masters, but helpers; they are not to make religion, but to shew it'.[53]

Westcott is aware of Whichcote's defects, and laments the fact that he had little permanent influence on English thought. He is convinced, however, that the principles he taught need to be applied widely in the contemporary world.

It is not difficult to see why Whichcote appealed to Westcott. His optimistic view of human nature, in sharp contrast to what the Calvinists taught, his positive attitude towards reason and human knowledge, and his emphasis on moral goodness as the *summum bonum* all found an echo in Westcott's own theology. Behind him, as with all the Cambridge Platonists, stood the ancient philosopher, whose teaching they believed was 'the most consistent and coherent *Metaphysicall Hypothesis*, that has yet been found out by the wit of man'.[54]

The other inspiration for Westcott's Platonism was the contemporary poet, Robert Browning. He discovered the poet in 1866,[55] when Browning's poetry was becoming immensely popular throughout the country. David Newsome points out that after 1868 'Browning Societies began to spring up like mushrooms in the night'.[56] Westcott soon became an enthusiast for his poetry, often quoting him in his sermons and addresses. In April 1884, when he received an Hon. D.D. at Edinburgh University, he was thrilled that the poet stood behind him at the ceremony, and spoke with him afterwards.[57] By a strange coincidence his last duty as Canon of Westminster was attending Browning's funeral.

His essay, 'On Some Points in Browning's View of Life', originated as a paper read to the Cambridge Browning Society. It begins with the definition of a poet as one 'who sees the infinite in things'.[58] It was clearly this aspect of Browning's art that appealed to him: the ability to see a vision of the eternal within the material and everyday, which is the essence of the Platonic outlook. 'There is an infinite, an eternal, meaning in all, and it is his office to make this intelligible to his students.'[59] Westcott argues that, like Wordsworth, Browning asserted the supremacy of feeling over knowledge, and that the keynote of his whole teaching is 'not knowledge, but love'.[60] He then quotes the well known lines from 'Death in the Desert', which was his favourite passage in Browning, as a kind of text for the whole essay:

> . . . Life, with all it yields of joy and woe,
> And hope and fear . . .
> Is just our chance o' the prize of learning love
> How love might be, hath been indeed, and is.[61]

Here, for him, is the kernel of Browning's view of life.

The remainder of the essay is a summary of what he saw as the most significant elements in Browning's philosophy of life. He pinpoints his conviction that life is a unity, within which each stage and each element in human nature contributes to the growth and maturing of the individual. He cites the poet's celebrated lines about old age as illustrative of this positive attitude:

> Grow old along with me!
> The best is yet to be,
> The last of life for which the first was made.[62]

Growth is the law of life, and the capacity for moral progress the essential characteristic of human beings. Our very limitations – our growing old, our doubts, our failures – can be the means by which we progress morally and spiritually. Westcott is appreciative of Browning's positive attitude towards doubt, and quotes again from 'Rabbi Ben Ezra':

> I prize the doubt,
> Low kinds exist without,
> Finished and finite clods, untroubled by a spark.[63]

The other aspect of Browning's thought which he dwells on is his optimism and hope. Browning is frank about the imperfections of human nature, and yet 'he still finds a spiritual power in him . . . which restores assurance as to the destiny of creation'.[64] He is convinced that life continues beyond death, and that therefore nothing good can be lost, as he expressed in another of his best-known passages:

> There never shall be one lost good! What was shall live as before;
> The evil is null, is nought, is silence implying sound . . .
> On earth the broken arcs: in heaven a perfect round.[65]

Surprisingly, he does not quote here the passage which perhaps encapsulates Browning's optimism about the goodness of life better than any other, and which was another of his favourite Browning quotations:

> This world's no blot for us
> Nor blank: it means intensely, and means good:
> To find its meaning is my meat and drink.[66]

Undergirding all these convictions for Browning is 'that Divine Love, of which love in man is at once the offspring and the evidence'.[67] The purpose of life is 'the learning love – the learning God – and that in a large degree through human fellowship'.[68]

[63]

It is apparent, as Newsome points out, that Westcott was selective in his reading of Browning, and in particular did not see, or refrained from commenting on, his strong revolt against some of the Victorian conventions.[69] Nor did he draw out in this essay Browning's conviction that the central truth of all history and experience is the incarnation. He does, however, emphasize the crucial role of the incarnation in the development of Christian art in the essay on 'The Relation of Christianity to Art', in which Browning has an important place. 'Christian Art is the interpretation of beauty in life under the light of the Incarnation. The ministry of the beautiful in every shape, in sound, in form, in colour, is claimed for God through man.'[70] One study of Browning's work claims that the incarnation is 'a central unifying concept' in his poetry,[71] which echoes William Temple – like Westcott a lover of Plato and Browning – who said of Browning that 'the climax of history, the crown of philosophy, and the consummation of poetry is unquestionably the Incarnation.'[72]

Sir William Richmond, who painted Westcott's portrait, made the interesting observation that there was a real affinity between the minds of the two men: 'the same love of the transcendental, the same effort to express thoughts scarcely touchable in so clumsy a vehicle as language relatively is, the same passionate love for all that belongs to our race – its faults, its struggles, enterprises, and failures – and the same keenness to unravel difficult knots'. He added that he perceived genius in Westcott in that 'the intuitive, the instinct, almost childlike, was allied in him to self mastery'.[73] This is a significant insight because in Browning's poems great importance is attached to people who experience life intuitively. A study of religious language in Browning's poems expresses his conviction in this way: 'to a few men, to those who can see deeper and to whom more is revealed . . . to the bard, the seer, the prophet, the saint, the lover, the painter, and the poet, to each God whispers something of his truth in a visionary moment of inspiration'.[74]

One final word must be said about Browning's optimism. In his old age Thomas Hardy mused on this aspect of his fellow poet: 'The longer

I live the more does Browning's character seem the literary puzzle of the nineteenth century. How could smug Christian optimism worthy of a dissenting grocer find a place inside a man who was so vast a seer and feeler when on neutral ground?'[75] It was not surprising that the great pessimist should find it hard to understand this aspect of Browning, but many literary critics of the later twentieth century, too, have struggled to account for his hopefulness and buoyancy in the face of life's struggles and challenges. It is one of the remarkable qualities of his work. What we may note in passing is that Westcott found in Browning, as in Origen and Whichcote, confirmation of that optimism about human nature that is so central a feature of his theological outlook.

It is impossible to overestimate the effect of the Platonic tradition on Westcott's thought. It helped to shape his theology and spirituality, and had a profound influence on his attitude to missiology and the other world faiths. His linking of Plato and St John – 'the Word for which Plato longed . . . has been given to us in Him Whom St John has made known'[76] – gave a breadth and an optimism to his outlook which was at odds with that of many of his Christian contemporaries. It was his sympathy with this strand in the Christian tradition that led him to reject the pessimism of the Augustinianism that had dominated the Christian imagination for so long, and to offer a very different model.

There was, however, a downside to this. The abstract and speculative nature of the Platonic tradition may have contributed to that impreciseness of thought which contemporaries sometimes levelled against Westcott. One of these, William Bright, recalled Westcott taking his reader 'through a golden Platonic mist; I was not sure where I stood, or what definite objects were within view'.[77] It is perhaps significant that two of Westcott's mentors in this tradition were accused of a similar obscurity of thought. Westcott himself quotes Whichcote's tutor at Emmanuel as saying of the young undergraduate, 'I remember I then thought you somewhat cloudy and obscure in your expressions',[78] while Sir William Richmond believed that the remarkable similarity between Browning and Westcott 'rendered to the writing of the poet as well as the theologian a certain air of symbolic obscurity – a style difficult to follow because the ideas were so remote and so unusual'.[79]

The whole question of Westcott's style and alleged impreciseness of thought is one of the important issues in his life and work, and it becomes crucial as we turn to consider his theology.

4

THEOLOGY: MYSTERY, INCARNATION, FULFILMENT

Those who are fortunate enough to think of truth and error as white and black, and as no less easily distinguishable, do not take kindly to people who seem to believe in varying shades of grey.[1]

1 Under a cloud

Of all Westcott's contributions to Christian thought it is his theological output which is the most difficult to evaluate. This is partly because the most acute and wounding criticisms of him have focused on this aspect of his work. His reputation as a theologian has never really recovered from the celebrated observation of one of his contemporaries, H. P. Liddon: 'When there was a dense fog in London, Liddon remarked that "it is commonly attributed to Dr Westcott having opened his study window in Westminster".'[2]

The author of this jibe was the leader of the Tractarian party in the Church of England, whose theological convictions and style were poles apart from Westcott's. There were other contemporaries, however, even amongst his admirers who believed that Westcott could be obscure and difficult in the expression of his thought. It is Liddon's wounding dictum which has been used to put the crucial question mark against Westcott's reputation as a theologian.

The cloud – or we might say, the fog – has never really lifted. When the Westcott Memorial lectures were arranged fifty or so years after his death to evaluate his general reputation, there was no lecture in the series on his theology – a highly significant omission. Indeed, one lecture in the series contained a criticism of his theology which was almost as dismissive as that of Liddon: 'His theology is a mystery to me in the highest, as well as in a lower, sense . . . to my mind in comparison with Westcott Maurice is clarity and coherence incarnate'.[3] Since then, there have been two attempts to rehabilitate Westcott as a theologian.[4] Both contain helpful insights, but they have not affected the general perception of him as a flawed theologian. Thus, when a leading Evangelical theologian at the end of the twentieth century published his *Handbook of Anglican Theologians*,[5] Westcott was among those omitted.

It is very necessary, then, that there should be a re-evaluation of Westcott's contribution to English theology. The difficulties which some have perceived must not be glossed over, but an attempt must be made to be fair to the originality and depth of his thought in its nineteenth-century context, and to his influence on the later Church.

It is also important, however, to recognize the development in his theological thinking. His appointment to Westminster Abbey, and then later to Durham, profoundly affected his theological perspective. His theology now becomes much more contextual, to use contemporary jargon, and the style and content changes radically. This shift in his thinking has often been ignored. We shall take it seriously by devoting a separate chapter to what may be termed his practical theology. His contribution to theological thought cannot be fairly judged without taking into account its wide-ranging nature, the academic and the practical.

2 The limitations of theology

Westcott's distinctive theological outlook was shaped by certain fundamental convictions about the nature of theology. It is important to grasp these before we look at his exposition of the central Christian doctrines.

He was convinced, first of all, of the limitations of systematic theology. From an early age he formed the opinion that the Bible was misused as a body of dogma. At the age of twenty-one he wrote to his future wife about his unhappiness with the Thirty-Nine Articles:

> I have at times fancied that it is presumptuous in us to attempt to define, and to determine what Scripture has not defined; to limit when Scripture has placed no boundary; to exact what the Apostles did not require; to preach explicitly what they applied practically. The whole tenor of Scripture seems to me opposed to all dogmatism, and full of all application; to furnish us with rules of life, and not food for reason . . . I only wish men would pay more attention to acting and less to dogmatising.[6]

The background to this is his growing familiarity at this time with the teaching of the two main parties in the Church of England. Both Evangelicals and Tractarians had a well-developed and coherent doctrinal system, and the tension between the two would be a significant feature of the life of the Church of England over the coming forty years. The young Westcott, struggling at the time with his doubts about the Christian faith itself, concludes that neither of these parties can satisfy him since they have both constructed theological systems which are inconsistent with the spirit of Scripture. An important aspect of his critique is that theology must be directed towards practical ends rather than being purely speculative – another of his strongest beliefs.

He was influenced in this fundamental conviction about the nature of theology by a remark made at a lecture in Birmingham when he was a schoolboy at King Edward's School. The headmaster, Prince Lee, encouraged senior boys to attend lectures on a wide variety of subjects in the city. Westcott later recalled a series of lectures on painting by a man called Haydon, in one of which the lecturer pointed to a beautiful chalk-drawing of Dentatus by his pupil: 'Look, it has no outline. There is no outline in nature.' Westcott repeats this saying and adds: 'Is it not a parable worth pondering?'[7]

He never forgot this epigram and repeated it in later life in contexts which show that it reinforced his early scepticism about dogmatic systems. He wrote in a letter of 1882: 'The Truth seems to me to be so overwhelmingly vast and manifold that I shrink from drawing any outline except provisionally, lest I should exclude something or add something in opposition to Divine teaching.'[8] There is another echo of the phrase in his Westminster Abbey sermons of 1885–6, in which he focuses on the doctrine of the incarnation and its implications for contemporary life and thought. He nevertheless disclaims any attempt at a full, systematic treatment of the doctrine:

> We shall not strive to gain any completeness of technical definition on the doctrine of the Incarnation. We acknowledge indeed that outlines are a necessity for man's representation of the truth of things; but they are a concession to his weakness and a symbol of it. There is no outline in nature, and no form of words can adequately express a spiritual reality.[9]

Westcott remained remarkably faithful to his early intuition. He never formulated his thought into any kind of systematic theology because such systems claimed too much for what was only one formulation of the truth, and often became lifeless formulae, unrelated to real life and experience. His theology was essentially biblical in character rather than dogmatic. The closest he came to setting his theology out in a systematic way was in *The Gospel of Life*, but it is very significant that in the preface he disclaims any such pretension: 'My desire has been to encourage patient reflection, to suggest lines of enquiry, to indicate necessary limits to knowledge, and not to convey formulas or ready-made arguments. Thoughts cannot be transferred: they must be appropriated.'[10] The final sentence indicates that he believed it is never possible to eliminate personal considerations from theological reflection. It is very characteristic of him that for the most part his theology is set out in the more personal, intimate forms of sermons and addresses rather than in lengthy theological books.

A very significant factor in all this is his early concentration upon the New Testament in his studies. It is here that we find the seedbed of his later theological development. He found within the New Testament that the essence of religion lies in relationships, between human beings and God, and between human beings themselves. This was true, above all, of the Johannine writings which became a special source and inspiration for his theology. It was precisely this personal note which he believed was missing when theology was formulated into dogmatic systems: knowledge of facts replaced a relationship with the living Christ, which is at the very heart of authentic religious faith. This comes out in a passage on the appearance of the risen Jesus to Thomas in John 20.24ff. in which he comments on the words, 'Blessed are they who have not seen and yet have believed' (20.19): 'The substance of faith is not a fact which we cannot explain away, or a conclusion which we cannot escape, but the personal apprehension of a living, loving Friend.'[11]

The point is made even more acutely in a remarkable passage about the purpose of studying Christian doctrine:

Christian Doctrine is designed to direct and sustain us in our efforts to hold a personal and living intercourse with a personal and living Lord. True doctrine is not an end in itself: it cannot carry us beyond the region of the intellect; and religion belongs to the whole life, our will answering to the will of God.

The passage goes on to contrast personal faith with the clinging to doctrinal formulae:

All formulas are of the nature of outlines: they define by exclusion as well as by comprehension; and no object in life is isolated. Our premisses in spiritual subjects therefore are necessarily incomplete and even logical deductions from them may be false. Thus the scholastic theology of the 13th and of the 17th century was found to fail in view of the facts of life; and systems of doctrine must fail so far as they do not minister to the present fellowship of the believer with his Lord.[12]

We find that the primacy of this personal relationship is affirmed in his earliest essay in theology, *The Gospel of the Resurrection* (1866). He argues that no student of the New Testament can deny that

> the earliest known description of a Christian is 'one who *believes in Christ*', and not 'one who *believes Christ*' . . . a Christian is essentially one who throws himself with absolute trust upon a living Lord, and not simply one who endeavours to obey the commands and follow the example of a dead Teacher.

Through the study of the Scriptures and of the history of the Church, the discovery will be made 'that we are the inheritors of a life and not of a system, of a life which is a pledge of the unity of all that is seen and temporal with that which is unseen and eternal'.[13]

Just six months before he died Westcott drew out the distinction between personal faith and taking refuge in systems in an amusing aside to one of his archdeacons. Explaining why he had entrusted delivery of a letter to a person rather than to the postal system, he commented: 'Faith in persons is stronger than faith in systems'![14]

Any interpretation of Westcott's theology must take seriously his misgivings about the whole theological enterprise. It is ironic therefore that the only published study[15] flies in the face of this fundamental tenet, and treats Westcott as a systematic theologian of almost Barthian subtlety and complexity.

A second deep conviction of Westcott was that theology must be free from the spirit of controversy. As an undergraduate at Cambridge in the 1840s he soon became aware of the polarization of theological opinions within the Church of England, and of the tensions between Anglicans and Roman Catholics at this time. His immediate reaction was one of revulsion. He wrote to his future wife in 1846:

> I cannot myself reconcile the spirit of controversy and that of Christian faith. No two things seem more opposed, and I earnestly

pray that we may be kept from its influence. Many of our noblest spirits have become gradually absorbed in its stream, and from earnest, active ministers turned to be shrewd, conceited debaters.[16]

He held firmly to this conviction throughout his life. The spirit of controversy, he believed, was damaging both to the cause of theology and to the wider mission of the Church.

In 1877 he wrote to his close friend, A. S. Farrar: 'I am sure that, as charged with the office of teachers, our duty is to speak with simplicity as we see the truth – a very little of the truth – and to refuse to enter into controversy. Let Scripture slowly speak its full message.'[17] Two years later in the 'Notice' to the fourth edition of his *The Gospel of the Resurrection*, he acknowledges certain changes he has made in the book in response to the arguments of his critics. He then adds:

But I have made the changes silently, for I cannot think that the pursuit of the highest Truth is a matter for personal controversy. No one, I feel, has a monopoly of Truth. It is enough that in defending the Truth which we know, we never consciously underrate or neglect the objections of opponents.[18]

In 1897, speaking to a Diocesan Conference on the hopes for the reunion of Christendom, he says of the relationship between the Church of England and other churches:

Above all things we shall avoid theological controversy. Controversy always accentuates details and generally turns upon them. But we shall spare no pains to understand the difficulties of those who differ from us and to present our own Faith in its completeness *living the Truth in love* (Eph. iv.15).[19]

As we saw in the previous chapter, he had been deeply influenced by the Platonic dictum that opposing views were always closer to one another than was supposed, and this spirit informed his whole theological outlook. For him it was almost an article of faith that 'a mere controversialist cannot be a real Theologian'.[20] The truth was to be found rather in the combination of insights arrived at by those in opposing theological camps. From his days at Harrow onwards he saw his role as a mediator between opposing theological parties on one hand, and between Christian orthodoxy and contemporary scepticism on the other, and in the conflicts and controversies which punctuated the life of the Church of England in the second half of the nineteenth century he is usually to be found in a reconciling role. There are, indeed, few major theologians of this period who are as eirenical as Westcott, a fact which has rarely ever been recognized.

This aspect of his theology is illuminated by his use of the word 'sympathy'. In his unpublished study of Westcott, O'Dea goes so far as to argue that this was for him a 'theological principle'.[21] He sees this in Westcott's early Cambridge days, where he is looking for points of connection with other people and other thinkers, and he also quotes from an unpublished sermon of 1894 in which he recommends 'a sympathy which entered into the feelings of another', so that it became one's own.[22] Westcott certainly used the word in several significant contexts. It was the word which came to him when he was trying to define the secret of the teaching method of his old headmaster, Prince Lee – 'sympathy as the spring of the teacher's influence'.[23] More significantly, he saw it as a *sine qua non* for the student of Christian doctrine, who

> will be filled with sympathy for every genuine endeavour towards the embodiment of right opinion . . . It is easier and . . . more impressive to make a peremptory and exclusive statement and to refuse to allow any place beside it to divergent expositions; but this show of clearness and power is dearly purchased at the cost of the ennobling conviction that the whole truth is far greater than our individual minds. He who believes that every judgment on the highest matters different from his own is simply a heresy must have a mean idea of the Faith.[24]

[74]

The Cambridge spirit embodied this eirenical outlook: there were no sharp divisions between disciplines and schools of thought:

> A Cambridge man, if he enters into the spirit of the place, can easily gain a sympathetic apprehension of opinions which he does not hold, and of studies which he does not pursue. Moving in a society where thought is fullest he is enabled to overcome the temptation to be one-sided or arrogant.[25]

He saw universities as 'schools of sympathy and enthusiasm',[26] and therefore as the right context for theological training of ordinands. Finally, we may note that Westcott regarded this as a biblical principle, implicit, for example, in the New Testament narratives of the resurrection where the risen Christ is recognized only by disciples: 'The revelation of the Risen Christ . . . is of necessity a revelation to believers. Sympathy is the imperative condition of apprehending the Divine Presence.'[27]

One of the most obvious examples of this principle in Westcott's own theology is his positive attitude towards apparently hostile, atheistic movements like Comtism, from which he endeavoured to learn lessons for the contemporary Church.

The third principle which underlies Westcott's theological work is the recognition of the element of mystery in religion. This is of crucial significance since it touches on the issue of his alleged obscurity.

O'Dea provides an important insight here by showing that Westcott was helped through the period of his doubts as an undergraduate by an acceptance of the necessity of mystery. He quotes from an unpublished diary which Westcott kept in these Cambridge years:

> a mind cannot comprehend the counsels of infinity . . . we humanize divine things: by lowering them to the standard of human credibility.
>
> (17 January 1847)

How utterly false the dogma, 'where mystery begins, religion ends'
... Just the reverse is the case, I feel.

(16 May 1849)

Wild as my doubts are, I cannot but feel that the NT 'finds' me; and
that with its deepest mysteries – but as mysteries, not as dogmas.

(20 May 1849)[28]

This discovery was to inform and shape his whole theological outlook.
If it was impossible for the human mind fully to grasp divine truth,
then there were inevitably limits to what theology could achieve. In the
preface to *The Gospel of Life* he writes of how in his years as a university
teacher he has been constantly aware of 'the trials, the dangers, the
hopes, of teachers. The world is not clear or intelligible. If we are to
deliver our message as Christians we must face the riddles of life and
consider how others have faced them.' He repeats the point later: 'we
"walk by faith" in the face of riddles which remain to the last un-
answered'.[29] A similar point is made in the first of a series of addresses
given to ordinands in 1888. Expounding the Collect for Ordination,
which speaks of Christians being 'regenerate and forgiven', he comments:

> Life has secrets which we cannot explain. We do not divest our lives
> of mystery when we set aside the teaching of our Faith. We are
> beset by that we in one sense, if I may use the paradox, transcends
> experience.[30]

There is an early sermon of his on the Trinity which acknowledges
the mystery of God. It contains – unusually for Westcott – two stories,
one of which tells of a king who asked the wisest man in his kingdom to
tell him what God is. The wise man asked for a day to think over the
answer, then two more days. At last he said to the king: 'Ah, sire, the
more I think of God, the harder do I find it to understand Him.'[31]
Much later in his life, in an address on the spirit in which Christian

[76]

doctrine must be studied, he urges the necessity for a vivid awareness at all times 'of the difficulty, the mysteriousness, the inexhaustible fulness, the practical significance of the subject with which he deals'.[32] It is highly characteristic of Westcott that a recognition of the 'practical significance' of doctrine should sit alongside his emphatic awareness of the difficulty of the whole task.

An important consequence of recognizing the essential mystery at the heart of existence is an acceptance of the inadequacy of language to express this mystery. Every human attempt to express the infinite must be flawed. Words must never be identified with the reality to which they point: they always fall short. These are principles which Westcott reiterated throughout his life and work. It will be recalled that when he was writing of Origen's theological unorthodoxy he defended him by claiming that he was merely trying to express the inexpressible: 'Thought must break down soon in the attempt to co-ordinate the finite and the infinite.'[33] This was something of which Westcott himself was continually aware.

It is expressed in his earliest published essay. In a passage on the way in which our understanding of God changes as knowledge grows, he comments: 'On such a subject all language, all thought, is necessarily inadequate and figurative.'[34] In an exposition of the doctrine of the incarnation in the 1880s he is aware, as we have seen, of the inadequacy of the language he uses fully to express this most important of all the Christian doctrines: 'We shall not strive to gain any completeness of technical definition on the doctrine of the Incarnation . . . There is no outline in nature.'[35] Above all, it is expressed most memorably in the address he gave at Cambridge in 1882 and at Durham in 1891 on the spirit in which doctrine should be studied. After insisting on the need for precision in the use of theological language he speaks of the necessary corollary of this for the student:

he will soon be profoundly impressed by a sense of the inadequacy of human language to express without defect and without exaggeration

[77]

the infinite Truth for which he is feeling . . . Our vision is not direct but mediate. The image on which we look conveys some features of the reflected object, but it cannot convey others. It represents in two dimensions . . . what is in three.

There must be caution in all attempts to attain clarity of language lest words be identified with the reality to which they point:

> I do not wish to encourage the too seductive belief that we can use any words as coextensive with the things which they indicate. On the contrary the very clearness which we gain at the price of limitation constrains us to look beyond all present words and thoughts to that which underlies and reaches beyond them.[36]

This whole passage is crucial for our understanding of Westcott's deep sense of the inadequacy of theological language to express the mystery at the heart of the universe. It permeates his written work and explains his reticence to define, and to some degree his lack of clarity at times. It is an important factor to remember in any evaluation of his alleged obscurity in theology.

It should be clear now that there was a sense in which Westcott was a reluctant theologian. He was sceptical of the value of any kind of systematic theology, unhappy about the polarization of opinion amongst theologians, and most important of all he was aware of the limitations of theological language. Academic theology, he believed, too easily obscured that personal relationship between the Creator and human beings which was at the heart of biblical faith. It also overlooked the fundamental biblical principle that faith must be expressed in practice rather than in speculation.

Westcott's distinctive perspective on theology is well set out in an ordination sermon on the call of the prophet Isaiah, in which he argues for a sense of awe and wonder in contemporary devotion and life:

> There is, I think, great danger lest the realism, the externality, the earthliness which have spread over modern life and thought should

dominate our religion. We are impatient of indefiniteness, of obscurity, of indecision; we are impatient of mystery, of reserve, of silence. We are tempted to treat divine things with a strange familiarity, to use human modes of conception and feeling and representation . . . We draw sharp outlines which can have no existence in the brightness which is about the throne. So it comes to pass that symbols, outward acts, formulas, the Holy Sacraments themselves in many cases, tend to confine and narrow the devotion which they were designed to enlarge. But we cannot rest with impunity in that which is of this world. So to rest is to lose the highest.[37]

3 *The central truth: incarnation*

We have argued that it is a misunderstanding of Westcott's whole approach to attempt to reconstruct a systematic theology from his work. He himself did not believe there was any value in such an enterprise, and any exposition of his theology which treats him as a systematic theologian is necessarily flawed. In this respect Olofsson's lengthy work is of limited value, although there are aspects of Westcott's thought which he illuminates.

In order to gain a snapshot of his particular theological style and tone, however, we will look at his exposition of the three central Christological affirmations in the Christian tradition: incarnation, atonement, and resurrection. The New Testament was always the starting point for his theological reflection, and he has something distinctive to say on each of these central doctrines.

It is significant that when he attempts to define what Christian doctrine is he virtually equates it with the exposition of the truth of the incarnation:

Christian Doctrine is . . . the partial and progressive approximation towards the complete intellectual expression of the Truth manifested to men once for all in the Incarnation. That one Supreme Fact contains all Christian Doctrine; and all separate dogmas contribute towards the understanding of it.

This is reiterated with greater clarity later in the same address: 'Christian Doctrine . . . is an interpretation of the facts of life in the light of the Incarnation, and of the Incarnation in the light of the facts of life.'[38]

In Westcott's writings the incarnation is variously described as the 'central fact' or the 'central event' in the life of the world, as '*the* fact of human life', as 'the central truth in the experience of men', and as 'the master-truth of life'.[39] It is important to note, however, that his use of the term 'incarnation' is not always consistent. He uses it most often in the accepted sense, as referring to the belief that in Jesus Christ God assumes our human nature. There are times, however, when it refers to the whole Christ event, not only his birth and life but also his death and resurrection. There is an imprecision in his use of language which is very typical of him.

It was the incarnation in the narrower sense which was the basis for his deep conviction that Christianity was at heart a personal relationship rather than a body of dogma:

> *The Word was God, and the Word became flesh.* This being so, it is clear that Christianity is not essentially a law for the regulation of our conduct: not a philosophy for the harmonious co-ordination of the facts of experience under our present forms of thought: not a system of worship by which men can approach their Maker in reverent devotion . . . But Christ Himself, His Person and His Life, in time and beyond time, and not any scheme of doctrine which He delivered, is the central object and support of Faith.[40]

As we have seen earlier, it was this personal dimension to faith which he believed had been lost in the theological controversies of the age, and which he was concerned to recover. It is this concern which lies behind his frequent characterization of the incarnation as a 'fact' as opposed to a speculation or a dogma.

The incarnation was also important to Westcott as the supreme example of the reconciliation of opposing and seemingly irreconcilable elements in human life.

> In that fact the three antitheses which underlie all human existence are seen to be reconciled, the antithesis of the seen and the unseen . . . the antithesis of the finite and the infinite . . . the antithesis of man and God . . . and it does not appear that any other reconciliation would have been possible.[41]

The same point is made in his exposition of the 'The Word became flesh' (John 1.14) in his commentary on John's Gospel, a phrase which 'affirms once for all the reconciliation of the opposite elements of the final antithesis of life and thought, the finite and the infinite'.[42] 'Reconciliation' is a key word if we are to understand Westcott's theology, and indeed his whole life, and it is clear that he saw this doctrine as a supreme illustration of this.

Reconciliation is the key motif in his exposition of the meaning of incarnation. First, it embodied the supreme truth that God had reconciled human beings to himself by bridging the gulf between the divine and the human. In an address given in the 1880s he relates Jesus' words, 'I am the Way' (John 14.6), to the general loss of a sense of purpose amongst religious people:

> We may not be able to tell whither we are going, but it is enough that Christ has bridged over the chasm between earth and heaven, and that as we advance along the way which He made, and which He is, we shall sooner or later be admitted to the vision of God and reflect the brightness of His glory.[43]

[81]

We may note the image of the bridge here, which recalls Westcott's intense interest in and knowledge of the bridges in his diocese and elsewhere, and which we have suggested is of symbolic significance if we are to understand the man and his work. The image is also implied in a passage in *The Gospel of Life*, where he asserts that the broken connection between God and humanity is re-established by the incarnation of the Logos, which is an absolutely unique idea, without parallel in any other religious tradition: 'The essence of the idea of the Incarnation lies not in the recognition of a distinct divine person, but in the personal and final union of the Godhead and humanity.'[44] In an ordination address in 1888 the point is made that God's taking of humanity to himself means that all nature and history are capable of becoming a means of revelation, and the address concludes with the well-known dicta of Irenaeus: 'The vision of God is the life of man: that is the fountain of knowledge. A living man is the glory of God: that is the inspiration of godliness.'[45] Here we are reminded that in his insistence on the reconciliation of the divine and human in Christ Westcott is indebted not only to the fourth Gospel but to the Greek theological tradition.

The second great truth expressed in the doctrine of incarnation was that a new relationship had been made possible between human beings. As a consequence of the divine initiative they are now bound together in a new solidarity. This has wide and far-reaching consequences for Christian practice. The conviction, however, is based firmly on the 'fact' of the incarnation:

> If then we pass from the intuitional to the historical elements of religion, in order to realise the practical effect of belief upon conduct, it becomes evident that if we hold that the Son of God took man's nature upon Him, we recognise a new and ineffaceable relation between man and man. We are assured by that fact that what binds us together is stronger than all that tends to separate us . . . that the unity of the race is something more than an abstraction.[46]

Westcott would spend the last two decades of his life working out the implications of this conviction in the arena of national and international events, and we shall evaluate his achievements in the discussion of his practical theology. One aspect of this solidarity was the new relationship between human beings and the natural world which contemporary scientific discoveries were pointing towards, and this too Westcott would explore in his later years.

It was these two aspects of the incarnation which he dwelt on to the exclusion of almost everything else. He had no interest in the more speculative aspects of the doctrine. He never concerned himself, for instance, with the question of the relationship between the divine and human natures in Christ, which had preoccupied the early Fathers, nor with the idea of incarnation as a self-limitation or *kenosis* of the divine Logos, which his former pupil, Charles Gore, developed in the 1890s. It is true that Westcott once set out a programme for a detailed study of the New Testament Christology,[47] but none of his works contains this kind of systematic enquiry. He also shows relatively little interest in either the life or teaching of Jesus in the Synoptic Gospels, and seems to have been quite unaffected by the vogue in the 1860s and 1870s for lives or biographies of Jesus. One of his students at Auckland later remembered that he had been 'very clear that the Sermon on the Mount was not, as so many people say, the essence of the Gospel . . . "it is not a Gospel, but a Law . . . there is nothing in it to lift a man outside himself, to teach him that he is dependent or that the work has been done for him"'.[48]

His Jesus was emphatically the Jesus of the fourth Gospel. There is a strong affirmation of the reality of the Word made flesh, even of a living person walking the earth, but the major theme in his teaching is the presentation of the living Christ who calls us into a relationship with him in the present. Knowing what Jesus said or did is no substitute for this personal relationship. So in an exposition of the saying of Jesus in John 14.9, 'He that hath seen me hath seen the Father', he affirms that the life, works and words of Jesus are 'not only to describe the object of

[83]

our love and worship and faith, but actually to present Him, so that we may never lose His living Presence'.[49]

His presentation of the doctrine of the incarnation and its centrality in his teaching sets him aside from the two main parties in the Victorian Church. In general, the Evangelicals had little feeling for an incarnational theology, centring very strongly on the atonement and work of Christ. On the other hand, the Tractarians did value the incarnation as a reaction against Evangelical teaching, but dwelt much more on the divinity rather than on the humanity of Christ.

In fact, in his constant repetition of the incarnation as a twofold reconciliation, Westcott was focusing on the two aspects of the doctrine which he believed had been neglected by contemporary theologians. Some have criticized him for being so repetitive. He would have replied that it is valid to go on repeating the two or three central beliefs which really matter. The overriding importance of understanding faith as a personal relationship with a living Lord, and of working out the practical implications of the divine taking of our human nature, became almost obsessions which gave his theology a very distinctive tone.

Two other aspects of his perspective on the incarnation must be mentioned: the influence upon him of the medieval theologian, Duns Scotus, and the concept of 'Christus Consummator'. In a sermon preached in Durham Cathedral a few months after Westcott's death, his lifelong friend, A. S. Farrar, recalled a conversation in the examination room at Peterborough twenty-five years earlier in which Westcott was enthusing about Duns Scotus' view of the incarnation. When Farrar expressed the view that it could not be squared with the views of St Paul, Westcott paused, absorbed in thought for a moment and then said, 'But does it not embody the ideas of St John?'[50] Farrar expressed the view that the medieval Franciscan was 'one great philosophical stimulant' to Westcott's mind, and that his influence is seen in the way in which in his later years the incarnation became the centre of his theology.

Most Western theology since Augustine had understood the

incarnation as being a response to the fall of man. It was a divine restoration of the original harmonious relationship between God and human beings. Hence, the saying *felix culpa* of the fall: sin had necessitated the incarnation, and so was a blessing in disguise. This was the view of Aquinas, for instance. Duns Scotus (1264–1308), a near contemporary of Aquinas, was one of the first to set out an alternative view. He believed that the incarnation was independent of the fall. Even if man had never sinned, God the Son would still have become incarnate in order to perfect humanity by elevating it into union with God. God's love alone is the explanation of the incarnation: he simply wills to have co-lovers in his love. He found biblical support for this in Colossians and Ephesians, but its origin was in the teaching of St Francis, and it was to become a distinguishing feature of Franciscan theology and spirituality.

Westcott sets out the support for this view in the essay, 'The Gospel of Creation', appended to his commentary on the Johannine epistles.[51] In a careful, exhaustive review of the evidence he shows that the idea is first found in the twelfth century, and is debated in the schools of theology in the thirteenth century and again in the Reformation period. It is the Franciscans, however, who champion the belief. He alludes only briefly to Duns Scotus, whom he quotes as saying: 'The Incarnation of Christ was not foreseen as a contingent event . . . but was seen by God directly . . . as an end from eternity . . .'; and 'from the first He wills the glory of the soul of Christ before He foresees that Adam will fall'.[52] Westcott argues that recent scientific discoveries about the origin of the universe and the age of man have made it an important issue again: 'We must look to the perfection and not only to the redemption of man . . . We cannot conceive that a being capable of knowing God and of being united with him should not have been destined to gain that knowledge, to realise that union.'[53] He has to concede that there is very little biblical support for such a view – he does not develop his earlier suggestion that it is the Johannine teaching – but significantly he finds support for it in some of the Greek Fathers.

[85]

Westcott soon came to believe that this view of the incarnation made possible a Copernican revolution in theological understanding. He tried to define this in his Westminster Abbey sermons of 1885–86. Contemporary teaching on the person of Christ was inadequate, he claimed: 'The Incarnation is commonly made to depend upon the Fall. And the whole tenour [*sic*] of revelation, as I conceive, leads us to regard the Incarnation as inherently involved in the Creation . . . The fitness and the necessity of the Incarnation exist therefore from the moment when man was made.'[54] The conclusion he draws is that there must be a radical shift in theological emphasis:

> Looking to the Incarnation as the crown of Creation we have found the true centre of the system in which we are set to work, even God and not man, love and not sin, the Creation which was the expression of the Father's will, and not the Fall which was alien from it.[55]

He was quite clear that this represented a major break with much traditional theology:

> So at last our Theology gains a transformation like that which was achieved in astronomy by the conception of Copernicus; it becomes Theocentric, while before it was anthropocentric: the ruling idea is not the self-assertion of man but the loving will of God.[56]

He once remarked that the real difference between Cambridge and Oxford theology was that 'We . . . are Scotists by nature . . . they are Thomists.'[57]

It is now clear that A. S. Farrar was accurate in his observation about the influence of Duns Scotus on Westcott. It may be remarked that in all this Westcott was engaging in the kind of theological speculation which we have claimed he usually avoided. He was himself aware of this charge, and closes the essay referred to earlier by affirming that this was in effect a very practical doctrine, very closely related to the 'great

[86]

problems which seem likely to grow more urgent every day'.[58] If this is a typically vague allusion by Westcott, it is nevertheless clear that moving the centre of theology from man's sinfulness to God's love would have profound consequences. This was the position taken by F. D. Maurice. With both men it led to accusations that they did not take the fact of sin seriously enough.

We see Westcott's optimism about human nature in his development of the concept of 'Christus Consummator', which is the other distinctive aspect of his understanding of incarnation. He expounded this in his Westminster sermons of 1885–86, which are based on an exposition of the Letter to the Hebrews. He sees the challenges facing the recipients of the Letter as corresponding with contemporary challenges to faith. These must be faced with a quiet confidence and with a willingness to surrender some earlier convictions if the new revelation which Christ brings is to be received. In this situation he claims that the special word the Spirit of God is speaking to the Church is not as in earlier days 'Christus Consolator' but rather 'Christus Consummator':

> Sin, suffering, sorrow, are not the ultimate facts of life. These are the work of an enemy; and the work of our God and Saviour lies deeper. The Creation stands behind the Fall, the counsel of the Father's love behind the self-assertion of man's wilfulness. And I believe that if we are to do our work we must learn to think, not only of the redemption of man, but also of the accomplishment of the Divine purpose for all that God made. We must learn to think of that *summing up of all things in Christ,* in the phrase of St Paul, which crowns the last aspirations of physicist and historian with a final benediction. We must dare . . . to look beyond Christ the Consoler to Christ the Fulfiller.[59]

Behind the idea is the conviction that Jesus is the archetype of man, the true Man. He has realized human life as it was meant to be and offered a perfect life to God. A key verse is Hebrews 2.10: 'For it became him, for whom are all things, and through whom are all things, in bringing many sons unto glory, to make the author of their salvation perfect through sufferings' (RV). In an additional note on this verse, Westcott claims that in his life as a human being Christ 'fulfilled in a true human life the destiny of man personally', and in his life as Son of Man he 'fulfilled in His life, as Head of the race, the destiny of humanity by redemption and consummation'.[60] Olofsson finds another source of the concept in the Letter to the Ephesians, especially in Ephesians 1.10, in which Paul speaks of God's purpose 'to sum up all things in Christ, the things in the heavens, and the things upon the earth' (RV).[61] The key Greek word here is ἀνακεφαλαιώσθαι, a word beloved of the Greek Fathers, and of Irenaeus in particular, for whom it is a central theological concept. In his exegesis of Ephesians 1.10, Westcott refers to Tertullian, Irenaeus, Jerome, Justin Martyr, and Origen, suggesting that these were all sources of the concept.

In the second series of his Westminster sermons he attempts to draw out the implications of this belief for the life of the Church. It is, he argues, a positive belief which should give Christians confidence and hope when faced with trials and challenges to their faith. Christ the Fulfiller is an image 'not only to give comfort, but to enlarge hope'. For those 'who will raise their eyes to Christ the Fulfiller . . . nothing in human experience can come as an unwelcome surprise. He, Son of man, Son of God, will bear, He has borne, though we see it not through the mists of days and years, all things to their goal, *Christus Consummator*'.[62]

One of the positive things about this idea for Westcott was that it enabled him to respond positively to the challenge of evolution. In his sermon on 'Incarnation and Nature' he pointed out how the new scientific teaching had revealed in quite new ways the fact of our union with the whole of creation, and had shed new light on the biblical doctrine of man as the crown and king of creation.[63] The humanity of Christ had to be understood as an inclusive one: his acts as Consummator include all living creatures, and not merely human

[88]

beings. Through him the whole of creation attains its goal. Here was a way of toning down the more negative aspects of evolution, the survival of the fittest, for example, and of stressing its positive aspects.

The difficulty of 'Christus Consummator' as a concept was that it was not as comprehensible as the concept it was intended to supplant. 'Christus Consolator' might be too negative an image for the Church of the 1880s, facing as it was challenges from many quarters, but at least it was an image most people could identify with. The notion of Christ as a 'Fulfiller' was more difficult to relate to. It seems that Westcott himself was aware of this. In the opening sermon of his 1885 series he admits that his ideas might seem 'strange . . . and removed from the familiar circle of religious reflection', and that they might 'require devout patience for their mastering'.[64] His cause was not enhanced by the fact that clarity of expression was not his greatest gift. There are passages in *Christus Consummator* in which he voices vague generalizations which do not advance his cause. One thinks, for example, of the final sermon on 'The Incarnation and Life', in which his intention is to deal with the practical implications of the concept, but in which he does little more than expound the phrase from John's Prologue, 'Out of his fulness have we all received, and grace for grace' (John 1.16). It is a disappointing end to the series, giving ammunition to those critics who berated him for his obscurity. Geoffrey Rowell's comment is apposite: 'the emphasis on Christ the Fulfiller and the social hope of man could easily degenerate into the cloudy phraseology of aspiration'.[65]

The twentieth century theologian whom one thinks of as having developed the 'Christus Consummator' idea in his writings is Teilhard de Chardin (1881–1955). His concept of Christ as the 'omega point' of history has some affinity with Westcott's use of fulfilment in Christ. As a priest and a scientist de Chardin was attempting to reconcile Christian teaching with contemporary scientific culture, and he developed a theory of evolution which incorporated the risen Christ as the present personal centre of the cosmos and the future focal centre of all human history and progress. It was an optimistic view of history which used quite novel concepts to express its vision, and an attempt to relate faith more radically to the world of the scientists. Christ for him was he who animates and gathers up all the biological and spiritual energies developed by the universe: 'physically and literally he is he who consummates ... the whole universe is ipse facto stamped with his character, shaped according to his direction, and animated by his form'.[66]

It is significant that de Chardin was regarded as unorthodox and obscure by many of his contemporaries, and it was only after his death that his writings reached a wider audience. Like Westcott he discovered that Christian orthodoxy does not take kindly to those who are searching for a new language to express their vision of an evolving and changing world.

4 Sin and atonement

If the incarnation was the central truth of the Christian faith, and part of the divine plan of creation rather than a response to the fall, what place was there for human sinfulness and Christ's redemptive death in Westcott's theology?

There are places in his published work where he does speak emphatically about the seriousness of human sin. There is, for instance, an early sermon preached at Harrow in 1869 in which he seems to take a sombre view of the human condition:

> His image is defaced, His glory veiled, His working hindered by some hostile power in man, and that power is sin – a selfish and wilful rebellion against His sovereignty ... There is something amiss ... which depends upon ourselves and not upon our circumstances, something in which we have been disloyal, something in which we are blameworthy.[67]

This sinfulness is 'like a disease', and its essence is the 'idolisation of self', living for ourselves and not for God. When we do this we also cut ourselves off from other people, which is a denial of our essential dependence upon one another. Our nature is not to be solitary but to live in relationships with others. Sin, therefore, is not solely rebellion against God; it has a social dimension, which affects our national and social life.[68]

Westcott alludes to this in an earlier sermon from 1852 in which he speaks with feeling of the plight of the homeless, the sick, the lonely and those for whom no one cares in contemporary society. The ultimate cause of the evil in the world is human sinfulness: 'there is an ever-present, ever-active source of sin in the wide world – in our own homes and in our own hearts, which is ready to check and hinder every good design we make, which is always at hand to fill our lives with unholy thoughts and words and deeds'.[69]

There are also places where he affirms his belief in the fall of man. He does so, for example, in his 1880 lectures on the Apostles' Creed. He finds this belief implicit in the Christian doctrine of redemption: 'The idea of Christ's sufferings, the idea of redemption, presupposes the idea of a Fall. Such an idea is, I will venture to say, a necessary condition of human hope. No view of life can be so inexpressibly sad as that which denies the Fall.'[70] As we shall see, there were clergy in the Durham diocese who would later accuse their bishop of doing precisely that – of denying the fall. He does not do so here, however. Elsewhere, Westcott makes it clear that he regards the fall as 'symbolical and not as historical', and draws attention to the 'remarkable silence' of the rest of the Old Testament about the fall.[71] For him, there are two essential truths enshrined in the narrative of Genesis 2:

> . . . the power of evil and the prerogative of personal responsibility. There is we feel a 'baseness in our blood', and we feel also that we have embodied the corruption 'by our fault, by our own fault, by our own great fault'. The tendency indeed is our inheritance, but we have made the issues our own by deed, we are actually . . . guilty, enthralled, alienated from God.[72]

The qualification which he is continually making, however, is that this sinfulness is not of the essence of human nature. It is a disease which has come in, so to speak, from outside. We see this in the passage preceding his affirmation of the fall in the 1880 lectures:

> The presence of evil amongst us and in us . . . is a reality which no ingenuity can hide or dissemble. Revelation did not cause this terrible affliction, but it shews that it does not belong to the essence of creation or to the essence of man. It shews therefore that it is remediable: that it can be removed from man without destroying his true nature, nay rather that his true nature is vindicated by the removal.[73]

The same point is made more concisely in a letter of 1881: 'Sin is separable from man because it is not of his essence, as he was made in the image of God.'[74] The fall and its consequences must not be forgotten, but it is also true that 'we must not exaggerate the change which it brought to man'.[75] 'Man did not lose the image of God by the Fall. His essential nature still remained capable of union with God, but it was burdened and hampered.'[76]

It is clear, then, that linking the incarnation with creation rather than with the fall, in the Scotist tradition, inevitably shifted the centre of gravity of Westcott's theology. He might on occasion speak of the seriousness of sin and of the necessity of believing in the fall, but in truth these are muted themes in his work as a whole. His major themes are incarnation and fulfilment. When he commented, as we noted earlier, on the theological differences between Oxford and Cambridge, he said of one of his former students: 'I am grieved to hear that Holland follows Mylne in making sin the centre of his philosophy. Surely the true centre is "in the image of God made He him".'[77]

A more significant testimony to Westcott's views on sin and the fall than his written work is the opinion of some of his friends and contemporaries. There is remarkable unanimity here on his lack of appreciation of the depth of human sinfulness and evil. One of his

Archdeacons in the Durham diocese, C. H. Boutflower, tells of Westcott's anguish, and disbelief that it could really have happened, when he had to deal with a serious case of clerical immorality: 'It was almost a refusal to believe in deliberate wickedness in men. "It shakes one's faith in human nature" was the painful remark such moments would wring from him.' It is Boutflower who quotes the telling remark made by some of Westcott's diocesan clergy in this context: 'The Bishop does not seem to believe in the Fall!'[78] Another significant testimony comes from Henry Scott Holland, mentioned above, who recalled his master's strange reticence in this darker side of human life:

> There was one department of human life which was strange and unfamiliar to him, and in which he moved with rare and doubtful steps. It was the world of sin. He told us little about it. It was alien to him . . . He loathed it; and passed it by, wherever it was possible. He preferred to uplift the ideal, and leave it to work its own victory . . . Somehow, that dark world is more tenacious and persistent than he quite allowed for.[79]

Holland goes on to note a 'certain white intensity of optimism' which characterizes Westcott's writings.

A similar point is made in the conclusion to a moving tribute to Westcott by one of his closest friends, A. S. Farrar:

> He had a surprising belief in Optimism. He could not realize the depth of human depravity and selfishness, he disbelieved the omnipotence of material and economic conditions as barriers to social improvement, and firmly held the power of mankind to mould circumstances, and was sanguine as to their willingness to do so. The future of the world . . . was to him a sphere of boundless hope.[80]

One other contemporary testimony may be cited, that of the astute A. C. Benson: 'He lived on so high and austere a level of thought himself that neither through experience nor imagination could he sound the depths of human nature. Wickedness, cruelty, sensuality, meanness, were not only horrible to him – they were inconceivable.'[81]

Such unanimity by those who knew and admired Westcott cannot be set aside. It confirms the tentative impression gained from his writings that he was essentially optimistic about our human potential, and did not engage deeply with biblical teaching about human sinfulness and depravity.

Olofsson concludes that so far as his writings are concerned there is only 'a formal acknowledgement of the existence of the dark aspects of life and the human race', and that overall there is 'no dimension of depth in evil and no struggle with evil' in Westcott's thought. He believes that Anselm's famous rebuke of his opponent is relevant to Westcott: 'You have not as yet estimated the great burden of sin.'[82]

To what do we attribute this optimism? Was it linked with his personality and temperament, as Benson appeared to suggest, or were there other factors? It is important to remember that Westcott was reacting against contemporary Evangelical teaching that human nature was totally depraved and incapable of realizing the divine image without supernatural intervention. He was also, as we saw in the last chapter, profoundly influenced by the optimism of the Christian Platonist tradition, with its very positive assessment of our human rational and spiritual capabilities. His optimism also owes a great deal to the 'paradigm shift' in theology which is generally attributed to F. D. Maurice, who grounded his theology in the nature of God rather than in human sinfulness: 'mankind stands not in Adam but in Christ'.[83] Whether or not he himself was directly influenced by Maurice, many of his friends were Mauricians, and his close friend and colleague, Hort, shared Westcott's views on sin as a 'disease' which is not a proper part of human nature, but an intruder. Most significantly, a recent survey of the work of his other great friend, J. B. Lightfoot, shows that the absence of any discussion of the fall in his work is highly revealing, and

concludes that his selective reading of the Bible ' blocked a full appreciation of the depth and extent of evil in history'.[84]

Some of the next generation concluded that their masters had reacted too sharply against extreme views of human depravity. One of
these was Charles Gore, Westcott's former pupil, who was deeply
influenced by the latter's sermon on the devout life. He came to reject
the Scotist view of the incarnation, and to hold a much more pessi-
mistic view of the reality of sin and of human nature than his master.
A. M. Ramsey wrote of Gore that, unlike Westcott, 'he would feel that,
humanly speaking, the outlook of the world was utterly bleak'.[85]

When we turn to Westcott's understanding of the remedy for human
sinfulness, we find only scattered hints as to how the atonement of
Christ might be understood. There is a clear rejection of contemporary
theories, however, and a deep scepticism as to the adequacy of any
theory fully to express the range of Christ's redemptive work. Penal and
substitutionary views of the atonement dominated English theology in
the middle and later Victorian period. In an article on the influence of
F. D. Maurice and his disciples, W. Moore Ede recalled the theological
ethos of the mid-century period: 'Few today realize how the theology
which started from human depravity prevailed at that time. I am old
enough to remember how crude theories of the Atonement dominated
popular theology, and can recall many weary hours in which I wrestled
with the doctrine of the Fall, as commonly expounded, which I felt to be
untrue.'[86]

Westcott was convinced at an early age that all such theories were
inadequate. In 1855 he comments in a letter to his wife on the fact that
the Hulsean lecturer at Cambridge had not appreciated the 'great
difficulties of the notion of sacrifice and vicarious punishment'.[87] Five
years later he is convinced of the inappropriateness of all controversy
about the atonement:

There seems to me to be something unspeakably sad in controversy
on such a subject as the Atonement. It is worse than a popular

[95]

discussion about Transubstantiation. Have we the slightest hope to expect to gain an intelligible theory of the fact? Is it not enough to say that the death of our Blessed Lord was necessary for our redemption? and that we are saved by it? Is it not absurd to expect that we can conceive how it is necessary – since the necessity is divine?[88]

This is the view he held virtually throughout his life. Even in his Hereford sermons, *The Victory of the Cross*, there is the telling sentence: 'A theory of the Atonement may be a minister of faith, but the fact of the Atonement is the inspiration of faith.'[89]

By the 1880s Westcott is aware that traditional views of the atonement are still held by many people, and he is seeking for 'surer ground'[90] upon which to build an alternative view. The 1888 sermons in Hereford Cathedral gave him the opportunity to set out such a view. He does not mince his words in dismissing popular theories as 'modes of exposition which belong to an earlier age', 'materialising fancies', and human constructs which 'fall immeasurably below the sublime simplicity of the apostle's teaching'.[91] In their place, however, there is no one theory, but rather some tentative suggestions as to what a biblical view of the atonement would include. One conviction, set out in the opening sermon, is that human beings cannot be saved in isolation. There is a solidarity in failure, sorrow, and sin, and in salvation.[92] This would become one of the main themes of his social teaching in the 1890s. Another theme is of Christ's death as a sacrifice,[93] which was central to F. D. Maurice's understanding of atonement. He describes sacrifice as the 'central truth of Christianity',[94] and nature and history both bear witness to its centrality. In his view it always strengthens, matures and blesses human beings. He does not develop the idea in any detail, however.

A third strand develops the thought of the Letter to the Hebrews that Christ 'was made perfect through suffering' (Heb. 2.10). The sufferings of Christ were taken upon himself voluntarily, and were felt in their full intensity, and it is through them that the whole human race could receive the power of new life. As he expresses it elsewhere: 'Christ fulfilled perfectly the destiny of man, fulfilled through suffering the destiny of man fallen, realising at every stage and through death itself union with God: there lies for the whole race in Him the promise of forgiveness.'[95] Again, there is no suggestion that this might be in any way a 'theory of the atonement'; it is seen as just one more strand in the biblical teaching.

Finally, there are places where Westcott hints at what we might call an Abelardian view of the atonement – the belief that the death of Jesus was above all an expression of divine love: 'The Passion as it was borne is a revelation of the inexorable sternness of infinite love . . . in the events of this Holy week, crowning the discipline of a holy life, we have an assurance of Divine love which is adequate for our utmost needs.'[96] This was a Johannine theme, of course, but at this time it was in no way a widely accepted view of the atonement.

These are some of the hints which Westcott throws out in these difficult sermons, but he makes no attempt to formulate any systematic 'theories' which might replace those he had criticized. There were those who clung firmly to the traditional penal substitutionary understanding of the death of Christ, and lamented the criticism which a person of Westcott's influence and stature made of their deeply held beliefs. In 1892 Revd J. Bennett, Vicar of St George's, Worthing, ventured into print to censure the saintly and eminent biblical scholar and bishop whose later writings convey 'a view of the atoning work of our Lord which I am compelled to regard as sadly defective'.[97]

In 1894 it was to Westcott that the Archbishop of Canterbury, E. W. Benson, turned when asked what new view of the atonement had replaced the old substitutionary theory. He asked him for extracts from his books, and for another book to help him to answer the question.[98] We do not know how Westcott responded to this request. We may only guess that the Archbishop did not receive an unambiguous answer to his question!

5 The resurrection

One of Westcott's earliest books addressed the question of the resurrection of Christ. *The Gospel of the Resurrection* (1866) was written while he was at Harrow but it contained 'very old thoughts', namely, answers which he had arrived at when wrestling with doubts in his undergraduate days.[99] It was written partly in response to Newman's *Apologia Pro Vita Sua*, which Westcott found wanting in its concentration on the relationship between God and the individual, to the virtual exclusion of the element of the world. He later described this work as the 'only one of my little books which I really care much about'.[100] In 1881 he published *The Revelation of the Risen Lord*, a careful examination and exegesis of the New Testament narratives of the resurrection. Together, these two works show that the resurrection had a special place in his theology, and they reveal his very distinctive perspective on this central New Testament doctrine.

The earlier work addresses contemporary scepticism about the possibility of miracles, and argues strongly for the possibility that a God who is both creator of the world and continually active within his creation can perform miracles as vehicles of his self-disclosure. Of these the resurrection is 'the fundamental and crowning Miracle of the Gospel'[101] since it combines all the miracles Jesus ever did. The resurrection is therefore historical, a fact, verified by the testimonies of the empty tomb and the encounters with the risen Christ. As such it can be subjected to historical investigation.

It is, however, more than a belief in an event in the past. Westcott uses the terminology of the fourth Gospel and describes the resurrection as 'the crowning "sign" of the counsel of God for men'.[102] A sign is something which needs interpreting in order to reveal the deeper meaning of an event. The risen Christ is revealed only to believers, to those who are spiritually discerning. The essence of the doctrine is this encounter with a living person, who became 'a spring of energy' in the lives of the disciples. For Westcott 'the Apostolic conception of the Resurrection is rather "the Lord lives", than "the Lord was raised" '.[103] The only 'proof' of the resurrection was this encounter with the risen Lord. Olofsson expresses this particular emphasis by suggesting that Westcott spoke about 'the resurrected one' rather than 'the resurrection'.[104]

Perhaps the most striking element in his treatment of the resurrection is the way in which he places it within the whole sweep of history. In *The Gospel of the Resurrection* he has a whole chapter on 'The Resurrection and History'. He sees it as the point at which all former history converges, and from which all subsequent history flows. The development of Judaism and of Greek and Roman civilization converges in this momentous event, and from it all later history flows as from a 'life-giving spring'.[105] He also relates it to the new revelations about the natural world thrown up by contemporary scientists. These threw light on the suggestions in the Pauline epistles, especially in Ephesians and Colossians, that the unity of all things had been summed up in Christ.

> They felt and they expressed, what we have not yet come to understand, that the belief in the Resurrection 'in Christ' carries with it a belief in the continuity, the solidarity, the totality of creation. The unity of being, of which science is slowly shaping a conception, was for them a unity of life tending to an issue of unimaginable glory.[106]

What Westcott seems to be arguing is that the resurrection should be seen not only as the climax of the story of redemption, but also as the climax of the story of creation. It is the fulfilment of the divine plan worked out through the long processes of history and nature:

> It is not properly an overwhelming fact attesting doctrines separate from itself, but a revelation which illuminates the whole range of human experience . . . . The Incarnation gives the absolute pledge of the fulfilment of man's destiny: the Resurrection shews that fulfilment already attained . . . We see in the Risen Christ the end for

[99]

which man was made and the assurance that the end is within reach. The Resurrection, if we may so speak, shews us the change which would have passed over the earthly life of man, if sin had not brought in death.[107]

This close linking of the incarnation with the resurrection is a distinctive insight of Westcott. For him the risen Christ is the first representative of the created order to attain the God-given goal. He is the perfect man, the guarantee that human beings can realize the likeness of God. The resurrection is nothing less than God's vindication of his creation. Here again were grounds for that optimism about human nature which was so characteristic of his theology.

A. M. Ramsey is one of the very few people to have seen the significance of Westcott's contribution here. He believed that his perspective on the resurrection was of permanent value. In particular, in the post-war period it provided an important corrective to the one-sided supernaturalism of the Barthian theologians. It vindicated his own feeling that their emphasis on the 'wholly otherness' of the gospel had gone too far and that the gospel theme of life through death is not 'wholly other' but is woven into the pattern of both nature and history. 'Both the historical and the transcendental, both the humanism of the Gospel and its supernatural character, are authenticated by the Resurrection.'[108]

A good example of Westcott's distinctive understanding of the theology of the resurrection is found in a sermon he preached in Peterborough Cathedral in 1869, in which he argues that the resurrection both harmonizes and inspires human life. It sheds new light on 'the unity of the seen and unseen, of earth and heaven'. Christ's life shows us that 'all life is potentially divine', and that God is at work in our common life for those with the eye of faith. It also means, however, that we may draw energy from union with Christ and that the vision of God can transform us into his image.[109] Here again is the emphasis on the resurrection as at once a historical fact and a transcendent reality. As he argued in his early book, the resurrection 'harmonises in itself the objective and subjective elements of religion'.[110]

This linking of resurrection with creation and incarnation rather than with redemption was perhaps the inevitable result of his embracing the Scotist view of incarnation. Once again he is out of step with most contemporary theology. What is beyond dispute, however, is that the resurrection has a very central place in his thought. It is significant that he sometimes uses the same phrases about it that he uses of the incarnation. Thus it is 'the central point of history' and 'the crowning revelation of God'.[111] He strongly believed that it had been neglected in much contemporary teaching, and that if Christianity was to be authentic it must be placed in 'the very front of our confession'.[112] For him the empty cross was the supreme symbol of the Christian faith. It was 'most disastrous for our whole view of the Gospel that a late age placed upon the Cross the Figure of the Dead Christ, and that we have retained it there. The Early Church rightly proclaimed that He "reigned from the tree".'[113]

Olofsson describes the resurrection as the 'all-embracing title of his theology', while the incarnation is his 'great theme', and concludes that the resurrection has a 'quite special luminosity' in Westcott's theology.[114] In this we may see another example of the influence upon him of the fourth Gospel, and of the Greek Fathers, for whom the resurrection was always more central than for the Latin Fathers. Westcott also anticipates the conviction of much mid- and later twentieth century scholarship that the resurrection is the crucial event underlying all the New Testament documents, and the conviction by which the Church stands or falls.

6 Westcott's place in English theology

Westcott is part of that movement in English theology in the later nineteenth century which reacted against a narrow theology of depravity and redemption, and shifted the centre of gravity from the atonement to the incarnation, from a 'theology of the cross' to a 'theology of the cradle'. It was a significant shift in emphasis, and his role was a major one, as later commentators and critics alike would acknowledge. One consequence of this new focus was that it brought the Christian faith into genuine contact with the contemporary world.[115] If God had become incarnate in the material world, then all of life was in one sense hallowed by him. This had profound consequences for the application of faith to the problems of society, as we shall see in the next chapter. David Newsome argues that this incarnationalism also raised morale amongst the clergy and the educated classes, and stemmed the tide of unbelief during the later years of the nineteenth century.[116] On the other hand, the present Archbishop of Canterbury has criticized what he calls the 'incarnationalist consensus' for its uncritical attitude to the social order, and for its failure to discern the distinctiveness and separateness of the Church over and against the fallenness of the world. Such a consensus lays itself open to 'the charge of sacralizing what already exists', and gives 'very little *theological* ground for asking awkward questions about the social realities of belonging, let alone for suggesting that there is a rather fundamental Christian vocation of *not* belonging, in families, nations, patriarchal "organic" states'.[117]

It must be said however, that Westcott's incarnationalism has a very distinctive character, and is quite unlike anyone else's. There are the twin themes which run through all his theology that what matters most is not speculation about the incarnate Lord but a living relationship with him, and that the efficacy of theology is proved by its translation into Christian action. There is the close relationship between creation, incarnation and fulfilment in his thought, as well as the insistence that the resurrection must be at the very centre of theological reflection. It is not enough to categorize him as just another incarnationalist. His theology has a distinctive, even idiosyncratic tone.

The key question, which we have already touched on, is to what extent his theology is lacking in a sense of the seriousness of sin and of the need for redemption and atonement? How far is his a one-sided 'theology of the cradle'? This has been the most common criticism of him. As early as 1903 J. Denney took issue with him for his assumption that the incarnation is something which has a significance and function of its own, apart from the atonement: 'Not Bethlehem, but Calvary, is the focus of revelation, and any construction of Christianity which ignores or denies this distorts Christianity by putting it out of focus.' This judgment is quoted by Olofsson, who clearly endorses Denney's view.[118] Westcott's biographer, J. C. Clayton, repeated this criticism in his 1906 *Life*: 'Westcott preaches, not the crucified Jesus, but a Gospel of infinite possibilities opened to mankind through the fact that God had become man.'[119]

It may be retorted that not too much should be made of these criticisms since they come from people who stand within the Evangelical tradition, and whom we would hardly expect to be sympathetic to Westcott's very different theological orientation. More significant is the fact that his former pupil Charles Gore, who as part of the *Lux Mundi* group at Oxford shared the buoyancy and optimism of the incarnationalists, eventually came to see its limitations and to re-focus his theology. In an article published a few weeks before Westcott's death he wrote: 'Dr Westcott . . . is a theologian who, in the opinion of some of us, does somewhat lay himself open to the charge of minimizing the Atonement as distinct from the Incarnation.'[120] The criticism is tentative, but it was a conviction which grew, and after the First World War in particular Gore's theology became much more atonement-centred: 'Everything in the New Testament appears to depend on this initial sacrifice of atonement, reconciliation, and propitiation,' he wrote in 1930.[121]

This leads us to the factor which makes it very difficult to evaluate fairly Westcott's theology, namely, the cataclysmic history of the century which followed his death. The First World War had an immense impact on theology. William Temple, for instance, came to see that the great weakness of incarnational theology was that it tried to explain the world rather than to redeem it. This became even more apparent after the Second World War. The marked shift in theological emphasis is seen clearly in one of Westcott's successors as Bishop of Durham, Hensley Henson (1863–1947). Now in retirement, he furnished his library borrowing the design of the northern portal of Westminster Abbey, in which Westcott had made the incarnation the central feature. To this design, however, he made important changes: in the middle he placed a crucifix, above which he put the words of the earliest Christian creed ('Jesus is Lord') and below it the words of the Te Deum, 'We believe that Thou shalt come to be our judge'. His comment is illuminating:

> Westcott's scheme reflected the calm optimism of a peaceful time. Now the world, torn and broken by two fearful wars, and hardly staggering to its feet with the energy enough to put a hand to the task of cosmic recovery, finds the most winning Appeal of Christianity less in *the Cradle of Bethlehem* than in *the Crucifix of Calvary*.[122]

In the light of this, Westcott's optimism about the immense potential of the human race and his 'Christus Consummator' concept seem very dated and detached from reality. It may be thought that his theology has not stood the test of time.

It is also true, however, that he must be judged in his context and without the benefit of hindsight. The history of the twentieth century has indeed made Victorian optimism in general seem short-sighted and even distasteful. What it has not done is to invalidate the achievements and perspectives of the Victorian age. There is evidence, in fact, that in the twenty-first century respect for all things Victorian is growing, as seen in the many exhibitions staged in 2001 to mark the centenary of Queen Victoria's death. In this spirit there is still much to value in Westcott's theological achievement, not least in the practical expression of it which we shall explore in the next chapter.

The other important question is to what extent is Westcott to be regarded as a follower of F. D. Maurice in his theology? This is a much-discussed issue. There are clearly many similarities in the thought of Maurice and Westcott: the debt to Plato and St John, the distrust of theological systems, the centrality of the incarnation, the grounding of theology in the love of God rather than in human sinfulness, the willingness to recognize truth in the arguments of opponents, and the perception that theology must have practical expression if it is to be authentic. The conclusion would normally be drawn that the younger man was undoubtedly influenced by the older. In their case, however, the evidence is by no means so clear that this was the case.

Discussion of Westcott's debt to Maurice has usually focused upon the books of Maurice which he may have read. Here there is conflicting testimony from his contemporaries. Llewelyn Davies said that Westcott told a friend, who told him, that he had deliberately refrained from reading Maurice so that the development of his own thought might be more independent. He added: 'We did not know at Cambridge of this purpose of his, but it explains what was sometimes rather unintelligible to us.'[123] Another contemporary, W. Moore Ede, claimed that Westcott told him he had read just one book of Maurice's before deciding not to read any more.[124] In a judicious survey of the evidence Alec Vidler concluded that Westcott read at least three books by Maurice, and that the comment about one book refers to his youth when he made a resolution not to read more so as not to endanger his originality. Later in life he read others, one of which was *Social Morality*, which became one of his favourite books and greatly influenced his thinking.[125]

There is another factor, however, which is more important than that of which books he may or may not have read. This is the issue of the influence of his friends upon him. In his early Cambridge days almost all his friends were admirers of Maurice. One thinks of Macmillan the publisher, C. B. Scott, D. J. Vaughan, and Llewelyn Davies. It is impossible to believe that he could have been insulated from Maurice's ideas in such company. A remark of Llewelyn Davies confirms this intuition:

'His inner circle of friends was full of that theology and he could not help becoming acquainted from his early Cambridge days with the formative ideas of it. I, for one, was always Maurician; and Westcott and I almost always agreed with one another.'[126] Equally important, there was the influence of Hort, with whom he enjoyed a close friendship and collaboration over a very long period. Hort was a confessed and open admirer of Maurice, and it is hard to believe that the two never discussed him and his theology. There is, indeed, evidence that at one time Hort was trying to 'convert' his friend to the Maurician viewpoint by encouraging him to read *The Kingdom of Christ*.[127]

Another important fact is that Westcott lived close to Maurice for six years in St Peter's Terrace in Cambridge. When Westcott was appointed Regius Professor of Divinity in 1870 Hort received the news from Maurice, and wrote an interesting reply which suggests that Westcott was acknowledged as at least an admirer of Maurice:

> To yourself the help of his presence will, I am sure, be great. You must often feel as if you were uttering words in a strange tongue; and now you will have the certainty of at least one coadjutor whose ears are opened. It is a special pleasure to think that you and he are at last to be really in contact.[128]

There was certainly correspondence between Westcott and Maurice on the latter's possible co-operation with the Divinity Professors, and there may have been some interchange between them on the subject of Comtism.[129] An unpublished letter to J. M. Ludlow, the Christian Socialist, written near the end of his life points to the reverence and affection Westcott had for Maurice in those days together in Cambridge: 'To be allowed to minister with Mr Maurice, whose countenance was a joy to me when I returned to Cambridge, was an exceedingly great reward.'[130]

All of this raises the question of whether Westcott deliberately played down his admiration for and dependence upon Maurice, in order to portray himself as an independent thinker. We know that he was always willing to learn from other people's ideas, but that he would always truly make those ideas his own. It is possible that in the case of Maurice he had found someone whose mind was all too similar to his own.

Certainly, later commentators had little doubt about the Maurician stamp of Westcott's theology. Writing of the Cambridge school of theology Hastings Rashdall acknowledged that Hort was more consciously under the influence of Maurice than his friend, but had no doubt that 'no one in our time has done more to carry on the work which Maurice began in this place' than Westcott.[131] A similar point was made by C. C. J. Webb: 'He may be said to have, more than anyone else, continued the tradition of the Maurician type of theology in the next generation.'[132] He is one of the key links in the chain which led to the revival of Maurice's thought in the mid-twentieth century.

Like his Cambridge colleagues he is not easy to place in the Anglican theological spectrum, for one stamp of a Maurician is the repudiation of church 'parties'. In some respects he stands within the 'liberal' Anglican tradition, of course, but as Rowan Williams has shown in his Westcott Centenary Lecture, he sits uneasily in that very broad coalition.[133]

7 An obscure theologian?

We return, finally, to the question posed earlier: to what extent was Westcott's theology obscure or difficult?[134]

Even his closest friends and admirers agree that in his written work his movement of thought is sometimes difficult to follow. Some contrasted the clarity of his textual and exegetical work with the difficulty sometimes found in his theological work,[135] and it is fair to say that few of those who found his theological works helpful believed that clarity of expression was one of his gifts. We have already noted places in his work where he is difficult to follow, and will point out others in later chapters.

Perhaps two examples of his literary style will illustrate the problem some had with his written work. In the introduction to his early book, *The Gospel of the Resurrection*, he establishes first that Christianity assumes the existence of an infinite personal God and a finite human will, and goes on to a discussion of the relation between the divine being and nature. Belief in a personal God means we must assume his influence in nature and the physical world. He then speaks of two errors to be guarded against:

> The one is the transference of the phenomena of succession and gradual growth and slow sequence, which are necessarily part of our observation of nature, to nature as the expression of the Divine will. The other is the supposition that 'laws' have in themselves (so to speak) a motive force: that the law, which declares the mode in which phenomena present themselves to us, has some virtue by which the phenomena *are* absolutely; or, in other words, that the Law not only declares how we see things, but *makes* them such as we see them.[136]

This is only a brief extract, of course, but the second sentence is a good example of the lack of clarity we sometimes find in his writings. It is not immediately clear what point he is making, and his use of 'so to speak' and 'in other words' show that he is struggling to express himself. A contemporary review of his lectures on the Apostles' Creed, *The Historic Faith*, mentions that there is 'sometimes a certain vagueness of touch, a mistiness of expression . . . as though the reality of the facts or incidents themselves were in some danger of evaporating,'[137] and this expresses well our reaction in this kind of passage.

A second example will illustrate another aspect of his style, its compressed nature. In his book on the atonement, *The Victory of the Cross*, his subject in the fifth sermon is 'The Virtue of Christ's Sacrifice'. He is making the point that Christ is able to communicate the virtue of his work, the reality of forgiveness, to all who are 'in him'. He gives as an example the story of the healing of the leper in Mark 1.40ff.:

The healing of the leper . . . opens the secret of His action. When the poor outcast, whose touch was defilement, fell prostrate at His feet, His answer was not the simple word of might . . . but *He took hold of him* (ἥψατο αὐτοῦ) with that firm, clinging grasp, with which the Magdalene would have kept the Lord Whom she had found again. He consumed with the fire of His love the impurity which He had removed. And so it is still: He gives the virtue of His own life to quicken the soul which rests on Him. True forgiveness is indeed the energy of love answered by love. The forgiveness which remits a punishment may leave the heart untouched. The forgiveness which remits a sin includes by its very nature the return of responsive grati- tude. The believer makes Christ's work His own, and God sees him in the Son of Man. He dies daily, dies into life.[138]

It is this passage which Sanday chose to illustrate the concentrated nature of Westcott's movement of thought, especially evident in his earlier work. He finds here a whole number of thoughts about atone- ment and forgiveness, but they are not in logical order nor is their link with the biblical passage made clear; each sentence merits longer explanation.[139] This point about literary style is interestingly voiced also by Lightfoot in an unpublished letter in which he comments on an essay of Westcott's he has been asked to read: 'I have marked some expressions and passages which seem obscure. The fault of the style is too great compression in parts. Your apophthegms read too much like enigmas because you do not lead up to them sufficiently.'[140]

There is, however, a wider issue here. We explored earlier the recog- nition which is central in his theology that there is mystery at the heart of existence, and that human language is always inadequate to express this mystery, always imprecise and indefinite. Any criticism of his style or his theology itself must take into account his own deep conviction about the inadequacy of human language. He himself was aware of the problems some had with his language and thought: 'to some I am a cloud; and I do not see how to help it'.[141] One of his students defended the 'indefiniteness' which is sometimes found in his theological thought: 'He was indefinite where he believed that definiteness could only be reached at present at the cost of a limitation which excluded some element of the truth.'[142] Equally illuminating is the reminiscence of one of his archdeacons, recalling a discussion about people's tendency to exaggerate a partial statement: '"Yes, of course there are two sides to everything", said someone. "Two sides!" said the Bishop, "You mean six – at least six! One cannot think of truth as less than a cube".'[143]

His attitude towards truth, then, cannot be divorced from the alleged obscurity of his thought. It was not surprising that churchmen who saw truth in terms of black and white found his wrestling with language and use of new concepts less than helpful. Like F. D. Maurice he was isolated from the main theological parties of the day, and at the same time he was attempting to break out of their traditional moulds and to find new language and new concepts to express a very different theological perspective. It was therefore inevitable that he would face criticism and misunderstanding. The criticism was sometimes justified. The more general difficulty of his theological thought, however, is 'an obscurity which ultimately bears witness to the difficulty of speaking of the ineffable'.[144]

5

PRACTICAL THEOLOGY

A friend was walking with him through a very poor part of London in 1883, discussing with him some academic issue in textual criticism or theology.

'On the narrow sidewalk we were dodging along, seeing at every step squalor and all manner of uncanny things. Something or other forced itself upon us more distinctly, and he said in substance, "But I cannot find the heart to busy myself with these questions when I see this life here. One must do something to make this better." '[1]

1 Seeds of change

In his 1964 lecture on 'Westcott's Christian Socialism' Alec Vidler argued that there were two distinct phases in Westcott's life, and that it was only in the latter phase, after 1883 and his appointment to Westminster, that he showed any interest in social questions. There was little or nothing in his pre-Westminster days, he claimed, to prepare us for the transformation which occurred in those later years.[2]

It is worth examining the evidence to see whether Westcott's life is to be divided quite so sharply as this. Our survey of his overall theological outlook has identified a recurrent emphasis on the need for theology to be given practical expression. Are there other seeds of the later change in him in his earlier years?

There is, first, the fact that he was born in Birmingham and as a boy witnessed the later stages of the Chartist demonstrations. In later years he was fond of recalling this and of claiming that it had had a profound and lifelong effect upon him. He told a Durham Diocesan Conference in 1891: 'The circumstances of my youth at Birmingham gave me a keen interest in the later stages of the Chartist movement. From that time forward I have followed as a Christian student the cause of social theories, revolutions, growths, at home and abroad.'[3] It may well be that in this Westcott was reading back into his earlier life an interest and concern which only developed fully later. As Vidler points out, it is the opinion of Westcott's son that it was only after 1883 that his father's interest in social questions 'first became manifest'.[4]

On the other hand it was the view of C. F. G. Masterman that his Birmingham origins had a permanent effect upon Westcott's mind and outlook: 'It was Birmingham that kept his scholar mind in touch with the realities of life, and that enabled him to keep the scholar's concentration while he conquered the scholar's aloofness.'[5] In support of this it has to be said that we are all profoundly influenced by the place of our birth, and by the things which we remember from our earliest years.

More significant than this, however, may be the people who helped to shape the young man's mind at King Edward's school. Foremost among these was his headmaster, Prince Lee, who passed on to Westcott that moral seriousness which would become one of the hallmarks of his life. As he later said of Lee's influence: 'our souls were touched, and we felt a little more of the claims of duty, a little more of the possibilities of life, a little more of the pricelessness of opportunity'.[6] Here, surely, were the origins of Westcott's social conscience, which was to develop fully only in those last two decades of his life. David Newsome sees Prince Lee and Dr Arnold, whom Westcott greatly admired, as the formative elements in the development of his social concern. In an illuminating discussion of the relationship between Westcott's Christian Socialism and his Platonism, he says of their influence: 'No high moral appeal could have left Westcott unmoved. Rigorous teachers had seized his youth . . . and if they had not purged his faith, they had plainly indicated that truth, although often simple, is never easily attained.'[7]

When we turn to the Cambridge years, there are occasional glimpses of this social conscience. In May 1848 he is reading the reports of the Government commissioners about poverty in the cities, and is clearly shocked by what he has read. 'Bad as I had esteemed the state of our poor to be, yet it is worse almost than imagination would have pictured it.'[8] The following year, in another letter to his wife, there is a reference to the deep divide between rich and poor within the country, in the context of the discussion in James 2 about the need for faith to be expressed in practical terms.[9] In an address given in London in 1893 Westcott confessed to having been haunted in his undergraduate days by Disraeli's picture of the 'the two Nations'.[10] Another letter from this period which discusses the Thirty-Nine Articles has, as we noted earlier, this very characteristic remark: 'I only wish men would pay more attention to acting and less to dogmatising.'[11]

The puzzling thing about these Cambridge years, as Vidler points out, is his apparent lack of interest in the Christian Socialist movement of 1848–54. His later friend and colleague, Hort, was by contrast deeply interested in the events of those years, even though he kept a critical distance. Much later in his life Westcott would claim that he was 'deeply interested' in the movement,[12] but it seems that this was another example of his reading back into his earlier life a concern which was only explicit much later. One explanation is that he kept his distance because of his desire to remain independent of F. D. Maurice, who was the dominant theological influence in the 1848–54 movement, but this is pure conjecture.

In his later Cambridge years and during his time at Harrow he became absorbed in his teaching duties and in writing works of scholarship. Even so, it is worthy of note that towards the end of his time at Harrow he discovers Auguste Comte's 'Politique Positive', and makes a special study of it in the summer of 1867. Two years later he reads Maurice's *Social Morality*. Both of these were academic studies, of course, but they would in time profoundly shape his social thought.[13] As early as 1869, in fact, there are signs that his theology is developing a social dimension. In a sermon preached in Peterborough Cathedral on the ascension he speaks of the importance of co-operation, of expressing our diversity in unity, within the life of a cathedral, in the wider

Church, and in the nation. Strength is to be found in co-operation: we need 'to strive towards the union of tasks and classes'. The times we live in 'call for unselfish and unreserved co-operation of class with class, and rank with rank . . . it is through mutual dependence that our personal powers are most operative'.[14] Here is an early statement of one of the major themes of his later years. In a sermon of the same year on the Good Samaritan he reiterates one of his earliest convictions: 'Religious truth cannot be of the intellect only. It must, if it is to be held vitally, show itself in life.' It is 'disastrous to cherish a creed which finds no expression of its characteristics in our lives'. It is an indictment of the Church that some of the best known social reformers come from outside its ranks: 'Some men who have been and are most active in reforming our criminals, in elevating our poor, in purifying the methods of government, in ennobling the aims of national policy, are without the all-constraining belief in the Gospel which we hold.'[15]

Even what we may call Westcott's academic theology at this period is not unaffected by this growing concern that the gospel should have practical and social expression. *The Gospel of the Resurrection*, first published in 1866, is especially significant in this respect. As we saw earlier, it was written partly in response to John Henry Newman's conviction, set out in his *Apologia*, that the essence of religious faith was the personal relationship between God and the individual. Westcott objected strongly to this because it left out the crucial element of the world, and so distorted theological understanding. It is for this reason that he presents the resurrection not only in relation to theology, but to history and to society. In the chapter on 'The Resurrection and Man', for instance, he argues that belief in Christ's resurrection has moral consequences and social implications: 'it hallows with a new sanction the idea of society at the same time and in the same way as it raises the dignity of the individual'.[16] He promises to address what he calls 'the social aspects of the Resurrection' in the final chapter, but his discussion is disappointing and does not really go beyond examination of some of the New Testament metaphors of the Church.

There is also a growing awareness on his part of the gap that existed between the Church's life and teaching and the life of the secular world. In the 1874 'Notice' to the book he writes:

> We have allowed questions of social and national right to be dis-cussed without reference to that infinite Truth which . . . is yet a light by which we can guide our course. We have stood as Christians so far aloof from secular speculation that we have almost forgotten that it must be through these lower studies that our apprehension of our own unchanging message is advanced.[17]

Thus we see that the seeds of Westcott's later total commitment to a social interpretation of the gospel are to be found in his early life, and in the development of his thought in the 1860s and 1870s. There are, in fact, very important continuities in his life and thought which are obscured if, like Vidler, we draw too sharp a contrast between the two phases of his life. The moves to Westminster and then to Durham were the catalysts which reshaped his outlook and transformed his priorities, but the fact that he was appointed to these two positions shows that there was a recognition that his interests were wider than the purely academic.

2 A steep learning curve

The move to the Westminster canonry in 1883 had a huge impact on Westcott's life and thought. For someone who, in Vidler's words, was 'remarkably sensitive and responsive to his immediate environment'[18] the combined effect of living close to a slum parish and of preaching in a church which was at the heart of the nation's life was enormous. The next seven years were to see a change in his priorities. This is well illus-trated by the remark he made to the American scholar, C. R. Gregory, while they were walking the London streets deep in theological conversation which is included in the epigraph to this chapter: 'But I cannot find the heart to busy myself with these questions when I see this life here. One must do something to make this better.' These years also see the evolution of a quite different theological style.

He soon becomes interested and involved in social and international issues. In 1885, for instance, he is impressed by a sermon preached by the Dean on the suffering of children in factories before Lord Shaftesbury's reforms.[19] In January 1887 he has become involved in and passionate about the movement for Imperial Federation.[20] At the same time he is involving himself in the growing concern about international disarmament. He makes a suggestion to Archbishop Benson about international arbitration in times of war in March 1887, and by 1889 he is chairing an international conference on disarmament and speaking at the Canterbury Diocesan conference on 'Christian Faith and War'.[21] Even while on holiday in Scotland, his conversation touches on the plight of the poor and the issue of immorality in society.[22] Then, in 1889, he becomes President of the Christian Social Union, and identifies himself with one of the important movements of the time. We shall discuss this later. For now it is enough to note that his identification with the Christian Socialist movement was the culmination of a growing personal interest and involvement in such issues during his Westminster years.

Alongside this involvement there was a deepening awareness that the Church, and in particular the Church of England, had neglected such questions in the past. After the Dean's sermon on children in factories he asks the question: 'And what was the Church doing? I wonder whether our eyes are open now.'[23] He is critical of the Church's unwillingness in the past to apply the lessons of the gospel to problems of international life:

During the last three centuries attention has been directed mainly to questions of personal conduct. But the time seems to have now come when Christians as Christians are required to realise and give effect to their creed in the discharge of the widest social duties – the duties not only of class to class, but also of nation to nation – as members of one race.[24]

On the issue of peace he is alarmed at the 'utter neglect of the question by churchmen'.[25] During 1889 and 1890 he is in dialogue with Archbishop Benson about the responsibility of the bishops to speak out on such issues, and about the need for the clergy to have some education in industrial economics.[26] He is hopeful that clergy will begin to discuss social questions in their meetings. 'But what is required is that we should feel that the Faith has something to say to Ethics.'[27]

There is little or no sign of Westcott's changed priorities in the first set of published sermons preached in the Abbey, dating from August 1885 and January 1886, and published as *Christus Consummator* (1886). The first five are expositions of themes in the Letter to the Hebrews. They begin with Scripture and expound biblical and theological themes, attempting to show the relevance of the Epistle to the contemporary world. The issues in the preacher's mind are not, however, the issues which were beginning to preoccupy him at this time, but what we might term the more 'academic' concerns such as the right understanding of Scripture, the problem of suffering, and the correct understanding of atonement. The second five sermons see him turning to the doctrine of the incarnation in order to illuminate some contemporary issues. Again, however, the treatment is academic rather than practical: the incarnation as a subject for study, and then considered in relation to creation, fall, nature and life. Our hopes are raised in the final sermon on 'The Incarnation and Life' in which he asserts at the outset that the noblest truths are not given to use 'for an intellectual luxury, still less for a moral opiate or a spiritual charm. They are for the inspiration of our whole being . . . for use in the busy fields of common duty.'[28] He then quotes Whichcote's dictum, 'I act, therefore I am', to support his contention that deeds are more important than words. The remainder of the sermon, however, does little to relate the incarnation to the 'busy fields of common duty', and is largely an exposition of Scripture.

There were, of course, close links between his concept of 'Christus Consummator' and his incarnational theology, and his new, active involvement in social questions. He would soon, in his early years at Durham, find in the incarnation the master key to the interpretation of the social and ethical ferment which he found in north-east England. In these addresses, however, he appears perhaps for the last time as the Cambridge professor, still engaging in essentially intellectual speculation.

It is in the second set of published sermons preached in the Abbey in August and December 1886 and published as *Social Aspects of Christianity* (1887), that we see for the first time the impact of his life at Westminster upon his theological thinking. In the preface he confesses to the huge impact upon him of his new environment: 'Of all places in the world "the Abbey", I think, proclaims the social Gospel of Christ with the most touching eloquence.' At the same time he says that it has reawakened in him 'the power of old thoughts'.[29] By this he means that the ideas in these sermons are not entirely new, but have been with him in some sense over the past thirty years. As we have remarked earlier, there are important continuities in Westcott's thought.

In the first group of sermons he attempts to show how faith in Christ 'guides, supports, encourages us in dealing with problems of social life'.[30] He deals in turn with the family, the nation, the race, and the Church, following fairly closely Maurice's sequence in *Social Morality*. The first sermon deals with the foundation on which society must rest, which is clearly stated to be the revelation of the living Christ, Son of man and Son of God. For him, this revelation has not yet found that social expression which sooner or later it must find. He sees three 'social lessons' of the person of Christ:

If the Word became flesh, the brotherhood of men is a reality for us.
If the Son of God was crucified, the fall, and with it the redemption, are realities for us.

> If the Son of man rose again from the dead, the eternal significance of our short space of labour is a reality for us.[31]

It is these which must be taken as 'the basis of our social scheme, and not as an appendage to it'.[32] Each is expounded in turn, but it must be said that they are related to personal life and relationships more than to the problems of society.

There is a strong conviction running through this address that the Church has failed to relate its faith to contemporary issues, of its having dwelt too much in the past on speculative and not enough on social issues. It is in the latter that the main challenge to the Church now lies: 'I do not think that our real controversies in the immediate future are likely to be speculative: they threaten to be terribly practical.'[33] Here is an assertion which reflects very clearly the changed priorities of Westcott's life and theology.

The second sermon discusses the family, which he describes as the 'first circle of social life', and which is a sign that we are not made to live solitary lives. 'The Family and not the individual is the unit of mankind.'[34] It is in a sense a reflection of the divine nature, and within it we learn the essential laws of all human fellowship: marriage, fatherhood and brotherhood. In the family we may find 'the principles at least of the right answers to many of the most urgent problems of society'.[35]

Then follows his reflections on national life, in which he rejects those theories of the origins of the nation state which are purely material and argues that nations have a spiritual basis in that they reveal something of the divine will for human life. Through our national life we learn our mutual dependence upon others, our incompleteness without others, and are enabled to serve our neighbours. There is a defence of wide variation of wealth and class within a nation: 'There could be no true nation, as there could be no true family, without wide differences in power, in fortune, in duty, among those who compose it.'[36]

The fourth sermon is to a large extent a discussion of the problems and responsibilities of empire, which we shall consider in chapter six, and the fifth is a reflection upon the Church as a realization of human brotherhood. He poses the question, 'What is the social mission of the Church?', and appears to give three answers:

> The Church is the prophet of the eternal in the light of creation . . . The Church is the interpreter of the world in the light of the Incarnation . . . The Church is the quickener and sustainer of life in the light of the Redemption.[37]

The second of these would become the touchstone of all his later social teaching.

The second set of sermons is of less significance for us, but it may just be mentioned that in the first of these there is a very significant discussion of the Kingdom of God, in which Westcott asserts that three of the characteristics of the Kingdom in the New Testament, righteousness, peace and joy, are the Christian equivalents of the Socialist triad of 'equality, liberty and fraternity':

> In 'righteousness, peace, joy' we can recognise 'equality, liberty, fraternity', interpreted, purified, extended. They tell us that the community and not the individual is the central thought in the life of men. They tell us that the fulfilment of duties and not the assertion of rights is the foundation of the social structure. They tell us that the end of labour is not material well-being, but that larger, deeper, more abiding delight which comes from successfully ministering to the good of others.[38]

This suggestion attracted wide attention, and had a profound effect upon the Congregationalist leader, R. W. Dale, who was a great admirer of Westcott.

We have dwelt at some length upon those 1886 sermons because they are revealing of the change of emphasis in Westcott's preaching and theology. He is now quite deliberately attempting to engage with some of the issues which are exercizing his contemporaries, even if in a somewhat general way. The focus is now on social issues rather than on academic questions. There is a real sensitivity to the criticism that the Church has been too concerned with speculative issues and not enough with social concerns, as if his new circumstances have led to some soul-searching. (Westcott did, in fact, consider giving up his Cambridge professorship at one point during his Westminster years.)[39] There is also the statement of themes which will become very familiar in his Durham years: human solidarity as opposed to individualism, the sacredness of family life, and mutual dependence within the life of the nation.

3 The master key

Powerful as the effect upon him of the Westminster experience was, the move to Durham had an even stronger influence upon his life and thought. Between 1883 and 1890 Westcott lived for nine months of the year in Cambridge. With his appointment to Durham he was permanently resident in one of Britain's most heavily industrialized areas, where the problems of unemployment, urban overcrowding and poverty were as acute as anywhere in the country. Something of the effect this had upon him can be seen in some words written in 1893, in which he is reflecting upon his first three years in the north-east:

> It can very rarely happen that one who has spent long and busy years as student and teacher should be suddenly called at the close of life to the oversight of a Diocese in which the problems of modern life are presented in the most urgent and impressive form. Such a transition brings with it of necessity many strange experiences. It gives by its very unexpectedness a singular reality to earlier thoughts. The Faith which has been pondered in quiet must without preparation be brought into the market-place and vindicated as a power of action.[40]

He then goes on to relate how these new challenges and the new context of his work have sent him back to Scripture with fresh questions and perspectives, and of how he has found the message of the incarnation a fruitful source for interpreting these new experiences. After some typically deep theological reflections on the meaning of the prologue to John's Gospel, he comes abruptly back to earth with the words: 'The proof of these lofty assertions must be given in deed.'[41]

This expresses very clearly the new emphasis in Westcott's theology in the last decade of his life. The stress is now overwhelmingly upon 'action' and 'deed'. The faith which has hitherto been reflected upon in relative tranquillity must now, as he will often say, be brought 'into the market place'. There will even be times when he almost regrets the years spent in academia, so acute is the challenge to the Christian faith which he finds in this new context. In his 1891 address to the Diocesan conference, for instance, he challenges the teachers of the Church to turn to the 'fundamental questions of national life', and then sounds a personal note:

> I know the attractions of the pursuit of speculative truth and of historical criticism, but these are wholly subsidiary to action, which is the characteristic of man. The Gospel which is committed to believers claims to have the power to deal with every practical question of human conduct for the manifestation of God's glory; and friends and foes alike have a right to demand that this claim should be vindicated on the broad fields of life.[42]

There is a reference here to Whichcote's maxim, 'I act therefore I am', which he had used in his first set of Westminster sermons and which had become an important principle for him since he repeated it in an address given in 1892 in Peterborough Cathedral, in which he appears to perceive the dangers inherent in an ivory tower existence:

> we bring back the conviction, which Whichcote was never weary of affirming, that the mark of man is action, and not thought. The

lesson is precious, both for guidance and for quickening. It saves the pursuit of knowledge from becoming selfish curiosity; and it saves the attainment of knowledge from becoming passive contemplation.[43]

The key to this significant shift of emphasis in Westcott's theology, which we see developing in his 1886 Westminster sermons, is the way in which he interprets the doctrine of the incarnation. This is the link between his earlier more academic theology and the 'practical theology' of the 1890s. In his later Cambridge years he had come increasingly to regard the incarnation as the pivotal Christian doctrine, although as we have seen earlier this was not in isolation from the other Christological affirmations. Now, facing new challenges and responsibilities, he finds this doctrine the master key to interpreting this new and very different world.

We see this in the 1890 'Notice' to the third edition of his Westminster sermons: 'the first experience of new work brings a fresh assurance that the solution of our Social Problems will be found in Him who is the Son of man, as He is the Son of God, *Christus Consummator*'.[44] Two years later the preface to his Cambridge lectures contains this significant affirmation:

> For no Christian doctrine is purely speculative. No opinion as to the facts of the world . . . can fail to influence conduct, least of all the message of the Gospel. The Incarnation binds all action, all experience, all creation to God; and supplies at once the motive and the power of service.[45]

Westcott had always emphasized the practical implications of theological study and reflection. Now, however, that conviction carried a new urgency and cutting edge.

In these early years at Durham we find him always and everywhere attempting to draw out the social and practical implications of the fact that in Jesus God had entered human history. The leading idea, which

[123]

he constantly reiterates, is that the Christ-event has established a solidarity or brotherhood of the members of the human race – a belief which clearly has important ethical and social implications. In an 1892 address he draws out the implications of Jesus' teaching in the Lord's Prayer that we should call God 'Our Father':

> The words . . . point to a personal relation between God and man which each man is set to realise in life: they shew that we share this potentially with all other men . . . So then we face our work, sons of God, brothers of men; and this double master-thought . . . will help us in dealing with our personal duties in regard to ourselves and in regard to others.[46]

He later points out that this is a very familiar insight, but one which has not been applied practically by Christians:

> For when seen in this light, as the application to men individually of the message that the *Word became flesh*, the assertion of the Divine sonship of each man, of the human brotherhood of all men in Christ, is fitted to chasten, to guide, to inspire us: to furnish at once a solid foundation and a touchstone for our theories of social intercourse.[47]

This conviction is set out equally clearly in the 1891 Diocesan conference address:

> However feebly we realise the fact, the truth, of the Incarnation, we find in it the inexhaustible spring of brotherhood. No difference which finds expression in terms of earth can stay it . . . man is bound to man, in virtue of his humanity, by that which is infinitely stronger than anything which tends to separate one from another: that in the reckoning of the great account the loss of one cannot be another's gain . . . Christ – such is the formal confession of each one of us – took me to Himself when He took humanity to Himself, and I owe myself to those with whom He has united me.[48]

In an address delivered in London in the same year on 'A Gospel for the Poor' he uses the incarnation as the motive for recognizing the mutual responsibilities of rich and poor to one another within the life of the nation:

The Gospel of Christ the Word Incarnate declares with a pathetic and irresistible power the unity of mankind, so that we cannot for one moment separate ourselves from any who share with us that nature which He has taken to Himself . . . The Gospel of Christ the Word Incarnate, of God entering into our life, is indeed good tidings, *good tidings to the poor*, good tidings in its essence to man, simply as man, reaching down to the lowest depths where humanity still lingers, and growing with man's growth to the utmost bound of his possible attainment.[49]

This doctrine was also the inspiration for Westcott's involvement in the movement for international peace and arbitration, and he re-affirmed his commitment to this in his Durham years: 'If nations are, as history has proved them to be, factors in human progress, the Incarnation proclaims a brotherhood of nations no less than a brother-hood of men.'[50] In an 1897 address on 'International Arbitration' he repeats his familiar theme: 'We have been enabled to recognise that the Incarnation . . . offers to us a revelation of the true relations of man to man, of class to class, of nation to nation, in the ideal unity of mankind in Christ; and we must bring the truth into life.'[51]

Westcott takes it for granted that this brotherhood and solidarity should be embodied and realized in a special sense in the Christian community. He sees St Paul's metaphor of the Church as Christ's body as an important expression of this solidarity:

Just so soon and so far as we regard ourselves and others 'in Christ', to use St. Paul's phrase, according to the Divine counsel, we shall strive to secure for each man, as for ourselves, the opportunity of fulfilling his part in a Divine society, for developing a corresponding character, for attaining in his measure to the Divine likeness. The apostolic picture will be constantly before us as our charter and our law.[52]

The Church was founded in order to embody the ideal brotherhood which is seen in the Son of Man. The Incarnation

> offers to us two fundamental thoughts unimagined before, the thought of the inherent value of each man as man, and the thought of the social destination of all men ... In order to realise them and to bring them to bear upon the world, the brotherhood of believers, the Church, was founded.[53]

At the same time, as we have seen, he is very much aware that the Church in the past has not been true to its calling, and has failed to put into practice the brotherhood it has proclaimed. Hence, his repetition almost *ad nauseam* during these years of the urgent need for Christians to embody in their lives and in their fellowship the 'brotherhood of men, of classes, of nations': 'If I am a Christian, I must for my own part acknowledge the widest issues of the Incarnation and strive to establish them.'[54]

The other great lesson which he is continually drawing from the Johannine affirmation that the Word became flesh is that it 'touches life at every point'.[55] The Son of God's bearing of our human nature and taking of it into heaven means that the whole of human life is hallowed and consecrated, and that there is a divine presence to be detected in every sphere of life. The incarnation 'affirms a Divine purpose and presence to be looked for and recognised everywhere ... transforms the simplest powers and opportunities which are given to us into means of making God better known.'[56] Encounters with the divine are not confined to so-called sacred places:

The office and the shop and the factory and the ship-yard and the pit, the municipal council-chamber and the board-room of 'the Union', are meeting-places with God where He can be honoured, if those whose duty lies there enter them as having welcomed the message of the Incarnation.[57]

This is the teaching of St Paul when he says that Christians are to do all 'to the glory of God' or 'in the name of the Lord Jesus':

We are charged to realise, as we may be enabled, and to show the Divine presence even in the commonest things. We are taught that we shall obtain our end by calling to remembrance in every action the truth of the Incarnation. This truth, this fact, adds an element of infinity to all that is of earth.[58]

This conviction is well expressed in a sermon preached in Birmingham in 1893 on 'Citizenship, Human and Divine'. He quotes the saying of Socrates in Plato's 'Republic' that a pattern for our earthly citizenship is laid up in heaven:

The Divine event, for which the great teacher half-unconsciously looked, has come to pass. Through the Incarnation every relation and circumstance of life has received a new meaning. The simple joys and sorrows, the little duties and occupations of an obscure position have been brought into direct connection with God. In the record of the Saviour's work we learn to recognize an eternal element in commonest things: behind all is the Divine . . . The pattern laid up in heaven has been brought to earth. If, then, we accept this pattern . . . [we] shall see that all human work is, from the nature of the case, potentially Christian work; that social, commercial, municipal, national activity, is part of the one human life which Christ lived, an expression in due measure of the nature which He has borne to His Father's throne.[59]

In his Westcott Memorial lecture Vidler quotes in this connection the well known reminiscence of C. F. Andrews, who recalled walking with Westcott on the moors near Robin Hood's Bay and the latter exclaiming: 'Remember, Andrews, nothing, *nothing* that is truly human can be left outside the Christian faith without destroying the very reason for its existence.'[60]

To sum up, Westcott turned to the Scriptures when faced with a totally new task in a new area, and to his favourite Johannine doctrine of the incarnation, and found there answers to the fresh questions he was compelled to ask. It is this central doctrine which is the link between his earlier theology and the 'practical theology' of the last decade of his life.

He was also, however, drawing on his knowledge of Auguste Comte's Positivist philosophy, of which he had made a special study in the 1860s. In his 1867 article on the relationship between Positivism and Christianity he argued that the two had three ideas in common: continuity, solidarity and totality. It is the second of these which is relevant to his exposition of incarnational theology. Comte saw the human race as an organic unity. To be human means to be part of the whole human race, and not an isolated individual. The actions of the individual affect the life and direction of the whole process: 'No one in any society works for himself. Each worker is a servant of the body. He does really co-operate with all for the good of all. It is only required that he should feel the destination and the source of what he does and of what he receives.' Society is the central concept, not the individual: 'If the individual be the centre, then he may have rights; but if the body be the centre, he can have only duties. It is possible that these complementary aspects may be reconciled, but there can be no doubt which we most frequently forget.'[61]

This organic view of society, which he had also found in the Greek Fathers, had a profound effect upon Westcott. The notion of solidarity became a key concept in his theology, and was an important factor in his Christian Socialism and in his sympathy with the co-operative movement and similar associations. It was characteristic of Westcott that the insights of St John and St Paul should be confirmed and underlined by the teaching of an atheistic philosophy. The solidarity of human beings in society would become one of his constant themes in the 1890s, repeated often in his sermons and speeches. There is a particularly good example of this in his 1890 Enthronement sermon, in which this is discussed in the context of intercessory prayer:

> We are not, we cannot be, alone. There is a larger life in which we are all bound to an irrevocable past and an immeasurable future . . . And there is also now a present life of the society in which we are all bound one to another, a life of the city, of the diocese, of the nation; a life which in these different relations is completed in many parts and fulfilled through many offices . . . a life in which each lives by all, through all, for all . . . We are not, we cannot be, alone.[62]

4 Christian Socialism

It was a significant moment when Westcott agreed to become President of the newly-founded Christian Social Union in 1889. His identification with the movement gave it respectability, and attracted many clergy who would not otherwise have joined such an organization. It was also a significant step for him, a kind of watershed in his life. It marked a resolve to earth his theology in practical commitment, and is the most striking example of the transition in his theology from thought to action.

Socialism was very much 'in the air' in England in the 1880s, and the CSU was one of the many movements which arose in response to the economic and social conditions of the time. The Victorians themselves believed there was a 'Great Depression' during the last two decades of the century, when there were falling prices and growing unemployment, especially amongst unskilled workers. Some economists now question whether this was in fact the case, but there was intense discussion about unemployment in the 1880s, and William Booth, in his 1883 *The Bitter Cry of Outcast London*, said that it was the main cause of poverty amongst able-bodied people. More and more people believed that only greater state intervention could cure such ills, and challenged traditional 'laissez-faire' attitudes. Tender consciences became concerned about such issues, as they did over the gradual realization among churchmen in these years that the great mass of working people were alienated from the churches. A census in the *British Weekly* in 1886, for instance, showed that four out of five people were either careless or hostile as regards public worship. Urban congregations were declining all over the country, and it was the Church of England which had suffered the heaviest losses. It was the conclusion of many churchmen at this time that Victorian religion had failed the poor and working classes, and that the condition of English cities was a great moral indictment of a 'Christian society'.

The 1880s therefore saw a great awakening of the social conscience of the middle classes. The 'condition of England' question was debated more intensely than at any time since the 1840s. Various governmental and private investigations into poverty and unemployment were undertaken. In 1884, the first Fabian Society tract was published, with the title, *Why are the Many Poor?*. It was against this background that, especially in the cities, many Christians discovered their social conscience and began addressing these issues. In Owen Chadwick's words, it was in the 1880s that 'the question of Christianity and socialism touched the churches'.[63]

Westcott was rarely ever influenced by the passing fashions or preoccupations of the day. It is impossible to believe, however, that he could not have been affected by the climate of society and the concerns of churchmen during the 1880s. Someone wrote of mid-1880s London:

In the parks and at street corners lecturers of the Socialist League and the Social Democratic Federation were at work – William Morris in the forefront. The Fabian Society was issuing leaflets to the middle classes, and the Rev Stewart D. Headlam and Mr Frederick Verrinder were raising consciences, through the Guild of St. Matthew and the Land Restoration League. Socialism was very much 'in the air' in London.[64]

The Canon of Westminster Abbey must have been aware of all this, and it was clearly against this background that he took the decision to identify himself with the CSU.

His contribution to the Christian Socialist movement needs re-assessing, as does the CSU's role in the history of the late Victorian Church. Alec Vidler's 1964 lecture on 'Westcott's Christian Socialism' was discerning in many ways, but it underestimated the continuity in Westcott's thought, and its judgment was affected by the author's self-confessed preference for the socialism of the Guild of St Matthew over that of the CSU. More recent assessments have been more sympathetic, both to the CSU and to Westcott's personal contribution, and the most recent developments within the Christian Socialist movement help us to see Westcott in a different light.

What exactly did Westcott's Christian Socialism amount to? To answer that question we turn to his famous lecture on 'Socialism' given to the Church Congress in Hull, on 1 October 1890.[65] His aim here is to isolate the 'essential idea' behind the many current types of socialism: 'The term Socialism has been discredited by its connection with many extravagant and revolutionary schemes, but it is a term which needs to be claimed for nobler uses.'[66] For him, it is 'a theory of life' and not only a theory of economics. It is 'the opposite of Individualism, and it is by contrast with Individualism that the true character of Socialism can best be discerned'.[67] The two terms, he believes, correspond to two quite opposing views of human life. Individualism regards life as essentially competitive, whereas socialism stresses co-operation as the ideal, and the need to organize society so that all work together for the welfare of all.

The central idea of socialism for Westcott is that 'the goal of human endeavour is the common well-being of all alike',[68] as opposed to the special development of one race or one class. This does not imply the equality of all, nor commitment to any one line of action. Rather, its aim is the evolution of a fairer society where all work together in the service of the state. He admits that such a goal may seem 'visionary', but points out the significance of the fact that 'dependence and solidarity and brotherhood' have become the watchwords of the time.[69]

This kind of 'true socialism', he argues, is found in Scripture:

> the thoughts that men are 'one man' in Christ, sons of God and brethren, suffering and rejoicing together, that each touches all and all touch each with an inevitable influence, that as we live by others we can find no rest till we live for others, are fundamental thoughts of the Law and the Prophets, of the Gospels and Epistles.[70]

It is the task of contemporary Christians to interpret and give practical expression to these beliefs: 'They must shew that Christianity, which has dealt hitherto with the individual, deals also with the State, with classes, with social conditions, and not only with personal character.'[71] The key to this is found in the doctrine of the incarnation, which we are to bring

> to bear upon the dealings of man with man and of nation with nation . . . We alone, I do not scruple to affirm it, we alone, who believe that 'The Word became flesh' can keep hope fresh in the face of the sorrows of the world, for we alone know that evil is intrusive and remediable; we alone know that the victory over the world has been won, and that we have to gather with patience the fruits of the victory.[72]

In brief, it is the incarnation which is the ultimate rationale of his Christian Socialism.

This doctrine, however, must be applied and worked out in the real world. Or as Westcott expresses it: 'it is here on the sordid field of selfish conflicts that we must prepare the kingdom of God'.[73] This means that Christians, and especially the clergy, must give serious study to contemporary social and economic issues such as the distribution of wealth and the moral significance of the poor, and gather as much information about them as a preparation for action.

> Zeal, enthusiasm, devotion are not enough to guide us in the perplexity of conduct; we need above all things knowledge as the basis of action . . . Meanwhile, our office as Christian teachers is to proclaim the ideal of the Gospel and to form opinion.[74]

This address contains the key characteristics of Westcott's Christian Socialism. Socialism is a philosophy of life rather than an economic theory, embodying his favourite motifs of interdependence, solidarity, and co-operation over and against a selfish, competitive individualism. As such, it derives not from modern socialist theory but from Scripture, and especially from the Gospels and Epistles, and its ultimate source is in his beloved doctrine of the incarnation. It recognizes that people's lives are affected by material conditions, but its main call is for a study and a gathering of information about these conditions rather than for direct action.

This has seemed to some to be a very mild and watered down restatement of socialism. It is important, however, to remember the context in which things are said; and critics of Westcott have not always done this. In the 1880s it was still regarded as highly dangerous to link the word 'Christian' with a word which in the popular mind was associated with atheism and immorality. Moreover, the speaker was a newly appointed bishop. Hence, the widespread criticism which the address provoked in the leading Conservative newspapers of the day: 'That a Bishop, of all people, should have a good word for "Socialism" seemed, in those days, to savour of treachery to his order – it was positively alarming.'[75]

[133]

Further light on Westcott's conception of the principles and aims of the CSU is shed by an address he gave at its annual meeting in 1894. He told his audience that the Christian has a duty to speak about the ethical and social concerns of the day, and should 'take his full part in preparing for the amelioration of the conditions of men no less than for their conversion'. This cannot mean, however, the taking part 'in class movements on class grounds'.[76] The most urgent need is for

> unwearied study of the moral history, and of the present state, and of the possibilities of ourselves and of our fellow-men . . . for the present, at least, our corporate work is not action, but preparation for action . . . it is, I know, far more important to confess our great principle, and to gain for it wide and intelligent welcome, than to press forward special reforms which a majority may favour.[77]

In this, the clergy have a special role: to focus their study on the Scriptures, which will shed light on contemporary social life and problems. They will also, through their pastoral contacts, learn of the difficulties facing both workers and employers and will wherever possible bring together representatives of the different classes and urge upon people their responsibilities to one another. 'They will, in a word, maintain naturally in the fulfilment of their office the religious basis of all life, and lay upon the consciences of their hearers to determine the application of the Faith to the circumstances of their own daily work.'[78]

Here we find two features of the CSU which its critics have frequently highlighted. There is the insistence that its members should not be involved in particular socialist organizations, or in pursuing particular causes or reforms, as for instance the members of the Guild of St Matthew were. And there is the exhortation to study and to gain information rather than to be involved in direct action. Indeed, it is when Westcott attempts to define exactly what kind of practical Christian action members of the CSU could legitimately be involved in that he produces one of his most opaque statements:

Meanwhile, for ourselves personally the way of action can be made plain. Our influence lies in the giving of our life. But we can give ourselves only as (in one sense) we are our own and as we are. We must ascertain our highest duty by resolute questioning, and then face it. If, as I have maintained, no devotion to the highest private interests can absolve us from public service, it is no less true that no devotion to public service can absolve us from the obligation of private discipline. The single will touched by the Spirit of God is the only force.[79]

It is when reading such a passage that Scott Holland's celebrated comment about Westcott's address at the founding of the CSU comes to mind. It was

a famous address . . . which none who were present can ever forget. Yet none of us can ever recall, in the least, what was said. No one knows. Only we knew that we were lifted, kindled, transformed. We pledged ourselves; we committed ourselves; we were ready to die for the Cause; but if you asked us why, and for what, we could not tell you.[80]

On the other hand, as Alan Wilkinson remarks, such opaque language could be reassuring to some people.[81]

While study and publishing were the main activities of the CSU there were some branches which became involved in direct action, in spite of their President's admonitions. The London group were directly involved in the 1889 Dock strike, the 1892 London County Council elections, and in a Commons deputation in 1898–9 to demand revision of the Factory Acts. The Oxford group completed 'white lists' of good employers, and there was a successful campaign in the pottery industry in North Staffordshire. These, however, were the exception rather than the rule. It is generally agreed that one of the weaknesses of the CSU as a whole was that it was too cautious and mild in its aims and practice.

Peter d'A. Jones's comment is fair: 'Of all the Christian reform groups of the period, perhaps the CSU exhibited the widest gap between its critical rhetoric and its cautious policy.'[82] A much more trenchant criticism came from Conrad Noel, the so-called 'Red Vicar' of Thaxted, who asserted that the CSU 'seems to consider it a crime to arrive to at any economic conclusion . . . An unkind critic has described it as forever learning but never coming to a knowledge of the truth.'[83]

The other criticism most commonly made is that it failed to make contact with the working classes. Many of its members were from a public school, Oxbridge background, and this effectively shut them off from contact with ordinary working people. This meant that there was little or no contact with trade unions, nor with the Labour party itself. Its strength lay in the south and south-east, and it was relatively weak in the industrial north.

All this is in no way to deny, however, that the CSU did have a very positive influence upon the Church of England. It is not claiming too much to say that it helped to change the Church's attitude towards social questions and social action. Most historians agree that it both shaped the thinking of a whole generation of ordinands and challenged bishops and senior clergy to take the social application of the gospel more seriously. It also helped to create a minority of lay people with a social conscience. It is generally accepted that because of its influence the Church of the early twentieth century was much more socially aware than that of the 1870s.

Some historians of the Christian Socialist movement like d'A. Jones and Alan Wilkinson also believe that it did in fact make some contribution towards the development of the Labour movement. With other similar Christian groups it helped to make socialism more respectable by breaking down prejudices against it. As d'A. Jones concludes:

There is no doubt that many 'waverers', who might never have joined the ranks of socialism because of its association in the public mind with atheism, were swayed by seeing such a large number of

reverends, doctors of divinity, and church dignitaries attach themselves to labor organizations and adopt the title 'socialist'.[84]

This brings us to Westcott's own personal contribution to the CSU and
to the history of Christian Socialism. Edward Norman's summary is
admirably succinct: 'Perhaps more than any other it was Westcott who
gave Christian Socialism respectability, who legitimized its existence
within the Church, and who, in the process, diluted it.'[85] There is no
doubt that Westcott's identification with the CSU contributed greatly
to the prestige and respectability of Christian Socialism. For such a
widely revered scholar and Church leader to appear on public plat-
forms in the cause gave the movement an enormous boost in the eyes
of many Christians. It did not matter that his Christian Socialism was
of a rather generalized nature, or that his language could be opaque. In
this respect, his influence 'was due much more to what he was than to
what he said'.[86]

It was in his public association with the movement that he exercized
a profound influence on many people who would otherwise have been
hostile to this particular expression of socialism. One of the founders of
the CSU was Henry Scott Holland. An unpublished study of his life
shows not only how much Westcott had influenced his own 'conversion' to Christian Socialism, but also the huge impact upon him of
Westcott's acceptance of the Presidency of the CSU. His acceptance
was 'a matter of supreme importance to Holland, for he saw it as the
symbol of the final fusion of the great Cambridge tradition which
descended through Coleridge and Maurice to Westcott with the
new Oxford movement whose characteristic manifesto was "Lux
Mundi"'.[87]

Norman's charge that Westcott 'diluted' the content of Christian
Socialism has been widely accepted. As we have seen, his concept of
socialism was of the most general kind, a philosophy of life which saw
society not as a collection of individuals in competition with one
another, but in terms of solidarity, brotherhood and harmony. This

so-called dilution of the concept is put in perspective, however, by the most recent developments in the Christian Socialist movement. In his 1998 Scott Holland lectures Alan Wilkinson discusses its recent revival within the Labour party, which he describes as a 'new mutation' of Christian Socialism. He argues that Tony Blair has redefined socialism in terms rather similar to that of Westcott, and in sharp contrast to the dominant tradition since 1918. For him it is:

> A belief in society, working together, solidarity, cooperation, partnership . . . That is my socialism – and we should stop apologizing for using the word. It is not the socialism of Marx or state control . . . Socialism to me was never about nationalization or the power of the state; not just economics or politics even. It is a moral purpose to life; a set of values . . . It is how I try to live my life.[88]

Blair's vision of society is based upon the recognition of our duty to one another, rather than our rights, and the family is for him one of its key building blocks. Wilkinson's wry comment is: 'Sometimes Tony Blair sounds as if he had read Westcott'![89]

Norman's charge that Westcott diluted the Christian Socialist tradition will, of course, be endorsed by those socialists who disapprove of Blair's particular vision of socialism. The fact, however, that Westcott's particular understanding of the concept has resurfaced, so to speak, one hundred years after his death in a Labour Prime Minister should make us more cautious about dismissing it as 'vague' and 'generalized'. It puts Westcott's contribution to the Christian Socialist movement in a fresh perspective. It is part of Wilkinson's argument that the word 'socialism' has often been used in a broad and general sense, and that the CSU has a right to be included in the socialist tradition.[90] Westcott, too, has a place in that tradition, which should not be underestimated or minimized as has been the tendency in the past.

5 Contextual theology

It is common today to speak of 'contextual theology'. This is the conviction that authentic theology always arises out of its social and economic context rather than being an unchanging, *a priori* revelation which is brought to that context as a given. This understanding was pioneered by the so-called liberation theologians of Africa, Asia and South America, and has had a profound influence on western theology and on the Church's attitude to mission over the past two or three decades. In broad terms, this method of doing theology involves in any given situation, first of all a social and economic analysis, then a search for biblical paradigms with which to interpret the situation, and finally the practical application of these to the actual problems and issues of the time.

This model may be helpful in understanding the developments in Westcott's theology in his later years. There is evidence that in the 1880s and earlier, he was taking seriously the social and economic conditions in the country, and especially in London. Then, with the move to Durham, there is the overwhelming appeal to the model of incarnation as a tool for interpreting his new situation. Finally – and this is a simultaneous process to some degree – there is the practical application of this to the actual issues with which he is confronted when he moves to the north-east.

We see this third stage in Westcott's setting up of a series of conferences at Auckland Castle on some of the central social and economic issues of the time. The aim was to bring employers, workers, and other interested parties together to try to find a way forward. It may be helpful to list the major ones so as to give some idea of their range and scope.

1 Pensions and National Insurance provision for the aged: 6 and 7 January 1891. The aim of this first meeting was 'the necessity of securing a more satisfactory provision for the aged', and the outcome

was the recommendation of the principle of National Insurance expressed in a nine-point resolution, which was finally agreed in June 1891.[91]

2 Co-operation in local industries: 27 May 1891. This was resumed at Newcastle on 20 and 21 October, with one of the questions to be discussed: 'How far Co-operation should aim at making men and influencing character, and not at money-making'.[92] This sounds very much like Westcott's own question! There was a follow-up to this in June of the following year.

3 Profit-sharing within industry: June 1892.[93] There was another conference on this issue held at Newcastle in October 1899, which led to the introduction of a profit-sharing scheme at the Swan Hunter shipyard on the Tyne.[94]

4 The distribution of money to the unemployed: 25 and 26 October 1895. A five-point resolution was adopted, one of which recommended the setting up of a permanent committee in each trade union to be responsible for poor relief.[95]

5 Aged Miners' Homes: early 1899.[96]

6 Co-operation in industry: October 1899. This was held in Newcastle, and Westcott gave an address.[97]

7 Working class housing: October 1899.[98]

This gives some indication of the range of contemporary issues which Westcott was trying to address. Whatever the outcome of these conferences – and some have claimed that they achieved little or nothing – they show at least that he was attempting to apply his theological insights to some of the pressing practical concerns of the region.

His concern about the social conditions in which the people of his diocese lived is also reflected in the Visitation Returns which he sent out to his clergy. Along with the usual questions about parochial life, there are also questions about the social and economic conditions in the parishes. In 1892, for instance, he asked his clergy these two questions:

4 Have people in your Parish generally, adequate opportunities and helps for healthy recreation?

9 Can you suggest any way in which you think it possible to bring the Gospel to bear more effectively upon ordinary life?[99]

In the returns for 1900 the questions were divided into three sections: 1 Education, 2 Social Conditions, 3 Church Work. It is worth listing some of those in section 2:

2 Have you meetings for the direct purpose of mutual intercourse and conference? Does the Mothers' Union tend to bring different classes together?

4 How far do the conditions of labour leave opportunities for the cultivation of home life, and especially of religious home life?

5 Do you observe that the Christian faith is a real force in purifying methods of business? Do you in your teaching give instruction on the ethics of common life?

7 What conditions of life which lie within our control seem to you to hinder the causes of temperance, purity, and healthy recreation?

In the preface to the questions Westcott wrote: 'Before we can effectively help one another we need . . . a further knowledge than we yet possess of the conditions of life, the common opinions, the opportunities, the difficulties of the different classes of our population.' There were, in addition, four questions relating to education.[100]

Here is more evidence of the bishop taking seriously the context of his work, gathering information as he was always urging his fellow Christian Socialists to do.

Another significant example of his concern to apply his theological convictions in a practical way is his involvement in the co-operative movement. As we have seen, two of the major conferences were on this theme, and he was a frequent speaker at conferences and rallies of co-operative branches. There is an illuminating address on 'The

Co-Operative Ideal' given in Sunderland in 1894, in which he describes co-operation as 'a master principle of life' which 'defines the right relation . . . of men as men bound together in the fellowship of one nature, one life, one destiny. Co-operation is the harmonious action of men and classes and nations.'[101] He admits that this may be an unattainable ideal, but says that he himself desires 'the widest application' of the principle of co-operation. Co-operative production within industry is therefore truly about 'reconciling interests which appear to be conflicting, of developing trustful fellowship between those who have to fulfil different functions'.[102] It has a 'moral value which is even greater than its economic value' and ideally 'includes in one fellowship all who are engaged in any work, however different in function, and gives to all a proportionate share in the profits of the business, and in the control of the administration'.[103]

Interestingly, Westcott claims that he has been a student of the co-operative movement for twenty-five years, and goes on to express his belief that an extension of the co-operative principle can help to bridge the gulf between the classes in our society. He concludes with the observation that the family is the supreme example of this ideal with its 'subordination of individual to social instincts'.[104]

It is clear from this why the co-operative ideal was so congenial to Westcott. It reinforced his convictions about the solidarity and brotherhood of the human race. It also appealed to his strong instincts as a born reconciler. There may be some naivety about the extent of the gulf between the classes in late Victorian Durham. There is no doubt in his mind, however, that the ideal must be applied practically whenever the opportunity arose.

All this is very relevant to Westcott's celebrated intervention in the Miners' strike of 1892, which may fairly lay claim to be the most famous example of his doing theology in context. In his Westcott Memorial lecture, *Bishop Westcott and the Miners*, Geoffrey Best set Westcott's intervention in the context of the steadily worsening relations between employers and employees in the 1880s and 1890s. When recession came in 1891 things came to a head: the owners requested cuts in wages, which were refused by the unions, and the strike began. Given the bitterness which already existed between the two sides, the strike was inevitable. There was, Best claims, virtually a state of war between the two sides, which was the first sign of a new era in which confrontations between the two would become increasingly bitter. Westcott's offer of mediation gave both sides the opportunity to save face. The miners were desperate, and there is evidence that the owners were looking for the 10% reduction in wages which Westcott suggested. His intervention certainly brought about a settlement more quickly than would otherwise have occurred.[105]

What Best shows, however, is that the conciliation board which was set up to deal with future disputes, and which Westcott believed was the most important part of the agreement, was to be of limited value. It was soon unpopular with the miners, who voted to abolish it after only nine months, only to reinstate it again. It was, he argues, only a 'sanction of the sliding scale' which had existed for some years, and by which wages had gone up and down according to the cyclical boom and slump within the mining industry. It did not help the miners to achieve even the lowest of their essential needs, a minimum wage tied to the cost of living. This could only be done by more radical forms of industrial action, which the next generation of miners' leaders were already considering.[106]

This sets Westcott's mediation in a new light. Further, Best goes on to argue that his well-intentioned action with its very limited achievements typifies the bishop's overall work at Durham. He did not really understand the industrial world of the north-east and the social forces which shaped people's lives. In his continual emphasis on the importance of 'character' in his teaching he was offering a simplistic individual panacea for complex problems. Behind this, he claims, was 'that innocent inability to understand the actual strength of Sin upon which all who knew him closely commented'.[107] He concludes that Westcott's main contribution to the life of the diocese was the personal one of his humility and concern for people, so that the miners came to believe that he was honest and well-intentioned and had a genuine care and concern for them.[108]

Best's argument amounts to a considerable critique of Westcott's Durham years, and of his practical theology. The point about the limitations of his conciliation in the 1892 strike must be conceded. What is interesting is that the memory of his intervention in the strike soon became a powerful 'myth' which enabled him to achieve more in his remaining years at Durham than would otherwise have been the case. As is often the case it is not what happens which is the most important thing, but what people believe has happened. This 'myth' was to profoundly affect all Westcott's successors in the diocese. In August 1920, for instance, Hensley Henson was facing another miners' strike in the county. In agonizing as to whether or not he should intervene personally, he was haunted by the example of Westcott: 'The tradition of Westcott leads the public to think that much is possible in the way of episcopal mediation, which everybody with any real information on economic subjects today knows to be wholly beyond the limits of possibility.'[109]

Best's wider point about Westcott's naivety on social questions is much more debatable. He did speak frequently about the importance of 'character' in his Durham addresses, and was emphatic that legislation was not the ultimate solution to problems such as intemperance and immorality. Christian example was, for him, more lasting in its effects than government policies. It is quite unfair, however, to accuse him of offering this alone as the panacea for social injustice and evil. He states quite clearly in his 1890 lecture on socialism that it is the task of Christian teachers to show 'that Christianity, which has dealt hitherto with the individual, deals also with the State, with classes, with social conditions, and not only with personal character'.[110] Moreover, his own actions show that he took this seriously. His association with the Christian Socialist movement, and his initiation of the series of Auckland conferences on social and economic issues, refute the allegation that he could think only in terms of individualist solutions. It has been part of our argument in this chapter that Westcott took great pains to understand the context in which he lived and worked.

It is true that in engaging with these issues he was hampered, as Best points out, by his optimism about human nature. He was in some respects an 'innocent abroad', as when, for example, in an address on the co-operative ideal in Sunderland in 1894 he asserts that in England there is 'no sharp division of classes among us', and claims that the Church of England has 'united all classes by sympathetic contact'.[111] His family and friends were largely from an upper middle-class background, and he had led a comparatively sheltered life in the academic world until the move to Westminster. All this, it must be admitted, affected his attitude and approach to social issues.

Where Best's criticism is unfair is in the lack of recognition of the effort and energy Westcott devoted to earthing his theology in the local context in Durham. His priorities changed during this period. He turned his back on academic scholarship, unlike his predecessor, Lightfoot, and focused his attention on the social and economic problems of county and country, and how the incarnation might shed light on their solutions. It was a huge reorientation for one from his background, and it must not be minimized. To recognize this is in no way to gloss over his limitations.

It is instructive in this respect to read some words of his successor at Durham, H. G. C. Moule, written to the miners in December 1901 as an inaugural letter of greetings. They reveal something of the impression Westcott had made in the north-east, and how the priorities of an Evangelical bishop would be different:

I follow a great Bishop. The miners of Durham are not likely to forget him. I cannot be like him in his wonderful power of masterly dealing with the difficulties of life and labour. But my heart is warm with his devotion to his brothers ... My first work as a Christian man and a minister of the Gospel is to preach ... our Lord Jesus Christ as the Divine Saviour and eternal life of man, the Lord of our spiritual and immortal being. I have to remember that no outward improvement of society can ever be a substitute for the conversion of our hearts and the power of God in our lives.[112]

A more balanced and fair judgement on Westcott's Durham years was given by a later successor of his, A. M. Ramsey (1904–88), who was theologically much closer to him than to Moule:

> The obscurities in his thought . . . were offset by the appeal of his character with its blend of otherworldliness and practicality and by the concrete nature of his social teaching. His old age in the see of Durham was thus the crown and completion of his years of academic work.[113]

6

EMPIRE, WAR, AND THE
MISSION OF THE CHURCH

Basil had a singular gift of sympathy, and, what is rare in these later days, 'almost oriental courtesy', as a friend said. These endowments stood him in good stead in his work, and I looked forward confidently to the time when he would be a Hindoo to Hindoos.[1]

1 Attitudes to the empire

The last three decades of the nineteenth century witnessed the idea of empire taking an increasing hold upon the imagination of the British people.

Some historians would date this change of mood from Disraeli's famous speech at the Crystal Palace in June 1872 in which he extolled the pride of the nation in belonging to an imperial power, and expressed its resolve to maintain its empire. In 1875 he obtained for the government a controlling interest in the Suez Canal, and the following year made Queen Victoria Empress of India. Such actions were calculated to unite the nation at a time of economic depression and to encourage the quest for new markets for British goods. In the 1880s Gladstone was compelled by the strength of imperialist feeling to encourage initiatives which he had opposed in opposition. One result of this was the 'scramble for Africa' which added five million square miles to the territory of the British Empire.

This spirit and confidence was well expressed in a best-selling book of the time, J. R. Seeley's *The Expansion of England* (1883), which claimed that English history pointed to her destiny as a unique power

[147]

in the world if only she would throw off her native parochialism and look outwards to the extension of the English name into other countries of the world. The opportunity was there for her to become a 'Greater Britain'.

This 'New Imperialism' came to full fruition in the 1890s. The British Empire now covered one quarter of the earth's land mass and had one quarter of its population. There was an almost universal pride in what was held to be the greatest empire ever known. The British believed themselves to be the most powerful nation in the world, arbiters of the world's affairs. 'Supremacy, dominion, authority, size, were the watchwords of the time.'[2] The culmination of all this was the overwhelming spectacle of Queen Victoria's Diamond Jubilee procession on 22 June 1897, when 50,000 troops from all over the empire marched through the streets of London to St Paul's Cathedral for a thanksgiving service.

Religion and the imperialist spirit were closely linked. Many Christians believed that a spiritual destiny had called the British to their special position. They were 'a chosen people, divinely different, endowed with special gifts, but entrusted with special duties, too . . . Providence, Destiny, Judgement – all these were basic to the vocabulary of the New Imperialism.'[3] This belief in the superiority of British civilization was tempered, however, in the most sensitive imperialists by the conviction that the chief end of empire was not the acquisition of wealth or power but the communication and spread of Christian faith and morality. The empire could then be seen as a means of service to humankind. Such a spirit was the inspiration behind much missionary work in the far-flung dominions of the empire.

How did Westcott respond to this remarkable growth of imperialist fervour? There were times when he acquiesced wholeheartedly in the enthusiasm for expansion and domination. In a sermon preached in London in 1900 he argued that the emergence of the empire was an inevitable development in the realization of the 'solidarity of mankind'.

Imperialism is the practical advocacy of a fellowship of peoples with a view to the completeness of their separate development, a wide federation for the realisation in the members of their special character . . . an Empire is a step towards the attainment of the earthly destiny of man . . . a corporate fellowship of men as men.[4]

The development of empires, he believed, belongs to a late stage in human history, and the English experience of empire is unique.

Expansion is the essential characteristic of English national life. Our Colonies have been spread throughout the world not in obedience to any definite and far-seeing design, but by a natural overflow of an energetic population . . . They have remained, though far off, parts of the Mother State. In this lies the secret of their permanence. In the seventeenth and eighteenth centuries there was not only a Greater Britain: there was also a Greater France, a Greater Spain, a Greater Portugal, a Greater Holland, but now the Greater Britain alone remains.[5]

Here he is giving expression to that confident and optimistic spirit of the times, which developed during the 1890s. He has no doubts about the privileged position of the British in the world. In another address in 1900 he went so far as to describe the empire as an image of the Kingdom of God! 'A world-wide Empire is a faint earthly image of the Kingdom of God, even as the Roman Empire was in the Apostolic age. The unity established by ties of blood and character and history is a transitory sign of that eternal fellowship for which we were made.'[6] There is irony in the fact that both addresses we have referred to were given during the Boer War, which divided the nation and was the first step in the gradual undermining of this kind of confidence in empire.

Alongside this buoyant expression of the spirit of the times, however, we find Westcott frequently voicing doubts about the developing imperialism of the 80s and 90s. His tender conscience could not acquiesce in the cruder expressions of the imperial ideal which became increasingly common in the last years of Queen Victoria's reign. His strong convictions about the brotherhood of men, their essential equality before God, led him to question the assumption that the British were a superior people. In 1886 he preached a sermon in Westminster Abbey on the words of Paul at Athens: '[God] made of one every nation of men for to dwell on all the face of the earth, having determined their appointed seasons, and the bounds of their habitation; that they should seek God' (Acts 17.26–7 RV). He affirms the relevance of these words to the expanding empire, and points to the danger of claiming supremacy:

> To us perhaps the spirit of domination is peculiarly perilous from the force of individuality in the English nature and from the conditions of our island home. Our first impulse is to claim universal supremacy for our own customs and opinions and forms of government: to regard each variation from our own standards of thought and action as the result of ignorance or degeneracy . . . to press patriotism into arrogant self-assertion.[7]

Such a spirit must be countered by the affirmation of the unity of the human race which is implicit in Christ's incarnation, and by recalling St Paul's metaphor of the body in 1 Corinthians 12, which he applies to the diversity of the nations of the world who all have an important office in the one body of humanity. If such beliefs underlie our understanding of empire, we shall be careful 'not to make our power the counsellor of our designs, or our material interests the standard of our successes'.[8] Rather, we shall 'grow conscious of the limits of our powers, and so we shall better understand that God is preparing His Kingdom, not through one nation only but through many nations, and claiming from others ministries which we cannot render'.[9]

Westcott gives a vivid illustration of this spirit in citing the example of the Bishop of Minnesota, who in the face of much opposition pleaded the cause of the American Indians before the Convention of his church.[10] In view of the later twentieth-century concern for the plight of the American Indians it is interesting to note Westcott's interest in them as early as the mid-1880s!

His conclusion is that the burden of empire has been laid upon the British 'not for material aggrandisement, not for the accumulation of private wealth, not for the suppression of independent growth, but that we may educate to generous activity great peoples in the East and West for the fulfilment of one life'.[11]

One response to the challenge of empire, then, was to affirm the New Testament conviction that 'In Christ there is no East or West'. Another response was that it had been entrusted to the British as an opportunity for service. In one of his village sermons preached in 1876 he pleaded the cause of the English mission to Bengal, where a relative of his wife was a bishop. The empire was not for vain glory but for the service and benefit of mankind: here 'the master of all is servant of all'.[12] In the address from 1900 referred to earlier he makes the same point:

> The vital question for us all is, What shall be the aim of our Empire? To what end shall the Mother Country use her treasures of influence, of insight, of experience? . . . She will . . . assuredly use them, not for aggrandisement in power or wealth, not for making others instruments of her own will, but, in a word, for effectual service – for service, in the first place, to those who are bound to her in the unity of Empire, and then to those who are without, as fellow-servants with her of God for humanity.[13]

He was in no doubt that such service would be costly and sacrificial. 'Imperial duty corresponds with national sacrifice . . . The love of country, like all love, is sustained, not by gaining, but by giving.'[14] He then refers to the Old Testament conviction that the nation of Israel was called to service and sacrifice that all the nations of the earth should be blessed, implying that the English nation and Church were called to a similar mission.

In a paper written in June 1897 reflecting on the lessons of Queen Victoria's reign he asked the question, What have we learnt during the past sixty years? One conclusion stands out:

> Great wealth and wide empire, which commonly fill our thoughts when we begin to estimate national prosperity, are opportunities of service and nothing more: a blessing or a curse as they are used.[15]

There is no doubt, then, that although there were times when Westcott's attitudes to empire marked him out as a man of his time, his vision of what he frequently called Britain's 'Imperial duty' was informed and shaped by biblical principles. He felt increasingly that the spiritual needs of the people of the empire had been neglected, and that it was time to make reparation for this.

His disillusionment with the aggressive and materialistic imperialism of the 1890s is seen best in his response to the Queen's Jubilee procession in June 1897 with its impressive display of the empire's military might. Nine months after the event he sent a letter[16] to his diocesan clergy in which he reflected on the lessons of the Jubilee. The dominant note of the letter is one of uneasiness. He acknowledges that the procession had been an impressive spectacle, that it had shown clearly the unity and military strength of the empire, and that it had united the nation in admiration and pride. On reflection, however, it had only served to confirm some of his deepest concerns about the direction and ethos of national life over the past decade. It had brought home to him afresh that in the nation as a whole the Christian faith was regarded as remote from ordinary life:

> The Christian Faith is treated as the Greeks treated Philosophy, as something far removed from the ordinary affairs of life. Sermons are often listened to respectfully . . . but it appears to be assumed that the

definite motives to which the preacher appeals, the forces which he claims to lay open, the transcendent truths which he declares, belong to an ideal region unconnected with the conflicts, the anxieties, the interests of daily duties. To invoke Christian principles in dealing with domestic or international questions is by general consent held to be out of place.[17]

The letter goes on to argue that what the nation needed above all else was a rebirth of Christian faith and energy which would lead to a new sense of responsibility in political and economic affairs and in family and social life. The familiar themes of his Durham years are repeated: the importance of the witness of lay people in civic and business life, the limitations of mere legislative change, the need to bridge the gulf between the classes, the challenge of poverty, the call to embody 'the social power of the Gospel'.[18]

In brief, the Jubilee celebrations had led him to reflect on the life of the nation, and especially on how far the people who had built up a vast empire had strayed from its Christian ideals. He had been disturbed by the overwhelming military nature of the Jubilee celebrations. 'Is the army the nation? or the strength of the nation?' he wrote at the time.[19] Time had served only to confirm his misgivings: 'We have had a vision of the call of England, impressive at once and intelligible by the contrast it suggests with the actual organisation of our social life. Such a vision cannot but fill us with self-questionings and self-condemnations.'[20]

One of Westcott's early biographers accused him of complacency over the Queen's Jubilee celebrations: 'The ostentatious display of military force . . . which distressed many, did not so strike Westcott.'[21] This is unjust criticism. For once the latter's characteristic optimism deserted him, and he could reflect only on the ambiguity of the gift of empire.

2 *The practice and theology of mission*

It is against this background of the growth and rapid development of an empire that we must now explore Westcott's involvement in the world mission of the Church.

It is difficult today to write objectively about the missionary movement of the nineteenth century. The years 1800–1914 saw the greatest spread of Christianity across the world since the first century. The past half-century or more, however, has seen sustained criticism of the motives which inspired this movement. Historians have dismissed the whole enterprise as an adjunct to British imperialism, concerned largely with extending the interests of trade and profitability, while many former colonies have reacted with revulsion against the religious and cultural imperialism which inspired the missionary enterprise.

What is indisputable is that a huge variety of missionary societies and individuals were involved in the movement, each with its distinctive objectives based on a particular theology of mission. A just appraisal of what Latourette called the 'Great Century' will be greatly enhanced if an attempt is made to understand and differentiate between these varied and often contrasting strands.

It is therefore important to understand Westcott's very distinctive contribution to the practice and theology of mission, for he is an important figure in the late Victorian missionary expansion, as a recent ground-breaking study by Kenneth Cracknell of early twentieth-century missionary attitudes has recognized.[22]

We look first at his practical involvement and then at his theology of mission. India was his great passion, the focus of both practice and theology, and his later influence was greatest there. One explanation of this lies in his family history. His great-grandfather, Foss Westcott, was a notable member of the East India Company in Madras from 1741 to 1751, and his wife and son were both buried there.[23] When Westcott's son, Arthur, became a lecturer at St Augustine's College in Madras in 1887 he wrote a letter to his mother in which he said that he had found records of the Westcott family there dating from the eighteenth century.[24] Then, as we have noted earlier, Mrs Westcott had a brother-in-law who was involved in the Bengal mission. Eventually, four of their sons would serve in the Church in India.

The beginnings of his interest in India are discernible in a sermon preached at Cambridge in 1872 in which he was very critical of traditional missionary attitudes. He called for the founding by the university of 'some school of Indian students [which] should be formed and sustained to witness to her devotion and to represent her spirit in the East', which he hoped might become 'some new Alexandria'.[25] This would be part of a plan for the whole of the Asian continent:

> The conversion of Asia is the last and greatest problem which has been reserved for the Church of Christ. It is through India that the East can be approached. It is to England that the evangelizing of India has been entrusted by the providence of God.[26]

The possibility of establishing an Anglican brotherhood in India was first suggested to Westcott in 1876 by Thomas Valpy French, a long-serving CMS missionary in Lahore, and the Cambridge Brotherhood at Delhi was inaugurated the following year under the leadership of E. H. Bickersteth, a fellow of Pembroke College. In the years that followed Westcott's views were to shape its aims and ethos. He was also deeply involved in its financial and moral support. Published and unpublished letters reveal him receiving subscriptions for its work, arranging business and public meetings in Cambridge and London, and discussing the work of the Brotherhood. He used the platform of SPG and CMS meetings not only to set out his own distinctive theology of mission, but also to keep the Delhi work before the public. He also reminded the university of its responsibilities towards the mission.

His very personal commitment to this particular venture impressed many during his Durham years. The fact that four of his sons eventually offered for service in the Church in India underlined the depth of his own dedication to the mission of the Church. An unpublished letter of 7 June 1896 thanks him for his 'practical Christian writings' and 'more especially for sending forth your own sons to serve Christ in foreign missions'.[27] When Basil, who joined the Cambridge Brotherhood in 1896, died four years later from cholera, Westcott's dedication seemed even greater.

The regular letters of the four sons kept their parents in touch with the realities of life on the mission field. Over one hundred and eighty letters from Arthur in Madras over a sixteen-year period throw light on the difficulties facing English clergy stationed there: loneliness, cholera, drought, the problem of caste, the desperate shortage of money affecting all the missions, and the challenge of mastering the language and understanding the indigenous religions.[28] There is a wry comment in one of the letters to his mother on the costliness of English theological books: 'Father's books are quite beyond their reach'!

Westcott's own commitment to foreign missions meant that many of his diocesan clergy went to serve in the Church overseas. In 1895 he received a letter from some of his younger clergy which made the suggestion that men in his diocese could be encouraged to offer for home or foreign service as the need arose, and that the final decision as to deployment should be left with him. He gladly accepted this responsibility as part of the duty of his office, and because it recognized the 'one work' of the Church at home and overseas.[29] An anonymous tribute in the *Guardian* after his death, clearly by one of his closest colleagues, recognized the extreme care which he gave to evaluating whether men were suitable for foreign service: 'few knew how many he as unhesitatingly retained where they were and are'.[30]

He was also in demand for counsel on wider missionary matters. In 1891, for example, he joined a group of bishops and archbishops who were asked to give advice to the General Committee of the CMS on a dispute between a high church bishop and the society in Palestine. His role in this was a central one, and he subsequently wrote to the Archbishop of Canterbury with an evaluation and a recommendation, that the CMS should in future employ and use more indigenous lay people who would be able to represent Christianity with knowledge and intellectual ability.[31]

It was from this very practical involvement in the Church's missionary work that Westcott developed his theology of mission. Just as he was constantly attempting to relate his more general theological reflection to the real world of social and industrial problems, so his theology of mission derived from his regular contacts with the Cambridge Brotherhood, with his sons, and with other clergy serving in the Church overseas.

We saw earlier how his general theological position was worked out against a background of real dissatisfaction with current theological attitudes. In particular he was convinced that neither Evangelicals nor Tractarians could meet the needs of Church or society in the ferment of the 1880s and 1890s. In the same way he is deeply unhappy with traditional attitudes to mission. As early as 1872 he expresses some forceful criticisms which suggest that for some time he had been aware of the need for a more radical theology of mission. In the Cambridge sermon mentioned earlier he argues that missionary teaching has been 'too defined and traditional'.[32] Christians in the west have inherited a great treasure of doctrine but it is mistaken to offer it in that precise form to people of other cultures. In doing so, we 'do dishonour to the infinite fulness of the Gospel'.[33] If Greek and Latin and Teutonic Christianity each have their distinctive characteristics, can it be doubted that India 'is capable of adding some new element to the completer apprehension of the Faith?'[34] Missionary work is 'the communication of a life and not of a system'.[35]

His second criticism is that missionary work has been 'too individual'.[36] It has neglected the truth that the Christian faith is essentially social, the proclamation of a kingdom and the calling of individuals into a divine society. This is especially relevant in India, where the reality of the caste system can only be overcome by the Church's 'substituting the idea of divine brotherhood for the isolation of supposed

[157]

spiritual descent'.[37] In brief, there is 'need of something more than the personal message of the individual preacher'.[38]

It is his third criticism, however, which is the most trenchant. Missionary teaching has been 'denationalizing'.[39] It has not taken seriously enough the modes of thought and religious instincts of the indigenous people, and in this respect it has unconsciously repeated the mistake made by the Judaizers in the Early Church. If we are to proclaim a universal rather than a western gospel, 'we must keep ourselves and our modes of thought studiously in the background . . . We must follow the religious instincts and satisfy the religious wants of Hindu and Mohammedan through the experience of men from among themselves.'[40] This is only possible, he suggests, if a school of Indian students is founded after the model of Alexandria – and it is in this context that he makes his oft-quoted suggestion: 'And is it too much to hope that we may yet see on the Indus, or the Ganges, some new Alexandria?'[41]

This sermon, preached before the university, was designed to bring home to its members the fact that there was an important role for the university in missionary work. It also contains the seeds of his very distinctive theology of mission, which he was to develop over the next two decades and which was very much at odds with much traditional thinking. The fullest expression of his missiology is to be found in two addresses from the mid-1890s. Both are based on texts from St Paul, in which he speaks of his being entrusted with the mission to the Gentiles. The first, 'The Call of the English Nation and of the English Church', was preached in St Paul's Cathedral in May 1894. It takes as its starting point the words in Ephesians 3.8: 'Unto me, who am less than the least of all saints, is this grace given, that I should preach among the Gentiles the unsearchable riches of Christ' (AV). Westcott makes what seems to us the audacious claim that Paul's words about the Gentiles can be applied to the English Church and nation: they stand to the peoples of the world as Paul stood to the Gentiles in the first century. Here he reflects the 'new imperialism' of the 1890s, which as we saw earlier sometimes shapes his attitudes. At the same time, however, he is critical of the materialistic spirit of his native country, and emphasizes that the responsibility has been given for 'human ministry' and not for the satisfaction of our own interests or ambitions: 'God has set us to be not only conquerors, or pioneers, or masters, or furnishers of the materials of outward civilisation, but beyond all, evangelists.'[42]

This address is notable for its exposition of a striking new motive for engaging in mission. He argues that the nations of the empire have a contribution to make to the truth of the incarnation:

> There are great nations – China and India – inheritors of ancient and fruitful civilisations, endowed with intellectual and moral powers widely different from our own, which have yet . . . some characteristic offering to render for the fuller interpretation of the Faith. There are innumerable tribes in Asia and Africa and America, which seem likely to teach us with new force that the Spirit, sent in the name of the Son of Man, is able to give dignity to the forms of the simplest life. All these lessons have to be learnt; and when they are learnt, they will be both for the enrichment and for the illumination of our message, which is one at once and infinite.[43]

The great diversity found in these nations will in the end 'find in the Incarnation that which combines them harmoniously in the unity of one life, as each according to its capacity embodies part of that Divine likeness which man was created to gain'.[44] Each will find in the Christian gospel 'the strength which they require and at the same time disclose through the experience of life new mysteries in the Incarnation'.[45] Such a vision, Westcott believes, is implicit in the imagery of Revelation 22, which speaks of the nations walking amidst the light of the holy city and of the kings of the earth bringing their glory to it.

Westcott was not suggesting that the incarnation as a fact can be altered in any way but rather that the interpretation of its significance could be deepened by contacts with non-Christian peoples. 'Great

[159]

peoples become to us interpreters of the will of God.'[46] We are reminded of his prophecy that Indian thinkers would be able to fully interpret the thought of St John in years to come.[47]

Cracknell points out the significance of this argument in the nineteenth century context. It was a 'brand new motive for mission' which created 'sufficient space for the working out of patient inter-faith dialogue', and in its very positive view of the religious experience of the indigenous peoples it was worlds away from the theology which saw them as heathens needing to be rescued from everlasting damnation.[48]

Within this address two other motives for mission are mentioned, both of which are found elsewhere in his reflections on mission. It will be a means of renewal both for the life of the Church and for the nation, generating a renewal of interest in Christianity and a new enthusiasm and energy in the Church at home:

> For our world-wide witness to Christ . . . concerns ourselves most nearly. It reacts upon ourselves. The foreign Mission-field brings to us not only that larger conception of our faith . . . but also the immediate confirmation of it which we need. It shows us new proofs of the power of Christ to subdue all things to Himself . . . We all share the fulness of one growing life. As often as we hear of a soul surrendered to Christ amid the unfamiliar influences of a strange land we recognise the signs of a Divine Presence.[49]

It was for this reason that he encouraged parishes in the Durham diocese to have a link with an overseas diocese, and there was a special link with the diocese of Adelaide.

The other motive was that of brotherhood. We are all children of the one Father. This was a popular notion in the 1880s and 1890s with the growth of socialist ideas and aspirations. For Westcott there was only one foundation for such notions:

> The Faith which bears us to the Mission-field gives the one solid basis for their loftiest aspirations. For there can be no other sure

foundation for human brotherhood, no other adequate spring of love, than lies in the Christian Gospel of creation and redemption. To feel this . . . is the call of the missionary.[50]

The second key address was given in London in 1895 and is entitled 'Missions a Revelation of the Mystery of God'. The mystery referred to is that of which St Paul speaks in Colossians 2.2–3, the revelation that Christ dwells among the Gentiles and is not confined to the Jewish people. This, for Westcott, is the foundation of the whole missionary enterprise. Just as he had argued that the Logos of God was at work in the pagan world of Greece and Rome, so he was convinced of the same presence among the contemporary non-Christian nations of the empire.

The address is an attempt to outline a missionary strategy for a changing world. There is an acknowledgement that missions are entering a new phase. The past century has seen a great variety of approaches to evangelization and a huge growth in knowledge and appreciation of the non-Christian people of the empire and their scriptures. The challenge now is to discern the divine plan for the future. What are the priorities in this changing situation? The first, according to Westcott, is commitment to the mission in India which has a special place in the hearts of the English Church and people. The 'conversion of India' requires that we give our greatest teachers to her and establish strong missions with Christian brotherhoods which must ultimately become independent of our presence and support. As a result, 'by patience and tenderness and sympathy we may interpret and complete the thoughts of many races, and, taught by the Spirit sent in the Name of Christ, may confirm and satisfy the aspirations of many faiths'.[51]

A second priority is combining respect for other people's beliefs with the conviction that the Christian revelation is unique:

We shall . . . always feel and show tender and sympathetic regard for the partial truths, not untaught by the Word 'that lighteth every man', through which great faiths have preserved the life of nations

[161]

for long ages; but we shall not exaggerate them, and we shall not dissemble our own claims. We have committed to us 'a new thing in the earth', a revelation absolutely unique, essentially different in kind from all other religions.[52]

The belief in a unique revelation, however, was no excuse for disrespect. The hallmarks of the Christian mission must be 'patience and tenderness and sympathy'. It is significant how often the word 'sympathy', which we noted in an earlier chapter is a characteristic word in Westcott's theology, occurs in his missionary addresses.

A third priority is the willingness to emulate Christ's pattern of sacrifice and self-emptying. The great peril of the British missionary was a sense of social and intellectual superiority over those among whom he worked. This must give way to the realization that we are servants of the one who took the form of a servant: 'we must loyally and lovingly remember that we come among them "not to be ministered unto but to minister", yes, and if need be, to give our lives for those whom we serve. Sympathy was the mind of Christ, and sympathy is the soul of Missions.'[53]

A fourth priority is that Christians should display a spirit of unity and love in their dealings with one another. The background to this is the rivalry and competitiveness found amongst missionary societies. This, for Westcott, was a stumbling-block to the spread of the gospel. 'The unity of love, which we so feel after, is that which will, as the Lord has said, lead the world to believe in His Mission.'[54]

The address closes with a caution about 'success' in missionary work. Westcott believed that there could be no 'quick fixes':

Meanwhile we shall not look anxiously for large results. Results will answer to the wise counsel of God. Of the immeasurable scheme of His working we can see little, but we see enough to determine our duty and to support our faith . . . success . . . as we count success . . . is no measure of the power of God that is with us.[55]

Reflecting on his missionary theology, it is the radical nature of his teaching which impresses. At a time when conversionist attitudes were dominant he advocated a more open view which took seriously the contribution to the understanding of the gospel which the people of Asia might bring. In this respectful attitude towards other faiths he was influenced by Max Müller, the German Professor of Comparative Philology at Oxford, who did more than anyone to acquaint the late Victorian age with the knowledge of non-Christian religions.[56] In his lecture 'On Missions' delivered in Westminster Abbey in 1873, Müller argued that love is the key to success in missionary work, and that the essence of such work is 'parental' rather than 'controversial'. It is fruitless to attempt to win converts by argument, for argument alone achieves little in theological discussion. The final victory over other faiths will be gained by loving and respecting their followers, not by forcing our creeds upon them: 'The fundamentals of our religion are not in these poor Creeds; true Christianity lives, not in our belief, but in our love – *in our love of God, and in our love of man, founded on our love of God*.'[57] This kind of emphasis is found throughout Westcott's general theological work – the need always to give faith practical expression – so it is not surprising that his theology of mission bears the same stamp.

What was his influence upon the later missionary work of the Church? One of his students, A. G. B. West, later revealed that Westcott saw the strategic importance of Australia in the Church's mission. He claims that he regarded Sydney, Calcutta and London as the three outstanding positions in the Church of England, and that he once intended to go to Australia himself. The 'Bush Brotherhoods' were also his inspiration.[58] As we have seen there was a special link between the Durham and Adelaide dioceses during his episcopacy. It is worth mentioning also that in recent years Australian scholars have shown more interest in Westcott and his Cambridge colleagues than their English counterparts![59]

It is in India, however, that his influence can be most clearly traced.

The direct descendant of the Cambridge Delhi Brotherhood is the Brotherhood of the Ascended Christ, given its new name in 1967. A portrait of Westcott still hangs above the fireplace in one of the rooms. Over the past thirty years it has given sustained commitment to the service of the poor in Delhi through clinics, community centres and schools. It has continued the earlier tradition of seeking to promote religious harmony, and in the 1990s focused in particular upon the needs and special plight of children in the city.[60] In addition to this link, the 'Westcott lectures' were endowed by William Teape, providing from 1955 for a yearly exchange of lecturers between India and Britain dealing with themes in the relationship between Hinduism and Christianity. The lectures were given at St Stephen's College, Delhi and at Cambridge, giving a range of well-known Christian thinkers over a number of years an opportunity to share reflections on interreligious situations.[61] They still continue today.

Westcott's vision of Christian mission was perhaps most notably embodied in the life and career of one of his Cambridge students, who became one of the most remarkable missionaries of the twentieth century. Charles Freer Andrews discovered the intellectual foundations for his faith in the teachings of Westcott and the *Lux Mundi* circle. When, prior to his ordination, he went to the Durham diocese as a lay worker at Monkwearmouth, he became part of the Westcott family circle through his friendship with Basil Westcott. He soon formed a close friendship with the Bishop, whose enthusiasm for social questions and love of the Greek Fathers had a profound influence upon the young man. He later remembered the parallel he drew between Greece and India:

> He placed India side by side with Greece – these, he said, were the two great *thinking* nations who had made the history of the world. As Greece had been the leader of Europe, India would always be the leader of Asia. One of his great hopes was that Indian thinkers would be able to interpret fully the Gospel of St. John.[62]

[164]

Andrews went out to Delhi with the SPG in 1904, joining the Delhi Brotherhood, and remained in India until 1940. Inspired by Westcott's dream of an Alexandria on the banks of the Jamna he was soon meeting Muslim and other scholars in dialogues in Delhi Public Library, and believed that he was encountering the presence of God in Sikhs, Muslims and Hindus. In 1908 he wrote 'North India', in which he argued for a change in missionary theology: Christianity needed to be stripped bare of its foreign accretions if it was to become indigenous. In 1911 he argued for the disestablishment of the Anglican Church in India.

His radical views led to increasing alienation from the Brotherhood and from the Church as a whole, which he felt was too complacently colonialist. He became friendly with the famous Hindu scholar, Rabindranath Tagore, and in 1914 repudiated his priestly orders and went to live in Tagore's ashram at Santineketan, where he remained for twenty-five years. He mingled with all kinds of Hindu groups, and through them became an intimate friend and advisor of Mahatma Ghandi. In this way he played an important role in the evolution of Indian independence. It was largely through his influence that the practice of indenture was abolished in 1920, and he was the only Englishman to retain the trust of the Indians after the Amritsar massacre in 1919. When Louis Mountbatten was appointed Viceroy of India, Ghandi's advice to him was to act 'as C. F. Andrews had done'. Ghandi called Andrews 'the pattern of the ideal missionary' and 'love incarnate', even after he had left SPG, while Tagore said of him that nowhere had he seen 'such a triumph of Christianity'. In independent India, schools and other institutions were named after him, a postage stamp was issued in his honour, and a National Seminar held in north Delhi at the centenary of his birth. Westcott's son, Foss, Bishop of Calcutta, spoke at his funeral on the words from 2 Samuel 3.38, 'Know ye not that there is a prince . . . fallen in Israel?'[63]

His attitude to missionary work was always at odds with the dominant Evangelical stream of thought. In his essentially sympathetic or 'expectant' approach to other religious traditions he was very much the disciple of Westcott. Andrews himself always acknowledged his debt to his great teacher: 'He was by his nature more akin to Hindu India than to the Islamic East. It was about Hindu and Buddhist India that I always used to talk with him . . . When I look back I think I probably owe more to him than to anyone else my attraction for Hindu India.'[64] After almost thirty years in India he wrote that for him 'Christ has become not less central but more central; not less divine to me, but more so, because more universally human. I can see Him as the pattern of all that is best in Asia as well as in Europe.'[65]

Adrian Hastings regards Andrews as an example of the Anglican spiritual vision at its finest, still remembered where most others are forgotten. Like A. S. Cripps in Rhodesia he had the 'irresistible urge to find a new spiritual and human relationship with the non-western world. They had gone out to teach; they really did remain to learn.'[66]

3 Christianity and world religions

The career of C. F. Andrews leads us to a consideration of Westcott's view of the relationship between Christianity and the other world faiths. We have touched on this at a number of points already, but it merits more detailed examination simply because it is at the heart of his whole conception of what the world mission of the Church actually is.

The first half of the nineteenth century had seen Christians generally taking a very negative and hostile view of other religious traditions. Cracknell distinguishes six elements in the early nineteenth-century theology of religion prevalent in Britain and America, and, in each of these, other world faiths are regarded as idolatrous, superstitious or spurious.[67] One of the first people to challenge this negative assessment was F. D. Maurice. In 1847 he published *The Religions of the World and their Relations to Christianity*, in which he tried to establish the truths underlying the various forms in which people expressed their worship.

He concluded that Islam, Hinduism, Buddhism, and even modern scepticism, were divinely appointed witnesses both for the gospel and against error and indifference. All have lessons for Christians, who should be grateful for their witness that religion has vitality and lasting power.

Interest in other religions was kindled by the growth of the empire, especially India, and mere curiosity led eventually to greater sympathy for those religions. It was Max Müller, whose influence on attitudes to Christian mission we noted earlier, who did more than anyone to widen the views of educated people on the nature of religion. Through his massive edition of *The Sacred Books of the East* and through his four series of Gifford lectures between 1888 and 1892, he helped people to discern the values in other religions for the sake of understanding their own. He believed that nearly every faith contained sufficient truth to enable those who sought the deity to find him in their hour of need. It was necessary to know about those faiths if one was to know who Christ was.

By the 1890s the comparative study of religion had become, in Owen Chadwick's words, 'a little force in public education', and there was a 'new sense of the reality of non-Christian religion'.[68] Some Christians felt that their Christian life was enriched by knowledge of other world faiths. Many others, however, clung to the traditional view that the Christian way was the only way to salvation.

It was against this background that Westcott worked out his own theology of religion. In his commentary on John and in his theology lectures at Cambridge we see him wrestling with the challenge of the world religions to the age-old claim that the Christian faith was uniquely true.

His work on John's Gospel in the 1870s brought him face to face with the Logos doctrine, and there are some significant insights in his exposition of the prologue to the Gospel. In his exegesis of the phrase 'the life was the light of men' in John 1.4 he comments: 'Man as made in the image of God stood in a special relation to the Word.' He then

[167]

quotes some words which Thomas Aquinas found in Theophylact, the eleventh-century Byzantine exegete:

> He saith not the Light of the Jews only but of all men; for all of us, in so far as we have received intellect and reason from that Word which created us, are said to be illuminated by Him.[69]

There is a striking comment on John 1.5, 'And the light shineth in darkness; and the darkness comprehended it not.' It is not to be understood as referring solely to the Christian revelation:

> It embraces the experience of Judaism and Heathendom, of pre-Christian and post-Christian times. The truth which found its most signal fulfilment in the historical Presence of Christ, was established in various ways both before and after it.[70]

Even more significant is his exegesis of 1.9 where the affirmation is made that the pre-existent Christ is the 'true Light, which lighteth every man that cometh into the world'. He interprets Christ's coming into the world

> as describing a coming which was progressive, slowly accomplished, combined with a permanent being . . . The mission of John was one and definite; but all along up to his time 'the Light' of which he came to witness continued to shine, being revealed in many parts and in many ways.[71]

He finds evidence elsewhere in the Gospel for this idea of 'a constant, continuous coming of the Word to men', and then makes this striking observation:

> Taken in relation to the context, the words declare that men were not left alone to interpret the manifestations of the Light in the Life

around them and in them. The Light from whom that Life flows made Himself known more directly. From the first He was (so to speak) on His way to the world, advancing towards the Incarnation by preparatory revelations.[72]

Finally, there is this pregnant comment on the words 'that lighteth every man': 'The words must be taken simply as they stand. No man is wholly destitute of the illumination of "the Light". In nature, and life, and conscience it makes itself felt in various degrees to all. The Word is the spiritual Sun.'[73]

Here, in his exposition of John's Logos theology, Westcott was laying the foundation for a theology of religion which would take a very positive attitude towards the pre-Christian world faiths.

What did Westcott make of the words of Jesus in John 14.6, which have always been a stumbling-block in inter-faith discussion and dialogue: 'I am the way, the truth, and the life: no man cometh unto the Father, but by me'? His exegesis of these words is highly significant. In his discussion of the first half of the sentence he refers to the use of the phrase 'the way' in the work of the Chinese philosopher Lao-tse (Taoism), and to the Jewish commentator Maimonides in his comment on 'the truth'. It is the final sentence of his comment on 'but by me', however, which is perhaps the most important of all his 'throwaway lines' about the validity of non-Christian approaches to God:

> It is only through Christ that we can . . . apprehend God as the Father, and so approach the Father . . . It does not follow that every one who is guided by Christ is directly conscious of His guidance.[74]

Cracknell claims that the final sentence 'was to prove seminal for Anglican thought on the significance of other religions'.[75]

That John's Gospel was crucial for Westcott's attitude to other faiths is seen also in a series of lectures he gave to theological students at Peterborough in 1876. There is an arresting comment on the promise of

Jesus in John 14.26 that the Holy Spirit 'shall teach you all things, and bring to your remembrance all that I said unto you'. He suggests that Jesus is saying that a full understanding of his words and of the incarnation itself lay in the future: 'His teaching shall be universal where mine has been partial . . . He shall bring me to the hearts of men. This is His work to the end of time; and every nation of the earth, every citizen in the federation of the world, shall contribute something to the completed apprehension of my Being.'[76] Also worth noting is his exposition of the words in John 15.5, 'apart from me ye can do nothing': 'Every act of sacrifice wherever and however wrought is an inspiration of the Word. He is obeyed, and may we thank God for the conviction, even where He is not known, and served where He has not openly revealed Himself.'[77] This is followed by a reference to the parable of the Sheep and the Goats in Matthew 25, with its acclamation for those who in serving the needy were serving the unknown Christ. There are similarities here with Karl Rahner's concept of the 'anonymous Christian', which gave theological support to the very positive pastoral attitude towards non-Christian faiths adopted by the Roman Catholic Church at Vatican II.[78]

A second important source for the development of Westcott's theology of religion was his concept of 'Christus Consummator'. In the book of that title he develops the teaching of the Letter to the Hebrews that human destiny is fulfilled and perfected in Christ in spite of human sinfulness. His optimism about human nature in the light of this is grounded in the conviction that creation, rather than the fall, is the starting-point of Christian theology. The most fundamental truth about human beings is that they bear the image of God. This is the clear teaching of Genesis 1.27: 'So God created man in His own image, in the image of God created he him':

In this august declaration of God's purpose and God's work we have set before us . . . the primal endowment and the final goal of humanity. We are taught that man received . . . a fitness for gaining, through growth and discipline and continuous benediction, union with God. God's image was given to him that he might gain God's likeness.[79]

This image is not effaced by the human propensity for sin: 'Man did not lose the image of God by the Fall. His essential nature still remained capable of union with God, but it was burdened and hampered.'[80]

Such a positive view of the human condition enabled Westcott to look much more favourably than, say, Calvinists, upon the non-Christian peoples of the world.

His belief in 'Christus Consummator' involves a hope or vision that all aspects of human aspiration would be fulfilled in Christ. He is especially thinking of the new scientific discoveries and how they are to be welcomed, not feared. There are, however, other references which suggest that he may also have been referring to the diversity of religious outlooks in the world, and how they too would be completed and fulfilled in him. There is a reference to the many different understandings of God's being. The gospel of creation 'teaches us to welcome and to use the imperfect conclusions of that Naturalism which offers a partial homage to the majestic progress of the physical order. It confirms the splendid visions which lend an unreal beauty to Pantheism by pointing to the end when *God shall be all in all*.'[81] This sermon ends with the vision of 'a holy unity passing knowledge – a holy unity which shall hereafter crown and fulfil creation as one revelation of Infinite Love, when the Father's will is accomplished and He has *summed up all things in Christ*'.[82]

Cracknell puts this in its nineteenth-century context: 'This God-centred vision of the place of Christ was incomparably different from the Jesus-centred focus of much late nineteenth-century Christianity, in which Jesus was viewed as a personal Redeemer offering private consolations and individualist spiritual experience.'[83] He also affirms the significance for his theology of religion of Westcott's paradigm shift from 'Christ the Consoler', who saves individuals from sin and suffering, to 'Christ the Fulfiller', whose concern is with the salvation of all people. This is a crucial change of emphasis because 'it is only possible to speak about other religious traditions positively when Christianity is made to concern the salvation of the whole world, and not just the individual's redemption from sin, suffering and sorrow'.[84]

The third source for Westcott's theology of religion is chapter four of his Cambridge lectures, *The Gospel of Life* (1892), where he sets out two important bases for the Christian interpretation of other religions. The first is the work of the pre-Christian nations in the Old and New Testaments in preparing the way for the Christian revelation. He argues that historical study of the development of religions is important for the Christian student. He sees parallels between the history of language and the history of religions: just as no one language tells us everything about the intellectual development of human beings, so the witness of many faiths is needed to inform us about their religious powers and needs. In particular the Old Testament witnesses to 'the part fulfilled by heathendom in the training of humanity for Christ'.[85] He cites the example of how Persian and Greek thought influenced Jewish life and organization:

> It can hardly be presumptuous to say that without the discipline of the Persian supremacy and the quickening impulse of Greek thought, a medium could not have been prepared to receive and record the revelation of the Gospel. The chosen people gathered to itself in due time the treasures which other races had won.[86]

This influence is acknowledged even within the pages of the Old Testament itself, where, for instance, Cyrus, the Persian king, is described as the Lord's anointed (Isaiah 45.1).

In the New Testament the preparation for the revelation of Christ is made more explicit. Paul's phrase 'the fulness of the time' (Gal. 4.4) is especially significant here. It is understood to mean that a whole range of historical circumstances had come together in order for the incarnation to take place and be understood. The whole process Westcott attributes to the work of the Logos of John's prologue. He also refers to the words of Jesus in John 10.16: 'Other sheep I have, which are not of this fold', who are 'not the less sheep because they had not yet recognised their shepherd'.[87]

Westcott's case, then, is that one important basis for the interpretation of the meaning of other faiths is an accurate understanding of the development of religion within the Bible itself. His implication is that Christians who based their view of the status of other religions on selected passages from Scripture had not really read the Bible correctly. Cracknell singles out for special mention his use of the Old Testament, and claims that Westcott was 'the first English theologian to invoke the pattern of Old Testament revelation against religious exclusivism or particularity in respect of other revelation'.[88]

The other basis for the Christian interpretation of other religions is the recognition by the Alexandrian Fathers, especially Justin and Clement, of the divine preparation for the incarnation in the heathen nations.

> These fathers and others, particularly men of the Alexandrine School, though they did not rise to the apprehension of the special office of Gentile nations in the divine economy, which a larger view of the relations of the parts of our vast human life enables us to gain, yet saw clearly that there was a work for and of God going on during the apparent isolation of the heathen from the region in which the Spirit revealed Him.[89]

He gives some space to an exposition of Justin's main ideas, singling out his assertion that the truths in Greek and Roman philosophy and poetry are due to the fact that 'a seed of the Word is implanted' (or rather 'inborn', ἔμφυτον) 'in every race of men', so that those who grasped the truth lived 'according to a part of the seminal Word' even as Christians live 'according to the knowledge and contemplation of the whole Word, that is Christ'.[90] Consequently, 'those who lived with the Word (with Reason) are Christians, even if they were accounted atheists, as among Greeks, Socrates and Heraclitus and those like them, and among non-Greeks, Abraham, and Ananias, Azarias and Misael, and Elias, and many others.'[91] The essence of Justin's teaching here is that there were 'Christians before Christ among the heathen'.[92]

He also mentions Clement's belief that Greek philosophy was 'a work of divine providence',[93] and that the Greek philosophers and poets were preparing the way for a greater revelation by the indwelling of the divine Logos. This was discussed fully in an earlier chapter. Its significance in this context is that it provides the foundation for a very positive evaluation of non-Christian religions.

In chapter five of *The Gospel of Life* Westcott gives a detailed exposition of 'The Religions of China' (Taoism and Confucianism), 'The Religions of India' (Hinduism and Buddhism), and Zoroastrianism. The overwhelming impression is of how generous and affirmative his evaluation of them is. He seems to be seeking what is good in each of them, and his criticisms are made against this background.

Of the Chinese religions, with their ancestor and imperial worship, he says that they

> deserve far more careful study than they have received . . . they present with unique force thoughts which at the present time seem to be essential for the interpretation of the Gospel to our own age, the solidarity of peoples and, in the end, of mankind, and the continuity of personal life in the family . . . For there is nothing which gave strength to China which does not find a fitting place in the Apostolic doctrine, while the Christian Faith guards against the evils which weakened the Empire.[94]

In the discussion of Hinduism, there is a long and remarkably sympathetic section on the idea of caste. He tries to understand it in its context within Hinduism, and suggests that it is founded on two great religious intuitions – 'that there is on the one hand a Divine element in humanity, and that this is realised by a spiritual fellowship; and on the other that society is based upon an organisation of unequal and distinct functions'.[95] These principles have been distorted and petrified by political and priestly pressures, but the institution has given permanence to Indian life: 'Caste is the outward expression of the belief that every detail of life is religious.'[96] He is similarly sympathetic towards the belief in reincarnation, which he had encountered, of course, in the myths of Plato. He claims that it bears testimony to two important beliefs: 'It affirms the vital connexion of all the forms of animated being. It affirms a possible, if indefinitely distant, reunion of every isolated existence with the one absolute existence.'[97]

Buddhism, with its sense of morality as an inherent obligation, is described as 'among the noblest as it is the vastest moral spectacle in history'.[98] Its central tenets – self-sacrifice, gentleness, reincarnation, nirvana – are again expounded with sympathy, making clear both where it has common ground with Christianity and where it diverges. Its greatest weakness for Westcott is in its denial of God in its purest form: 'It leaves no place for worship or for prayer or for a sacrifical priesthood: the believer has no support and no motive outside himself and his fellow creatures.'[99] His final sentence, however, affirms its permanent significance: 'The true vitality of Buddhism, and therefore its interest for us, lies in the moral principles of love and sacrifice.'[100]

Finally, he regards Zoroastrianism as 'a splendid attempt to deal with the world and man as integral parts of a divine scheme in their totality. Body and soul, the seen and the unseen, evil and good, were set over against one another, and some approach, at least, was made to reconcile them in a provisional synthesis.'[101] Its most important contribution to the religions of the world is, he believes, in its doctrine of the last things: 'Elsewhere a future existence was connected with the doctrine of transmigration. Zarathrusta fixed the ideas of a Heaven and a Hell as answering to man's conduct in his time of trial on earth.'[102]

Throughout these discussions of other religions Westcott frequently makes the point that a particular belief or principle is only truly realized in the Christian religion. For all his sympathy towards them he is convinced that Christianity is distinguished from all other faiths by the fact that it is 'absolute' and historical.[103] For him the incarnation is a unique idea 'wholly unapproached in earlier religious speculations or mythologies'.[104] What is remarkable, however, is that this does not prevent him from seeing what are the positive features in these faiths. He can even speak of 'the value of the prae-Christian Book-religions to the Christian student'![105] As we have seen, his exegesis of John's Gospel, especially the Prologue, and his understanding of the development of religion within the Bible enabled him to build bridges between the 'absolute' religion and the lesser revelations. Few, if any, treatments of systematic theology before his had adopted such a positive and sympathetic attitude towards other religions.

Finally, we may note that Westcott contributed an 'Appendix' to the *Cambridge Companion to the Bible* (1893) on the sacred books of the non-Christian religions, in which he set out in more systematic form the teaching of the religions he had described in his Cambridge lectures. That he was invited to contribute in this way to this popular handbook illustrates that he was regarded as an authority on such issues. In the concluding 'General Reflections' he is noticeably less sympathetic towards these scriptures than in his earlier lectures. He concludes that they are 'unhistorical', 'retrogressive', and 'partial', and he is emphatic that there is no comparison with the teaching of the Bible.[106] Whether this reflects the demands of the publishers or a changed perspective on his part it is impossible to say.

What of the later influence of Westcott's very liberal theology of religion upon the Church and the missionary movement? In part this can be seen in individuals who were profoundly affected by his lectures or by contact with him. The case of C. F. Andrews was mentioned earlier. Another example is J. E. C. Welldon, a student of Westcott at Cambridge, who later became Bishop of Calcutta. In a discussion of the difficulties he encountered in understanding the eastern religions, he acknowledges the influence of his former teacher in using one of his most characteristic words: 'I have schooled myself . . . into sympathy with other creeds and rituals than my own.'[107]

A more objective assessment of this influence is provided by Cracknell in his important study of the World Missionary Conference at Edinburgh held in 1910. In particular he made a close study of the report of the Commission on *The Missionary Message in Relation to Non-Christian Religions*. This was based on the replies of nearly 200 missionaries, who responded to a questionnaire which included these two questions:

1 What attitude should the Christian preacher take towards the religion of the people among whom he labours?
2 What are the elements in the said religion or religions which present points of contact with Christianity and may be regarded as a preparation for it?[108]

In his analysis of the replies Cracknell detects that a 'sea change' has taken place in the attitudes of missionaries towards people of other faiths. In a sample of 40 out of 187 replies he notes the constant use of the words 'sympathy' and 'appreciation'. While most of the comments acknowledged the fact that truth was mixed with error, or the need for that truth to be fulfilled, 'entirely missing is the note of condemnation of superstition and idolatry'.[109] Cracknell also noted a strong sense of solidarity with people of other faiths, and many references to personal friendship with their representatives. There was a strong emphasis on the importance of meeting such people rather than reading books about their religion, and a respect for the spirituality of the different peoples of the world.[110]

Cracknell goes on to ask what were the factors which had brought about this very significant change in attitudes. He concludes that one major factor was the teaching of five theologians who had had a major influence on the attitudes of this particular generation of missionaries.

Among the five was Westcott. He claims that F. D. Maurice was another key figure, as was A. V. Allen, an American Episcopalian theologian who was deeply influenced by Maurice, and possibly by Westcott too.[111]

Westcott's influence is traced in particular in his rediscovery of the Logos doctrine, which is explicit in the replies of numerous missionaries. This was a crucial factor since it enabled people, as we have seen, to speak of the presence of Christ within other religions. It was a pattern of thinking which was especially fruitful in India. John 1.9 ('the true Light, which lighteth every man') is mentioned explicitly by one missionary and implied by others, and there are two references to Clement of Alexandria's belief that the preparation for Christ's coming is to be found in the Greek philosophers. To be fair, the other four key theologians are also credited with rediscovering this doctrine.[112]

Westcott's concept of 'fulfilment' was also found to be useful in helping some of those who responded to the questionnaire to express the relationship between Christianity and other religions.[113] All were adamant about the finality of the Christian revelation, but they wanted also to affirm that other faiths were moving towards their fulfilment in Christ. There is, however, only one explicit reference to Westcott's 'Christus Consummator' theme, and this comes from C. F. Andrews. Others hint at it or are reaching towards it. Cracknell mentions in particular George Lefroy, the Anglican Bishop of Lahore, who acknowledges Westcott's influence in his conviction about the 'substantial contribution which the peoples, and . . . the Faiths, which are outside of Christ, can bring into the life of the Body when they are brought into the City of God'.[114]

A century after his death it is possible to see even more clearly than in 1910 the prophetic nature of Westcott's work in the theology of religion. In the mid-twentieth century the influence of Barthianism provoked sharp criticism of the kind of liberal attitudes which we have been discussing. In more recent years the strong conservative element in all the churches has reinforced scepticism about the status of non-

Christian religions, and reopened the debate which many had thought had been concluded. For all the wide geographical spread of religions and cultures in our time, the questions with which Westcott wrestled in the 1880s and 1890s are still being debated in the contemporary Church.

This was well illustrated by the January 2002 edition of the theological journal, the *Expository Times*, which included an article on 'Christian Theological Attitudes to Other Religious Traditions in a Plural World' by Frank Whaling, followed by a discussion of John 14.6, 'No One Comes to the Father but by Me', by R. E. O. White. In both there were reminders of Westcott's contribution to the debate over a century earlier. Whaling argued that one of the ways in which Christians have related their tradition to that of other faiths is by using the concept of 'fulfilment', which he describes as 'a time-honoured, ongoing, and eirenical attempt to combine respect for others with a sense of the fulness of Christ'.[115] White concludes that contrary to the popular conception, the words of Jesus in John 14.6 are not a denial of valid religious experience outside the Christian sphere, but rather affirm 'the far larger, more wonderful truth that *all* glimpses of divine reality come only through Christ . . . He is declaring the value, and by implication promising the success, of every genuine search for goodness and for God.'[116] It is impossible not to recall the pregnant final sentence of Westcott's exegesis of these words written one hundred and twenty years earlier: 'It does not follow that every one who is guided by Christ is directly conscious of His guidance.'[117]

4 War and peace: ideals and reality

We turn finally to examine Westcott's attitude towards war, and especially towards the Boer War which divided the nation at the turn of the century and put an early question mark against the permanence of the British Empire.

His first experience of war was of the Franco-Prussian war of 1870.

He took a chaplaincy in Germany in the summer of 1870, and in Cologne, Bonn and Darmstadt saw evidence of the conflict: soldiers being cheered off to the front, and the wounded arriving in railway carriages. He reflected on 'the two sides of the war picture'.[118]

Before he went out to Germany, but after the war had commenced, he preached two sermons in Peterborough Cathedral. In the first, 'Our Attitude Towards the War',[119] he laments it as a disaster in which no principle is at stake, the result of naked ambition. The important question for him, however, is what is our duty as spectators of the conflict? The first is to resist un-Christian attitudes. There must be care in interpreting the events in terms of divine retribution or providence since we are not able to read God's ways. He warns against thinking only of what we may gain from the struggle and not of the sufferings of those involved. He counsels against an unhealthy excitement about events which are overwhelming tragedies. The second duty is to pray for those who are directly affected by the war, and to believe in the efficacy of prayer.[120] Near the end of the sermon there is a sentence which in retrospect proved to be prophetic. It contained one of Westcott's favourite words, but pointed to the war which was to divide the nation and the churches almost thirty years later: 'It may be that in the active exercise of sympathy we shall be strengthening ourselves to bear the sacrifice which we in turn shall have to make.'[121]

The second sermon, 'A Sequel', was preached six weeks later when the conflict was well advanced. It breathes a 'European spirit' in its deep regret that such a calamity has come upon two countries 'both bound to us by the closest ties of mutual service, both charged with noble offices for the good of Europe and mankind'.[122] Again, his main concern is with evoking sympathy for those affected by the war. He discourages feelings of pride and superiority towards those involved, and the spirit which would glorify what is a tragedy. The most important response is expressing practical compassion towards those who suffer. (The bishop had ordered that a collection be taken to this effect in every church in the diocese.) There is, however, a recognition that war is sometimes necessary as a last resort. It is 'not an evil to be escaped at any cost, but a last necessity to be faced like death with solemn resolution, if that which is dearer to us than life itself is imperilled'.[123]

By the late 1880s Westcott had become involved as a leading spokesman in the movement for international peace and arbitration. He now changed his opinion that war might sometimes be an unavoidable necessity and came close to saying that it was a denial of the Christian gospel. He gave an address to the Canterbury Diocesan Conference in July 1889 on 'The Christian Faith and War' in which he asked: What does the Christian faith teach us about our international duties? He argues that 'the Incarnation proclaims a brotherhood of nations no less than a brotherhood of men'.[124] The consequence is clear:

> As Christians, then, we oppose war, not simply as wasteful of material wealth and fertile in suffering . . . but because it hinders what has been made known to us as the Divine counsel for the progress of man . . . It tends to give sanction to modes of action universally condemned in private life: it connects great virtues with unworthy or, at least, questionable motives: it is the extreme form of self-assertion maintained by force: it leaves behind a sad heritage of discontent to the vanquished and arrogance to the victor: it separates with a legacy of bitterness those through whose generous co-operation the end of creation must be reached.[125]

This insight, he claims, is one given uniquely to this generation. In the past war has been widely accepted as a necessary evil. Now, for the first time,

> that aspect of war is revealed through which its evil is seen in its full spiritual magnitude; that now, for the first time, the duty is laid on believers of applying the social power of the Gospel to hallow and fulfil the spontaneous aspirations of troubled hearts towards international concord.[126]

[181]

He challenges his audience to help to form public opinion on the issue, and to realize the unique role which the national Church has in doing this. He concludes with the vision of a 'confederation of the nations of the West' as a fulfilment of his hopes.[127]

Westcott, the born reconciler, was in his element as an advocate of international peace and brotherhood. He strikes an even more eirenical note in a paper given in Sunderland in 1895 on 'International Arbitration', arguing that 'Our view of war . . . is a crucial test of our view of Christianity'.[128] He urges again that the principle of brotherhood implicit in the doctrine of the incarnation should be applied not only to the social problems within the nation but also to international relations. If this is done, there is no doubt that war can be abolished. He uses the analogy of the abolition of slavery:

> We hold that war is no less opposed than slavery to the mind of Christ – to the ideas of our brotherhood and membership in Him. Therefore we can confidently look for its suppression in due time and work for this issue, though the end is not yet . . . The experience of the past does not limit the possibilities of the future . . . The instinct for justice is strong in the minds of the masses of men; and power is falling surely into their hands. We stand on the edge of a new world, charged with new promises and new hopes.[129]

He goes on to answer the charge that war can be beneficial to a nation socially and politically, conceding that in certain cases it may be the lesser of two evils. But it almost always creates more problems than it solves: 'War settles nothing except the immediate preponderance of force, and leaves a legacy of evils to the next generation.'[130] If the Christian principles of a brotherhood of nations and a common membership of the one human race are mastered, war will come to seem unnatural. He again repeats his 'dream' of 'a fellowship of nations in which each contributes of its wealth to all the others and receives of their fulness'.[131]

There are few better examples than this of that innate optimism about the human potential which we have noted frequently as one of Westcott's characteristic beliefs. His huge confidence about the prospects for breaking down the social and economic divisions within English society was matched by the earnest hope that a new dawn of international harmony and brotherhood was about to break.

It was not long, however, before the clouds of war were gathering, this time in South Africa, part of Britain's worldwide empire. The outbreak of the Boer War in 1899 was to split public opinion, divide politicians and churchmen, and shake Britain's imperial self-confidence. A new mood of self-doubt and questioning seized the nation. The optimism of the previous two decades was severely challenged. Chadwick comments: 'The Boer War gave a shock to the idea of general progress, and may have helped to open the eyes of churchmen to see that their faith outran the facts.'[132]

Christian opinion was sharply divided, although the majority in the churches supported the war. Many Christian Socialists, led by Gore and Scott Holland, denounced the war as an expression of British imperialist arrogance. Over 5,000 nonconformists signed a manifesto against the war in 1901. Some Church of England bishops, too, opposed it, notably Percival of Hereford and Winnington Ingram of Stepney.[133]

In the light of his work in the field of international peace and arbitration, it might have been thought that Westcott also would have been an opponent of the war. He was, in fact, a firm supporter of the British action against the Boers, seeing it as 'the fulfilment of our imperial obligations'.[134] In a letter to the Durham Artillery Militia, about to leave for South Africa, he expressed his unqualified support of their mission:

A great crisis has revealed the Empire to itself. We feel from one end of the world to the other, as we have never felt before, that we are one people, charged with a great mission, and united by a history which is our inspiration to noble deeds. All minor differences of class and opinion are lost in universal desire to fill Imperial obligations according to our opportunities, and to preserve unimpaired for the next generation the inheritance which we have ourselves received.[135]

He was aware that such a strongly pro-war tone was very much at odds with his recent very public profile as a spokesman for international peace and arbitration. In a preface to a sermon on 'The Obligation of Empire' he tried to meet the charge of inconsistency:

> For many years it has been my privilege to plead the cause of international peace and arbitration. I do not recall one word which I have spoken or abandon one hope which I have cherished. The duty of fulfilling a trust is not a matter for arbitration, and, if need be, must be preferred to the maintenance of peace.[136]

He believed, then, that the overriding duty was to fulfil the obligations of empire, which for him embodied the principles of brotherhood and service, we must remember. He was on occasion critical of the conduct of the war, condemning the Jameson Raid and criticizing Cecil Rhodes. He never seemed to doubt, however, that Britain was right to resist Boer aggression, and he believed that a by-product of the war would be a more united empire and a purified nation.

It is interesting to see him, in an address to the Church Congress at Newcastle in September 1900, trying to answer those like the Quakers who argued that war is inconsistent with the profession of Christianity. He himself had come close to adopting this position in his paper of 1895 at Sunderland. Now, however, he argues that Christianity must deal with the world as it is with all its violence, evil and selfish ambition in personal and national life. The supreme end of life is 'not peace, but righteousness – the fulfilment of personal and national duties to God and men, the repression, the extinction, if possible, of personal and national injustice'.[137] The maintenance of this righteousness, or justice, however, depends ultimately upon the use of force, whether in national life or in international relationships. There must then be, he argues,

[184]

the possibility of a 'just war'. He concedes that there is a need to determine carefully the conditions under which this might be the case, but there is no doubt 'that the Christian must acknowledge war as an ultimate means for maintaining a righteous cause'.[138]

He goes on to speak of the importance of international arbitration and of the need to understand the needs and aspirations of other nations. The address ends with the muted hope that the cause of peace is moving forward, however slowly. It is one of his least convincing addresses, full of contradictions and very revealing of the extreme difficulty he faced in the last two years of his life in reconciling his support for the war with his previous campaigning for peace.

The whole incident marks one of the least happy episodes in Westcott's life. His reputation was such that 'many looked to him for a lead when war broke out'.[139] He knew well that some were disappointed with the lead that he gave. He was, for instance, at odds with his Dean, Dr Kitchin, who spoke out from the first against the policy that led to war and protested against its continuance. In his defence it can be said that by this time he was a sick man.

It is, however, a significant incident. For all his important contribution to missiology and the theology of religion, he is revealed here as a man very much of his time. Aware as he was of the ambiguity of the gift of empire, it is his pride in membership of an imperial power which in the end overrides his oft-repeated belief in the brotherhood of man.

7

EDUCATION

We were discussing our Cambridge courses of study, when Dr. Westcott
with the utmost gravity remarked: 'I would give a man a degree for asking twelve good questions'. Of course he did not seriously regard this as
practicable. Yet the mock proposal meant a great deal.[1]

1 Godliness and good learning

To understand the nature of Westcott's contribution to educational
thought and practice it is necessary to go back to his years at King
Edward's School, Birmingham, where he sat at the feet of the headmaster, James Prince Lee.

In 1893 he returned to the city of his birth, to the Grammar School
for Girls, where he gave an address on the debt he owed to Lee. The
latter, who later became Bishop of Manchester, had spent eight years at
Rugby School before moving to King Edward's, where he profoundly
influenced a whole generation of pupils. Westcott attempted to explain
the secret of his influence, and singled out four of his characteristics.
The first was the importance of active participation in learning and of
independence in thought:

> He made us feel that in all learning we must not be receptive only but
> active; that he only learns who thinks, just as he only can teach who
> learns. He encouraged us to collect, to examine, to arrange such
> simple facts as lay within the range of our own reading, that he might
> use the results in dealing with some larger problem. In this way, little
> by little, we gained a direct acquaintance with the instruments and
> methods of criticism, and came to know something of confident
> delight in using them.[2]

He mentioned, secondly, Lee's 'intense belief in the exact force of language. A word, as he regarded it, had its own peculiar history and delivered its own precise message. A structural form conveyed for him a definite idea. In translating we were bound to see that every syllable gave its testimony.'[3] This aspect of Lee's influence upon Westcott was touched on in our discussion in Chapter 2 of the latter's interpretation of Scripture, where we noted that some people had felt that Westcott was over-subtle in his elucidation of the meaning of words, and that Lee's influence had been responsible for this.[4] The pupil himself, however, had no doubts that this belief in the force of language had been the most precious of all his teacher's gifts to him.

The third feature was Lee's encouragement to his pupils to read widely and to acquire the widest possible general knowledge. 'When we came back from the holidays the welcome question was, "Well, what have you read; what have you seen?"'[5] He threw open his library to his senior pupils, and enabled them to attend lectures in the city on art, archaeology, physics and painting. Westcott believed that such encouragement had its origin in Lee's belief in the essential goodness of the world, and in this context he quotes Browning's words about the world being 'no blot, nor blank, it meant intensely and meant good'.[6]

Finally, he mentions the faith which undergirded the whole of Lee's philosophy of education. He tells of a visit to his old teacher shortly before he died, in which he had spoken of the disappointments and failures in his life, and had finally said to Westcott, '"$\mu\acute{\eta}$ $\phi o\beta o\hat{u}$, $\mu\acute{o}\nu o\nu$ $\pi\acute{\iota}\sigma\tau\epsilon\upsilon\epsilon$ (fear not, only believe)". Those four words . . . were I think a perfect interpretation of life as the Master saw it, and as he taught his scholars to see it.'[7]

He then summarizes Lee's conception of the teacher's task and affirms its enduring value and relevance:

Methods may change, but these remain as the master powers of education: sympathy as the spring of the teacher's influence, service as the end of the scholar's effort – independence, conviction, largeness of view, faith.[8]

These principles underlie much of Westcott's own scholarship and teaching. It is remarkable, for example, how frequently in the prefaces to his books he emphasizes the fact that his aim has been to stimulate and encourage independent thought in his readers. He urges readers of his commentary on the Johannine epistles to spend time testing his conclusions:

A few hours spent in tracing out the use of a word or a form, in comparing phrases often held to be synonymous, in estimating the force of different senses of the same verb in regard to the contexts in which they are found, will bring assurance which no acceptance of another's work can give.[9]

A similar plea is made in the introduction to his commentary on Hebrews as we saw in Chapter 2:

I have endeavoured to suggest in the notes lines of thought which I have found to open light upon problems which we are required to face. In doing this it has throughout been my desire to induce my readers to become my fellow-students, and I have aimed at encouraging sustained reflection rather than at entering on the field of controversy. No conclusion is of real value to us till we have made it our own by serious work.[10]

The same point is made in his two theological works. In the chapter on his theology we quoted the very significant words in the preface to his major work: 'My desire has been to encourage patient reflection, to suggest lines of enquiry, to indicate necessary limits to knowledge, and not to convey formulas or ready-made arguments.'[11] In the 'Notice' to the second edition of the work there is a similar challenge to the readers: 'The truths which we hold are worth to us just what they cost us and no more.'[12] Then, in the 'Notice' to the third edition of the *The Gospel of the Resurrection* there is an admission of the limitations of all language in theological exploration, and then the justification for his work: 'it seems better to stir enquiry, if it may be, than to appear to anticipate and satisfy it'.[13]

Westcott always remained convinced that education was not about the imparting of information from the one who knows to the one who does not. Arthur Benson quotes him as saying: 'Information is of no value . . . The best teacher shows the boys where the ore is, encourages them to dig for it, and inspires them to do the coining for themselves.'[14]

Westcott also exemplified Lee's ideal of the educated man as someone who is widely read and of broad interests. His own students and his closest friends often remarked on this aspect of his mind. The remarkable breadth of his contribution to scholarship, which we have been tracing, is a fine example of his master's ideal.

It is important to see Prince Lee's influence upon his pupil in a wider context. Lee was not only an outstanding headmaster and teacher but he was also a good example of the early Victorian educational ideal of 'godliness and good learning'. David Newsome has shown that this ideal was based upon the conviction that 'education and religion were essentially allied', and that the essence of education was 'a combination of intellectual toughness, moral earnestness and deep spiritual conviction'.[15] It was this ideal which shaped Westcott's character and whole attitude to life, and which determines his own educational theory and practice.

By the 1870s this ideal was being replaced by the cult of 'muscular Christianity'. The moral earnestness of the earlier Victorian ideal was giving way to the belief in manliness and high spirits. Godliness was now associated with physical activity and patriotism.[16]

Westcott was less at home in this new world and was often critical of contemporary educational values in the last two decades of his life.

He remained to the end an unrepentant exemplar of that earlier educational ideal which had so deeply affected the mind and thought of early and mid-Victorian England.

2 *The teacher's vocation*

Westcott seriously considered becoming a schoolteacher himself. After a conversation with someone about his future career he wrote in his diary: 'A schoolmaster or a clergyman? I am fearful, if once I embrace the former profession, I shall again be absorbed in all the schemes of ambition and selfish distinction which used continually to haunt me; and yet I think the discipline as well as the leisure which such a life affords would be immensely useful in relation to my after duties.'[17] This was at a time when teaching was a highly regarded profession, and when clergy often became headmasters. Having chosen ordination he considered becoming a headmaster, but was dissuaded from this path by his friends and eventually became an assistant master at Harrow.

These seventeen years, 1852–69, were undoubtedly the unhappiest years of his life, for he was not suited to the task of a schoolteacher. His closest friend at this time, Lightfoot, clearly felt that he was making a mistake in going to Harrow. There is an unpublished letter in which he voices his apprehension at Westcott's appointment: 'I fear that you will find school teaching at Harrow too laborious. I believe you capable of more hard work than most men, but, if accounts be true, the work at one of the large schools must be complete drudgery.'[18]

Lightfoot's misgivings were to prove to be all too prophetic. Westcott had gained much from an outstanding teacher at King Edward's, but his own gifts did not equip him to inspire and emphathize with the average adolescent boy. There is a significant comment about schoolboys in a letter to Hort written only a few months after his appointment to Harrow: 'How much I should like to talk with you about boy-nature. Sometimes I am tempted to define a boy as "a being in whom the idea of honour exists only potentially". Truly one grows sad often at what experience teaches.'[19]

This was an ominous sign. The fact that he never really understood the boys at Harrow led to a growing feeling of inadequacy. One problem may have been the type of boy he found at a major public school like Harrow. O'Dea suggests that the problem lay in their background: unlike the boys at King Edward's, Birmingham, they were from very privileged backgrounds and were not motivated to work hard.[20] Westcott's personality, however, was also a factor. It has often been pointed out that his greatest success was with the more able boys. One of these, who spent seven years at Harrow in Westcott's time, later said that he had learned more from him socially than from formal education, and then made this significant comment about the man: 'He was far too good to be a schoolmaster, and every one of us in his house would have done anything for him, and why, because he trusted us and knew that not one of us would deceive him in any way and no one did.'[21]

As the years passed it was largely his sense of duty which kept him at Harrow, the conviction that the self-sacrifice and self-discipline required would be good training for whatever might lie ahead. The one consolation was that he was able to pursue his scholarly interests. As we have seen these were very fruitful years in this respect. Nevertheless, unpublished correspondence reveals that within four years of taking up his post at Harrow Lightfoot was encouraging him to look for an opportunity of moving to Cambridge, where he believed his friend's true work lay, and that over the next ten years he encouraged Westcott to apply for academic posts which came up, amongst which was the Hulsean Professorship of Divinity.[22] It was not until 1868, however, when his health and state of mind were causing concern to all his friends, that the opportunity came to move to the canonry at Peterborough. Lightfoot's emphatic advice to him to accept the offer of the canonry is eloquent of the concern he felt for his friend: 'If the vacant canonry at Peterborough *should* be offered to you ... accept it at once, if you see your way to this; but *do not by any means decline it*, until we have talked the matter over . . . If you are to decline it, I should never forgive you, nor would your other friends.'[23] At last came the opportunity to pursue what he and his friends believed was his true work – education within the wider Church rather than within a school.

At Harrow, then, Westcott was the proverbial 'square peg in a round hole'. Those years cost him a great deal in exhaustion and a feeling of inadequacy. They did, however, give him some experience of the classroom environment, which he used to good account in later years. They also brought him face to face with a sense of failure, and more especially of a sense of biding his time in preparation for something greater, which were to influence his spirituality profoundly. There is an illuminating sermon preached in 1866 on the words of Jesus in John 2.4, 'Mine hour is not yet come', in which he spoke of the significance of the thirty years Jesus spent in obscurity and isolation before his public ministry. These have deep lessons for us and encourage us to have patience, trust and watchfulness when we are in similar waiting situations. So, 'our hour will come and in a momentary crisis show the fulness of our nature'.[24] There can be little doubt that here he was reflecting on the lessons of the difficult years at Harrow.

Twenty-five years later, soon after his appointment to the see of Durham, Westcott gave an address at the Jubilee of Bede College in Durham. He spoke of the ideals for which a teacher must strive. He applied the words of Jesus in John 17.17, 'Sanctify them in the Truth', to the vocation of a teacher and argued that there are three marks of a dedicated teacher: self-surrender, transformation, service.[25] It is one of his most austere addresses, moving for the most part in the realm of abstract theology and hardly lit up at all by references to his own experience in a school. Towards the end he seems to realize that he has perhaps been over the heads of his audience, and at last refers to this:

Do I seem, my friends, to have set too high a standard for the spirit of your preparation? to have claimed too lofty a devotion for the fulfilment of a work which is often held to be – and so may often become – commonplace or even mechanical? I can only say that I speak from my own experience. I know that nothing is harder, even as nothing is more fruitful, than elementary teaching.[26]

The only occasion when he reflected more widely on the national education system and the questions it raised was in an address to the Christian Social Union in 1896. Here he looked back to the 1870 Education Act, which had for the first time created a national education system for children up to the age of ten, and on twenty-five years of the new system and the issues it had raised. He began with a general statement of the aims and object of education:

> to train for life, and not for a special occupation; to train the whole man for all life, for life seen and unseen, for the unseen through the seen and in the seen; to train *men* in a word and not *craftsmen*, to train citizens for the Kingdom of God.[27]

He then moved on to the 'proper work of a teacher', emphasizing strongly the development of a child's intuition and powers of observation. A teacher will encourage children to 'observe, and to describe what they observe, and not communicate at once his own observations: he will let things speak to them for themselves . . . even if at first they give an uncertain voice'.[28] He will also encourage observations from life and not only from books. A teacher will encourage children to value the inheritance of literature from the past, and the 'golden deeds of heroes and saints'.[29]

All this, he claims, will help his pupils to develop the graces of character, 'for if knowledge alone were the teacher's aim, he would foresee how soon differences of opportunity must hopelessly divide classes of men'. Rather, he will cherish in his pupils 'the graces of humility, and obedience, and tenderness, and gratitude, and generosity, and reverence'.[30]

It is clear, then, that education and religion are intimately related:

Education is a spiritual relationship. It becomes operative through sympathy. The personal element in it is supreme. Faith and love and religion can only be taught by those who possess them . . . His final appeal will be not to ambition, not to self-interest, but to love.[31]

This was an uncompromising statement of the older educational ideal of 'godliness and good learning' in which he himself had been schooled. He was well aware that in a rapidly changing world such an ideal was now very much out of fashion. The challenge came not only from the cult of 'muscular Christianity', but from the cry that education should be more closely related to the world of industry and the need for more 'vocational training', to use a much later twentieth-century watchword. He could only lament over the latest developments in the education system:

We grow more and more impatient of processes which do not yield speedy measurable results. The communication of information which can be reproduced with the most complete exactness and the least independent thought, is coming to be regarded as the teacher's supreme aim. The motives on which the surest reliance is placed are anti-social – personal emulation, and material interest. In some places competition threatens to invade the nursery.[32]

Westcott goes on to remind his audience that all this should be of great concern to them since the life of the nation is profoundly influenced by the way in which its children are educated. What was urgently needed was a clear view of the nature of education as 'the training of the whole man – body and soul and spirit – for social service through the harmonious cultivation and disciplining of his personal powers'.[33] He urged them to become managers of schools or members of school boards, to take a personal interest in the work of local schools. He concluded by reminding them that in all he had been saying he had been drawing on the lessons learned from his own schooldays, and from his own experience as a teacher.

It is not surprising that Westcott should have chosen to speak to the Christian Social Union about education. It had long been held that social reform and improvement were closely linked with improving educational standards. During the first phase of Christian Socialism between 1848 and 1854 it was F. D. Maurice who concluded that the co-operative ventures would fail unless working men were better educated, and he eventually founded the Working Men's College in London in 1854. The same year Maurice gave six lectures on the subject of adult education, and we know that Westcott had read these because he recommended them to his daughter in March 1892.[34] Apart from his own experience as a teacher, then, it is wholly consistent with his general interest in social questions that he should have remained passionate about educational ideals and concerned about the theory and practice of education to the end of his life. One of his students even said of him that he wished he could have spent his life as an inspector of schools![35]

In the years after he died there were some who believed that Westcott's educational ideals were a significant part of his inheritance to future generations. On 8 April 1903 a John Charles Medd of Cirencester wrote a letter to Arthur Westcott on the publication of his father's *Life and Letters*. He expressed the wish that there had been more in the latter about Westcott's views of education because he was 'far in advance of everyone who is officially responsible for it . . . in England – his ideas on it have now become the common property of every serious thinker'.[36] Then, quite by chance, I discovered that in a Founder's Day address preached just before the First World War at my old Grammar School in Suffolk a Canon Bindley used Westcott's summary of Prince Lee's philosophy of education to express the essence of education: 'sympathy as the spring of the teacher's influence, service as the end of the scholar's effort – independence, conviction, largeness of view, faith'.[37]

As we shall see, Westcott's educational legacy to future generations is to be found in the sphere of university reform and in the training of the clergy, rather than in primary or secondary education. It is nevertheless interesting to see how some of the issues in the latter about which he felt strongly are still debated in the educational ferment of our own time. His lament, for example, over the latest developments in the education system in his 1896 address to the CSU could well have been voiced by someone disillusioned with recent trends in education today. It is also worthy of note that the 'godliness and good learning' ideal, with its conviction that education and religion were essentially allied, was to influence educational ideals well into the second half of the twentieth century through its embodiment in the 1944 Education Act. One of the architects of the Act was William Temple, the Archbishop of Canterbury, who shared many of Westcott's ideals. A recent biography of Thomas Arnold, the famous mid-Victorian headmaster of Rugby, underlines the connection between Rugby – where Prince Lee had taught before moving to Birmingham – and the 1944 Act through William Temple's father, Frederick, who was a later headmaster of the school. In its fundamental conviction that all true education is religious in nature and intention it was 'pure Arnold, a third generation on'.[38]

3 University reform

Westcott was appointed Regius Professor of Divinity at Cambridge in late 1870, and took up his duties early in 1871. This was a significant moment in relations between the universities and the churches. It was in 1871 that Gladstone's government passed through Parliament the University Tests Act, which opened all degrees and offices (except those tied to holy orders) to men of any religion or none, at Cambridge, Oxford and Durham. The colleges were still obliged, however, to maintain Church of England services in their chapels and to provide religious instruction for undergraduates who were members of the established Church.

Pressure for university reform had been growing since the 1830s. Resentment amongst non-Anglicans that admission to degrees and the government of universities were restricted to Anglicans had been building up, as had a feeling that compulsory attendance at College chapel was no longer appropriate if undergraduates were to be treated as adults rather than children. Alongside this was a recognition that university degrees and courses were also in need of revision.

University reform was therefore very much 'in the air' when Westcott arrived in Cambridge. He soon became involved in the processes which were to effect some significant changes. He became a member of the Syndicate which was appointed to consider the whole question of theological examinations in the university, and in particular the special theological exam (the 'Voluntary') which candidates for ordination at Cambridge were required to pass. Many felt strongly that provision for divinity studies in the university was inadequate. There was a need both to deepen study and to introduce more specialized studies in language and history into the curriculum. The Syndicate framed new regulations for divinity degrees, and recommended to the university a scheme for the establishment of a theological tripos examination from January 1874. There were to be three papers on the Old Testament, two on the Greek New Testament, six on the history of the Church and its doctrines and one on 'modern theologians'. Owen Chadwick points out that the strong emphasis on history is due partly to the general climate of academic opinion, but also to the influence of Westcott and Lightfoot within the Syndicate.[39]

Westcott was also one of the prime movers in the other significant reform, the establishment of a new general theological examination conducted by the divinity professors for candidates for holy orders. This was to replace the old 'Voluntary', but this proved to be no easy task, largely because of the difficulty of convincing the bishops of the need for reform. We find him, for example, writing to Hort in

November 1871 urging him to accept an examining chaplaincy to the Bishop of Ely since this would help to gain the assistance of one more bishop in supporting the new scheme.[40] He eventually received, in June 1872, a letter from seven of the bishops expressing their approval of the new examination, and this ensured its eventual success. It took several years, however, to win over the majority of the bishops.

His main concern in this was to secure an examination of a high standard which would be uniform in all the dioceses. He was equally concerned that this examination should be moved from its traditional time in the days immediately preceding ordination. He felt very strongly that preparation for ordination should be given a more devotional emphasis.

For all this, Westcott's role in implementing these significant reforms must not be exaggerated. Treloar points out that the process of change and improvement had been started as early as 1858 and that it was Lightfoot who since 1865 had been the prime mover in sponsoring the new schemes.[41] As Chadwick puts it: 'Westcott's arrival as Regius Professor made less difference than is sometimes supposed, for the reason that Lightfoot was here already.'[42] There is no doubt, however, that his arrival strengthened the cause of reform. There were notable Anglicans at Cambridge, and still more at Oxford, who resisted these changes and gloried in the past. Westcott helped to give nerve and determination to those who believed there could be no going back to the old ways.

His attitude to the Tests Act and to the whole question of change and reform at Cambridge is set out in *On Some Points in the Religious Office of the Universities* (1873), which is a collection of addresses he gave between 1868 and 1872 on the role of universities in the spiritual life of the nation.

In an address given to the Church Congress at Leeds in October 1872 he made clear that he did not agree with those Anglicans who saw in Gladstone's University Tests Act the end of the Church's power and influence in the universities. It was rather an opportunity for grasping the nettle of change, for God was speaking to them through such intellectual and social changes:

> We loyally accept the legislation which regulates the mode of our future action. We confidently trust to the enactments which preserve inviolate the religious character of our society as a whole. If we recall the greater privileges which have been swept away, it is that we may profit by the sibylline warning, and show that we rightly value, and desire to rightly use, those which are as yet assured to us.[43]

The presence of nonconformist scholars and students will, he suggests, be beneficial to the university, and a salutary influence:

> This fresh element may in some degree counteract the growing luxury of our life, and bring back into due prominence the idea, which we have well-nigh lost, that the Universities are not clubs for the rich and indolent, but, above all things, places for devout self-denial and labour. In this respect we have much to learn from the social organisation of some of the isolated Christian societies around us.[44]

Here we remember his friendship with Methodist scholars like W. F. Moulton, with whom he had been working on the revision of the New Testament for the past two years. There is, he concludes, no reason why as a result of the new legislation the life of universities should be 'less spiritual' or less religious' than in the past.

Westcott's optimism in the face of change and reform is seen well in a sermon preached at Cambridge in Advent 1872. Taking as his text Paul's words in Romans 13.12, 'The day is at hand', he speaks of his belief that he and his contemporaries are standing 'upon the threshold of a new age'.[45] At such a time of transition universities had a vital role in helping people to come to terms with the demands of this new age. At a time of a growing divide between rich and poor, they were able to offer the vision of a simpler life which is not founded on material values. They must encourage the study of science alongside the older disciplines, for all truth is of God, and the incarnation enables us to see the new discoveries about the interdependence of human beings and the wider created world as a revelation of Christ. They must help people to hang on to their personal faith and ideals in a fast-changing world.[46]

Here was huge optimism about the power of a university to help people at a crucial time. In his view, a university has a social, an intellectual, and a spiritual office; the intellectual and the moral are closely related. It may be thought that he was over-sanguine about what a purely academic institution might achieve. His attitude, however, was very typical of that optimism which we have seen often was an integral part of his Christian faith. As Chadwick points out, this attitude was exactly what was needed at such a time:

there was something about his cast of mind which fitted the needs of the time ... he had no sense of gripping the past with his finger-nails, no retrospective utopianism, no anxiety for what was being lost. Christopher Wordsworth looked backward with yearning and faced the future with fear; Lightfoot and Westcott looked backward dispassionately and faced the future with equanimity and hope.[47]

Another sermon, 'The Universities as a Spiritual Power', sets out in more detail his view of the religious duty of a university. Preached in Trinity College Chapel in 1868, four years before his move to Cambridge, it reiterates his belief that universities have both a spiritual and an intellectual role in the contemporary world with all its challenges and changes:

They witness to continuity by an uninterrupted life which has found scope for a healthy development through every period of change. They witness to catholicity by the records of their foundation and the large scope of their teaching. They witness to the Christian

destination of all labour by claiming for every public act the consecration of a divine blessing.[48]

The first imperative was to 'teach the "relativity" of all human development'.[49] He argues here for the historical perspective in the teaching of
literature. He is critical of the neglect of history by some politicians,
and of its misuse by some churchmen who aim at 'regenerating society
by reproducing the past'[50] – a reference to the Tractarians.

The second was to 'openly recognize and teach the catholicity of
study'.[51] Here he is thinking about the study of science, and in particular of the great diversity in methods of approach in the different
branches of scientific study. He gives an example in the study of the
three fundamental existences, the self, the world and God: each is
tested by different proofs and investigated by different methods. These
methods are not mutually exclusive, but complementary. 'No one is
universal; but together they bring within an intelligible order whatever
man can learn of thought and action and being.'[52] If students remember this, they will recognize that their particular field of study has a permanent validity, but it is at the same time one amongst many subjects.

The third and final duty of a university was to teach 'the divine
destination of labour'.[53] This is a typically vague phrase of Westcott's
and he is not at his most lucid in developing this particular point. What
he seems to be drawing attention to here is the danger that increasing
specialization of study will isolate students from one another. To
counteract this we must recognize that we are all members of the one
body (his text is Ephesians 2.15–16 where Paul speaks of the Church as
a body, and Christ as the head). It was also important, however, to
respect other people's disciplines. The spiritual office of a university
was to enable people to see the unity of all knowledge:

The study of history shews the unity of life: the study of science
shews the unity of thought: the study of action shews the unity of
being: unities broken indeed by man's sin, but yet potentially

restored by Christ. To bring these out into a clearer and more commanding light is the highest work of education. To inspire men with the sense of their sovereign grandeur is the spiritual office of the Universities.[54]

How did Westcott's view of the religious office of the university compare with those of his contemporaries? In his Westcott Memorial lecture Owen Chadwick points out that he was firmly with the conservatives in his belief that it was the main purpose of a university to provide a general education, and not specialized courses or a multiplicity of new studies. This is the significance of his phrase 'catholicity of study'. For him, the innovators who were arguing that one went to university to acquire information or practical skills were misguided. He was in agreement with those like John Henry Newman who believed that universities were for the enlargement of mind, knowledge for its own sake rather than knowledge because it is useful.[55]

He was at the same time, however, very much at odds with the religious conservatives, notably those like Pusey and Wordsworth at Oxford, who believed that the first duty of the university was to teach the doctrines of the Christian faith. As we have seen, his view of the religious office of the university was far broader than this. Chadwick expresses it in this way:

> He said that the first religious duty of the university was to study man and his world, in science and in history, and so to inspire the student with 'the sense of their solemn grandeur' . . . The primary aim . . . was an elevation of the mental gaze as a means of creating a reverent spirit . . . In this way he denied the looming hiatus between a critical theology which was not religious, and a religious theology which was not critical.[56]

On the question of whether amidst the changes taking place universities still had a religious office, Westcott was emphatic that the answer must be in the affirmative. Another question, however, soon raised its head: were they adequate any longer for the training of the Anglican clergy?

4 *The education of the clergy*

Westcott at first believed that with the particular reforms in the scope and content of theological examinations which he had helped to bring about, the Church should continue to use the universities to train its clergy.

In an address to the Church Congress at Nottingham in 1871 he made it clear that he believed that the intellectual training provided by the university was entirely appropriate for ordinands. He conceded that there was also a need for pastoral training, but this was best done in the cathedrals.[57] The universities were unique in giving ordinands a wide view of knowledge, and a healthy attitude to the relationship between theology and other disciplines:

> The theologian who studies theology only, is really as liable to error, as unnaturally cramped, as imperfectly equipped for his work as a philologer would be who confined himself to the knowledge of a single language. It is his task to watch for the convergence of all the streams of truth, to gather every scattered ray of light, without hurry and without misgiving . . . without misgiving, for he knows, as no one else can know, that all truth, all light is one.[58]

The other great strength of a university education for the ordinand was that it gave him training in the historical method. A study of the Scriptures and of the history of the Church, with its glories and its failures, provided a firm foundation for his work. 'Nothing is more wanted, in order to extend and deepen the Divine life amongst us, than the profound study of the Bible, and of the progress of the Christian society.'[59]

[203]

In another address given in 1871 to the Ely Diocesan Conference he admitted that there was room for improvement in this area of historical study. He mentioned in particular the need for more time to be given to the study of biblical exegesis, the neglect of study of the medieval period in Church history, and the importance for the ordinand of studying the spiritual life of one of the saints.[60] What he was utterly convinced of was the fundamental importance of schooling in historical method for the would-be priest.

Chadwick defends Westcott and his colleagues against the charge that they were mistaken in their overwhelming emphasis on historical study in the new theological tripos.[61] Far from diverting theology from its true path into an irrelevant past, Westcott was reacting against the belief that religious training was essentially the transmission of revealed doctrines. His deep conviction was that credal formulas and the like could only be understood as arising from their historical context.[62] As Westcott himself expressed it, using an antithesis which is common in his theological writings, the ordinand is 'the inheritor of a life and not of a system'.[63]

To those who argued that training in the increasingly secular milieu of a university would be damaging to the faith and morals of candidates for holy orders, Westcott responded that faith must be exposed to the questions and challenges inherent in the university context. Nothing would be gained by attempting to protect them from the speculation and scepticism which was part of contemporary society. He admits that there might indeed be 'some shipwrecks of faith in this mental commerce: the great deeps of thought cannot, in our imperfect state, be traversed without peril'.[64] The risk is necessary, however. He then criticizes the Roman Catholic model for the training of the priesthood: 'No seminary walls can exclude their influence. Sooner or later, our clergy will have to contend with them; and it is better that they should be first met when they can be calmly interrogated than that they should come as a surprise.'[65]

There was, then, nothing inherently antagonistic to a healthy religious life in a university education. On the contrary, ordinands would be forced in such a context to face up to the great social questions which were being pressed upon them, and which many people were trying to ignore. His conclusion is that it would be 'a disastrous day for England, and for Christendom, if the candidates for the ministry of our Church were withdrawn in any large numbers from the chastening influences of wide and liberal discipline in a society as free and varied as that in which they will be called to exercise their ministry'.[66]

This optimism about the continuing suitability of a university for the education of the clergy proved to be misplaced. What is more, within eight years he had almost unwittingly helped to give birth to an institution whose very existence denied the principles he had been spelling out.

His own vision of clerical training was a predominantly intellectualized one. Almost all the benefits he had spoken of in his addresses were about broadening and deepening a man's mind. This was an important part of such training, but it was not the whole of it. There was the question of worship: undergraduates found that the worship provided by their college chapels was not adequate in itself. There was the need for training in what we today would call spirituality – prayer and the devotional life. This was a deep concern of Westcott's, as we shall see in the next chapter, but it could hardly have a place in the normal university undergraduate course. Then there was the issue of pastoral training, of which Westcott was aware and for which he believed special provision should be made. He had not foreseen what the wider needs of ordinands would be.

So it was that in May 1880 the first meeting took place of a private committee called together by him to give advice to ordinands, to help them prepare for pastoral training, and to provide them with regular services in addition to those held in their college chapels.[67] The purpose of the group was to assist graduates who were seeking ordination to prepare for their vocation without sacrificing the advantages of university residence.

Preparation was to be in three parts – devotional, doctrinal and practical, and lectures were to be given in each. He himself was involved in the first two areas. Additional services were held in the side chapel at King's College, and he sometimes gave an address on a devotional topic. He was one of the lecturers in the courses on doctrine, and practical preparation was made possible through links with parishes in Cambridge and the surrounding area.

Eventually, the whole project was given a name – the Clergy Training School; and in 1886 a public appeal was launched to provide stipends, bursaries, and a house which would be the centre for the work of the school. A constitution was adopted which provided that the divinity professors, the principal and vice principal of the school, and the lecturers should form the council of the school.

Westcott returned to Cambridge to dedicate the first group of buildings, which included a chapel, on 18 May 1899. In his speech he stressed firmly his continued commitment to what he called 'the master-thought in the whole of my work at Cambridge . . . that the training of the clergy and laity should be as far as possible conducted under the same conditions'.[68] The truth was, however, that the coming into being of the school was, in Chadwick's phrase, 'a monument to the failure of Westcott's plan!'[69] In spite of all he had said about the suitability of the university for the training of the clergy, he had helped to create an institution which would inevitably separate them from their lay colleagues, and would provide in time a very distinctive and different corporate life. For the time being the ordinands continued to reside in their colleges and to attend their college chapels, and the teaching continued to be done by members of the university Divinity School. Once created, however, an institution gathers a momentum of its own, and in time it would become the kind of institution he instinctively disliked.

It was not the only theological college, however, to which he helped to give birth. The Community of the Resurrection at Mirfield, founded in 1892 by Charles Gore, owes something to a sermon he preached at Harrow on 'Disciplined Life'.[70]

Education

In 1905 the Clergy Training School was named 'Westcott House' in memory of his contribution to its foundation. For the past hundred years it has provided training for Anglican ordinands and is today part of the ecumenical Cambridge Federation of Theological Colleges. If there is an irony in its still bearing his name today, it nevertheless stands as a reminder of his significant contribution to the practice and theory of education in the later nineteenth century.

8

SPIRITUALITY

The Cambridge Trio of biblical scholars, Lightfoot, Westcott, and Hort, should be studied for their spirituality as well as for their commentaries on the text of the New Testament. Their scholarly rigour was grounded in faith and devotion . . .There was no great gulf between the asceticism of the study and asceticism of the cell.[1]

1 Not only a scholar

Any account of Westcott's achievement must take into account the fact that in his lifetime he was valued not solely for his multifaceted contribution to scholarship, but also for his saintliness of character.

There is a wide range of testimony to this aspect of his influence. In the summer of 1872 the young Henry Scott Holland was preparing for ordination with Westcott at Peterborough. He wrote to a friend of the latter's reverence for John's Gospel but also of the impression made by the character of his teacher:

> We go three times a week to him, and bring him things written which he has set us to do. He is quite wonderful, of a pure earnest holiness of life, a humility, a gentleness, a saintliness, such as I have hardly met with before . . . He is the sort of man before whose high-toned purity and prayerfulness and intense religiousness I cower with shame. He prays with us when we come to him; so slowly, gently, whisperingly.[2]

One of Westcott's Cambridge students, W. R. Inge, later to become Dean of St Paul's, remembered the Sunday afternoon meetings in King's College, when undergraduates met with Westcott for informal discussion of religious questions. Inge recalled the difficulty he had in understanding his teacher's ideas of human solidarity, but he too spoke of the impact of the man: 'I remember that he spoke of the shame which he felt in reading of any horrible crime, as if he were in some way partly responsible for it himself. But whether we understood him or not, we always felt that we were in the presence of a saint, and that it did us good to see and hear him.'[3]

Another former student, G. R. Eden, who worked with Westcott in the Diocese of Durham also singles out this quality. He affirms that the bishop was 'not only a great scholar but a great saint', and refers to the teaching of a great seventeenth-century Anglican: 'he came nearest, I think, of anyone I have known for satisfying Jeremy Taylor's three conditions of holy living – Care of our time, Purity of intention, and the Practice of the Presence of God'.[4]

It is necessary, of course, in evaluating such testimonies to make allowances for the adulation of the young, and for the Victorian propensity for turning biography into hagiography. A century later we live in more cynical times when 'goodness' and 'holiness' and 'saintliness' are suspect terms. It is the range of testimony, however, to the personal impact which Westcott made upon people which cannot be lightly set aside.

It was not only former students who singled out this aspect of his influence. The American textual scholar, C. R. Gregory, highlights Westcott's humility as a feature of the man. He refers to a sermon in which Westcott's eldest son spoke of his father's being deeply troubled by his popularity in some quarters: 'there are times when I feel just overwhelmed by the kind things which are said, and the gratitude of men: it makes me quite afraid'.[5] Gregory remarks that it was this kind of humility, which is not in evidence in his later letters, which was the very essence of the man: 'That is the keynote of the spirit of the man.'[6] Gregory had a deep admiration for Westcott as a scholar, but in reviewing his career it was his compassion and humility which he wanted to underline.

Then there are the ecumenical tributes. The Congregationalist scholar, R. W. Dale, had a great respect for Westcott's scholarship, but even more for the man. During Dale's final illness he received a letter from Westcott which spoke appreciatively of Dale's recent *Lectures on Ephesians.* Dale's son comments: 'No other living man could have so cheered him. For Dr. Westcott, though they seldom met, he had the most profound admiration, and a reverence that learning by itself can never command.'[7] During Westcott's own final illness, the Wesleyan Methodist Conference, then meeting in Newcastle, sent him a letter of greetings. In proposing that the letter be sent, the Methodist President, Revd Dinsdale Young, said of Westcott, 'He is the Bishop of all the Christian Churches, and we are all indebted to his scholarship and his saintly influence.'[8] There is the same linking of these two aspects of his life in a tribute from the General Committee of the Church Missionary Society after his death. It speaks of the way in which he had enriched the life of the Church in every land 'not less by the sincere simplicity of a saintly life than by the rare stores of learning, as varied as they were profound'.[9]

In the light of all this, it is surprising that this aspect of Westcott's influence has been largely ignored, as has his own practice and teaching on the spiritual life. The truth is that there is here a large gap in the history and appreciation of nineteenth-century spirituality. Almost all surveys of Anglican spirituality in this period give ample coverage to the Evangelical movement and to the Oxford Movement, and then pass on to the twentieth century. The Cambridge trio are recognized as significant from the point of view of their scholarship, but their contribution to spirituality is rarely acknowledged.

There are a few exceptions to this: Gordon Wakefield, a Methodist, whose words about the Cambridge trio stand at the head of this chapter, and A. M. Allchin, who recognizes Westcott as someone in the recent Anglican tradition in whose teaching there is a 'deeply mystical element'.[10] Neither, however, has the space to develop his points. A recent anthology of Anglican spirituality does have one extract from

Westcott's writings, part of the essay in *The Epistles of St John* on the 'gospel of creation', but this may be contrasted with four extracts from the much more meagre literary output of his colleague, Hort.[11] Westcott has still not been accorded his true worth as a spiritual teacher. Finally, there is a recent major history of English spirituality by Gordon Mursell which at last recognizes the contribution to spirituality of what he terms the 'Liberal tradition'. The representatives chosen to represent this stand, however, are F. D. Maurice and Charles Kingsley, and there is no mention of Westcott or his Cambridge colleagues.[12]

An exploration of Westcott's spirituality is therefore long overdue. It will perhaps contribute towards a wider appreciation of the achievement of the Cambridge school, and provide further evidence of their unjust neglect in the history of the Victorian Church.

It is a commonplace that 'spirituality' is an elusive word, subject to varied definitions. For our purposes it describes 'those attitudes, beliefs, practices which animate people's lives and help them to reach out towards super-sensible realities'.[13]

2 A simple lifestyle

In Chapter 5 we attempted to show the close relationship between doctrine and practice in Westcott's thought. We argued that from an early age he was consistent in emphasizing the need for faith to be expressed in practical ways. This concern also shaped the pattern of his personal life. As early as 1852 he is critical of any mysticism which is not earthed in the world: 'It is not enough to frame fair visions of perfection and to dream in seclusion of the restoration of the world . . . Formality and mysticism find little encouragement in the Gospel . . . contemplation must be realised in practice.'[14] In a sermon preached in Durham Cathedral in 1891 there is a similar insistence. The supreme truth of the incarnation is given to us that it might be embodied and expressed in our lives: 'It is committed to us, not for idle contemplation but for active use. We are bound to make known through the fashioning of our own conduct the revelation which we have received.' Then comes a quotation from Tertullian: 'The evidence of the being of God is our whole character and our whole environment.'[15]

There is a real concern here that the contemplative life in itself is not enough. What Westcott consistently affirmed was that one of the marks of an authentic spirituality is a life which embodies Christian values and is not divorced from the social and economic challenges of the world around.

One of his strongest convictions was that crucial to this was the rediscovery by Christians in his time of a new simplicity of life. It was a constant theme of his teaching, and one that was most eloquently expressed in his own life and practice. Contemporaries often remarked on his austere lifestyle. His son tells us that he did not smoke, nor drink after his fiftieth year, and that if his family had allowed it he would have existed on dry toast and weak tea! He never liked spending money on himself, and wore threadbare coats very much against his family's will. Yet he gave away 25 per cent of his income in charity, and one of his last actions before his death was to summon up the energy to write a cheque which would allow a poor clergyman to have a summer holiday.[16] One of his students remarked on how often he spoke of the 'absolute disadvantage of great wealth', and of his questioning 'whether there was any real necessity for a Stock Exchange'.[17]

In spite of his reservations about a contemplative life detached from the challenges of the contemporary world, he turned to the history of monasticism for support of his teaching on simplicity. In particular, there was the 1868 sermon at Harrow on the lives of Antony, Benedict and St Francis, calling for a new type of disciplined life appropriate to the age:

History . . . teaches us that social evils must be met by a social organisation. A life of absolute and calculated sacrifice is a spring of immeasurable power. In the past it has worked marvels, and there is nothing to prove that its virtue is exhausted. God has blessed the spirit of ascetic devotion, and no less clearly has He shown that it must not be confined to one form.[18]

The sequel to this was preached two years later, with its suggestion of a *coenobium* or group of families living in communities committed to poverty, study and devotion. It is worth noting what he says about poverty: 'The obligation to poverty would aim at establishing extreme frugality in the material circumstances of living. The type would be absolute simplicity, not ostentatious asceticism.'[19] If the founding of the Community of the Resurrection in 1892 was in part a fulfilment of the first vision, that of the *coenobium* was to remain unfulfilled, although as David Newsome has pointed out, Charles Gore took up the idea in his 1903 pamphlet on the 'Social Doctrine of the Sermon on the Mount'.[20]

It was perhaps the example of St Francis which inspired him most of all. He devoted one of his Westminster sermons of 1886 to the Franciscan movement. He was not uncritical of it, but recognized in its history vital lessons for the contemporary Church. As we would expect he was deeply disturbed by the growing prosperity and materialism of the late Victorian age, and by the deepening awareness of the gap between rich and poor:

We need, from the highest to the lowest, to feel the perilous burden of wealth, the responsibility of stewardship, the cares of authority. Francis lost nothing of his grace and courtesy, nothing of his joyousness, nothing of his delight in Sun and Moon and Wind and Fire and Earth, because he had cast off every perishable help towards sustaining such gifts in their freshness . . . We need, in other words, to know the blessedness of *the poor, the poor in spirit*: to know that our life cometh not of our possessions in their abundance.[21]

[213]

It was the move to Durham in 1890 which brought a real challenge to his desire to lead a life of simplicity and self-sacrifice. The bishop's home was a huge castle in the centre of a mining area. This was a huge embarrassment to him. He came to terms with it in some degree by opening it up to the public, and welcoming groups of people from the diocese and beyond. It was, he was often saying, not solely his family's home but the common property of the diocese. There is little doubt that his embarrassment remained, however. One of his clergy went to read with him after being appointed to the diocese, and went on holiday with him. He later observed of the bishop: 'He loved simplicity of life and was delighted when we left the huge castle and went for a stay at a seaside cottage near Whitby. I sat and did my work in a cabbage garden. He and his papers occupied the little sitting room at the village shop and he remarked: "I have not had such a good morning's work since I left Cambridge".'[22]

There was a similar feeling about having to be transported as a bishop in a horse and carriage. He once received a letter from a miner chastising him for indulging in such luxury. It hurt him deeply. The truth was that he 'always felt that it was a degradation to be dragged about by horses . . . he would always sit miserably huddled up in a corner of the carriage with his back to the horses, as a protest against the horrid necessity'.[23] Scott Holland observed that he 'crept into his carriage as if it were a hearse'![24]

Nevertheless, he continued during his time at Durham to urge his clergy and lay people to live simpler, more frugal lives. He told his diocesan conference in 1891 'to dwell on the simplicity of the material conditions of the noblest manhood: on the austere side of the teaching of the New Testament: on the havoc wrought by luxury: on the moral value of the simplest acts of buying and selling'.[25] The use of money was for him a key issue. A London congregation in 1893 was told:

Our expenditure as Christians must from first to last be directed not to private gratification but to the good of the whole body, and it is in this good that we find our own highest satisfaction . . . There is need of sparing, of self-control, of reserve, for the possession of enduring joy no less than for the noblest exercise of genius.[26]

His annual address to the Christian Social Union in 1899 was on the subject of 'Expenditure', and they too were urged to 'seek to live on as little as will support the full vigour of our life and work'.[27]

It is clear, then, that what Christians in the second half of the twentieth century termed 'lifestyle' was an important aspect of Westcott's spirituality. He was often addressing the problem of the 'social inefficacy of the Christian faith':[28] the fact that there was little visible difference between the lives of believers and non-believers. Until people saw different values in the lives of believers the witness of the Church would suffer. In his call for a simpler, more sacrificial lifestyle his personal example was perhaps more eloquent than his teaching. Personal sacrifice and renunciation were for him an integral part of the spiritual life.

3 A creation-centred spirituality

There is a photograph of Westcott taken in the garden at Auckland shortly before he died. It is a St Peter's Day Reunion, and he is seated surrounded by 85 of the 'sons of the house'. He looks ill, an unwilling participant in this set piece. A dog is lying in front of one of the clergy on the front row, seemingly asleep on the lawn.[29]

His affection for animals was something which impressed his contemporaries. His son, who claims that he was not fond of dogs in general, tells of how he adopted his son's fox-terrier, Mep, when the latter went to Canada, and how he became his companion for many years. He once said of him: 'The dog is far more than a dog to me. He is a symbol.'[30] A. G. B. West tells us that the bishop adopted his dog too when he went to his first curacy, and it may be this one which is in the photograph. He adds a comment Westcott made about the status of animals within the Christian tradition, in which he refers to Pope Pius IX's refusal to permit a society for the protection of animals in Rome: 'The Bishop was horrified at the dictum of the Pope – that animals did not need to be baptised and therefore had no rights as Christians. Therefore cruelty to them was not a sin – a monstrous doctrine.'[31]

He used the famous park at Auckland which had traditionally been used for hunting with hounds 'as a resting-home for exhausted pit ponies, against whose hard usage in the pit he continually pleaded'.[32] He would not eat game which had been killed for sport, was uneasy about fox-hunting, and could hardly tolerate fishing as a sport.[33] 'Intense sympathy for every kind of suffering extended with him to all created things.'[34] Llewelyn Davies remembered his love of wild flowers, and how he kept them as memorials.[35]

This respect and reverence for all created things is expressed in a sermon preached at Sedbergh on 'Consider the Lilies' in 1896. It sheds interesting light on the concern for the environment which was 'in the air' as the nineteenth century neared its close, the consequence of rapid industrialization and the impact of urbanization on the countryside:

> Do we really hold that all the objects which fill the earth and sea and sky are as truly God's workmanship as our own bodies? . . . It does not seem possible that we should without one moment's thought defile the air and desolate the earth in the premature pursuit of gain if we really believed our own confession . . . The flower torn up and thrown upon the ground, the sea-bird shot upon the wing in the wantonness of skill, the dog tortured in vain curiosity show the same temper. And such actions, trivial as they may seem, profoundly affect the character of the doers. When we violate the reverence due to God's creatures we grow insensible to the joy which they can bring. We spoil and waste our heritage. On the other hand the spirit of devotion is strengthened by habitual tenderness.[36]

It is mistaken to see this concern as expressing mere sentiment. Underpinning this conviction about the oneness of the created order was his incarnational theology. The fact that in Christ God had taken our human nature meant that the material world could now be seen in a quite different light. He told a group of ordinands in 1889: 'God in His Son has taken humanity to Himself. All that really is, is in Him. All Creation, all History, is therefore capable of becoming to us a revelation of Him. Through Nature, through Life, we can enter into converse with Him. The Incarnation has, for the believer, lifted the veil from material things.'[37]

This belief was closely related to the scientific discoveries which for thirty years or so had been transforming people's view of the natural world. Many Christians found it hard to reconcile these discoveries with the biblical revelation. For Westcott there was no clash between the two. The scientists were revealing hitherto hidden aspects of divine truth. He told his Peterborough congregation that

> we may be unspeakably thankful, though many have found it a hard lesson, to these strange, unwilling, or at least unconscious prophets, who have taught us, more plainly than ever before, our dependence one on another, and upon our environment in nature. St Paul and St John taught the same truths, but men could not read their teaching without the commentary of outward experience.[38]

He was often saying that the new discoveries amounted to a divine revelation: in them the purpose of God or Christ was made clear. In the final year of his life, preaching in York Minster on the closing words of Matthew's Gospel, 'Lo, I am with you always, even unto the end of the world', he makes the point that the divine presence from time to time comes to us in some new form. In our time it is in the 'new renaissance of science . . . as momentous a crisis in the history of the world as the renaissance of letters. Never was an age more clearly marked by signs of Divine working, more full of opportunity and of peril, than our own. As Christ came in the past He is coming now.'[39]

[217]

His positive view of the impact of the new science upon Christian faith and devotion is set out most clearly in his Westminster sermon of 1886, 'The Incarnation and Nature'.[40] Scientists, he argues, have enabled us to realize with a vividness undreamed of in earlier times our 'common union with nature'. This illuminates the biblical doctrine of creation, and does not contradict it, for there man is the 'crown and king of Nature': 'He is neither above nor separated from the other works of God . . . His isolation from the realm committed to him is a doctrine of heathen philosophy and not of Judaism or of Christianity.'[41] He shows also how the discoveries of the scientists have helped Christians to understand the biblical vision of the renewal of nature in Isaiah and the book of Revelation, and also the words of St Paul in Romans 8.22, 'the whole creation groaneth and travaileth in pain together until now', which words formed part of the text of the sermon.

He goes on to deal with the question of pain and suffering in the natural world, the struggle for existence and the waste of life. This aspect of the theory of evolution – 'nature red in tooth and claw' – challenged the faith of many Christians. He takes this challenge seriously, but is at his most imprecise and unsatisfactory in answering it. We know that suffering in the animal world as in human society was a great problem for him, and here his argument seems to falter. All he can offer is the vague hope that from that 'which appears to us to be a confused struggle shall come a new and more perfect life. The pains which we witness are the very conditions of the birth of the new order.'[42]

The sermon concludes with a call to Christians not to cling to traditional beliefs and so fail to apprehend the lessons which science has been teaching.

This very positive interpretation of the significance of the teaching of Darwin and others was, then, one of the foundations of Westcott's intense reverence for all created things. For him, the gospel was not for human beings alone but for all creation, a truth proclaimed in Scripture but confirmed by the new discoveries. Gordon Mursell shows that there is a similar positive approach in the work of Charles

Kingsley, and that there is therefore a link between 'spirituality and science'.[43] Westcott's Cambridge colleagues, Lightfoot and Hort, both shared his positive approach here; indeed, the most moving and profound expression of the impact upon faith of Darwin and his contemporaries is to be found in Hort's Hulsean lectures of 1871, *The Way the Truth the Life*.[44]

We mentioned earlier in the chapter Westcott's admiration for St Francis of Assissi. It is worthy of note that in his address on the Franciscan movement he mentions Francis's 'sympathy with every living creature, his feeling for everything without life . . . the hallowing . . . of all natural science.'[45] Here was another aspect of that movement which corresponded with his own deepest convictions.

Finally, it is worthy of mention that the late twentieth century saw the development of a movement which desired to return to what it called a 'Creation-Centred Spirituality'. It stressed 'original blessing'[46] rather than original sin, looked to the eastern rather than to the western theological tradition, and numbered St Francis, George Fox, and Teilhard de Chardin amongst its forerunners. Without claiming that Westcott anticipated this movement, it is interesting to note how much they shared his concerns and beliefs.

4 The contemplative spirit

There was a strong contemplative streak in Westcott. One of his sons recalls his habit while at Peterborough of being alone in the cathedral in the evening: 'Ofttimes . . . he would go in the quiet of the evening, when all was dark and still, and taking his great key with him, make his way into the Church and sit there all alone.'[47] A. C. Benson thought that 'he was essentially lonely in spirit' and 'did not need people, though he suffered them gladly'.[48] Scott Holland in his vivid prose confirms that judgement: 'At Lambeth, he would hide himself away from the Archiepiscopal pomp, with a mutton-chop in the Lollard's Tower. He would retreat, to the very last, from Archidiaconal hot-joints to a cold corner of a railway station waiting-room . . . and sit there for an hour or two, huddled in a shawl, engrossed in meditation.'[49] It was this characteristic which contributed to his reputation as a 'mystic', a term he himself disliked.

It is striking to find this quality mirrored in his devotional writing, where there is strong emphasis on the importance of being still before God, of waiting for him in silence or in the tedious routine of everyday life, and of the blessings of a 'quiet life'.

Reference was made in the last chapter to a sermon preached in 1866 in which he speaks of the significance of the thirty years Jesus spent at Nazareth before his public ministry began. Probably drawing on his experience at Harrow, he shows how times of tedium in our lives can also be times of preparation for a greater task. 'Patience', 'trust' and 'watchfulness' are the lessons to be learned at such times.[50] Three years later a similar point is made in a sermon at Peterborough: 'it is in the silent, unnumbered, unnoticed trivialities . . . of daily business that character is formed which in due time a crisis will reveal'.[51]

It is in his exposition of John's Gospel, however, that he most convincingly develops the case for the contemplative spirit in the life of the believer and of the Church. He does this first in one of his 1871 Peterborough lectures by contrasting the life, character and message of St John with that of St Paul. The latter's sudden conversion and subsequent missionary zeal and enthusiasm are contrasted with the quiet reflectiveness of John who spent many years in relative seclusion before writing his Gospel. The contrast is significant for the contemporary Church:

There is still scope in the Church for the untiring enthusiasm of St Paul; there is still scope for the contemplative strength of St John. We have need of action and we have need of reflection . . . It is good to labour with much serving; it is still better to sit at the feet of Jesus. It was a glorious end which was granted to St Paul, that he should receive the martyr's crown; it was not less glorious for St John to tarry till his Lord came – left alone a stranger in a new world. His work was long delayed, but it came at last. Then he knew that not one hour of his three-score years of waiting was lost.[52]

The reference to the Lukan story of Mary and Martha is clear, as are Westcott's own sympathies.

There is another passage in an 1876 lecture on the vine metaphor in John 15 which is significant in this context. He is commenting on the words of Jesus, 'He that abideth in me, and I in him, the same beareth forth much fruit' (John 15.5): 'The figure of the Vine itself speaks of faithful waiting, of long growth, of slow maturity, of bud, and flower, and ripening cluster . . . He dwells on patient continuance as though he would warn us against the perils of haste and excitement, seasons of drought and scorching heat. There will be seasons of stillness and (to our eyes) of stationariness in the spiritual life . . . It cannot but be so. Such is the divine method in all things.'[53]

Westcott's most memorable mining of this rich biblical seam is to be found in his 1882 book on the resurrection narratives of the New Testament, *The Revelation of the Risen Lord*. Chapter 8 has the title 'The Revelation through Patient Waiting', and is an exposition of John 21.20–23, where Peter, after his meeting by the lakeside with the risen Christ, sees John and asks what will happen to him. Jesus replies, 'If I will that he tarry till I come, what is that to thee? Follow thou me' (21.22). He makes that saying the foundation for a contrast between Peter and John, not unlike the contrast he had drawn earlier between Paul and John. The two men

mark two types of service which must always be rendered, if the Church is to reconcile order with progress, the service of working and the service of waiting, the service of action and the service of thought, the service of outward effort fashioned after the likeness of Christ's Passion and the service of inward meditation directed to the vision of Christ's coming.[54]

Peter's proactive ministry as one of the leaders of the Church facing danger and persecution in the name of Christ is contrasted with John's 'tarrying' for thirty years in silence and obscurity before writing his Gospel. He concedes that it is the example of St Peter which is most congenial to the spirit of the present age. It is, however, the example of St John which is the more urgent need of the time:

> If, as we cannot but believe, the Lord is even now coming to His Church, we shall be ill prepared to meet Him unless there be some among us tarrying for Him in self-concentration and silence, looking to Him and lost in Him: men who dare to wait and stand outside the battle in which as yet they have no part, who dare to hold their peace till the meaning of the Spirit is clear.[55]

He concludes the chapter with a strong plea for the proper recognition of a Johannine type of faith and spirituality, which he believes has never been truly realized in the history of the Church. Christ calls some to work and others to wait:

> And waiting . . . is a sacrifice of self, a real martyrdom no less than working. St John by his long life, as truly as St. James by his early death, drank of the Lord's Cup and shared in the Lord's Baptism according to His own words. To win the soul in patience, to bear the trial of delays, to watch for the dawn through the chill hours which precede it . . . is a witness to the powers of the unseen world . . . It is a witness which we need at present.[56]

Here is a strong argument for the practice of the contemplative life in the midst of everyday existence rather than in the monastic cell. The Oxford Movement's nostalgia for the medieval world and its attempt to revive the monastic life hold no appeal for Westcott. Not that he believed there was nothing to learn from asceticism; as we saw earlier, he appealed to its witness on numerous occasions. He was arguing that the contemplative spirit was for most people to be cultivated in the midst of everyday life and not in detachment from it.

He found the example of his beloved St John much harder to emulate when he became a bishop. Easter eve, 1891, finds him reflecting on the busyness of his life and on 'the blessing of a still life'.[57] The same year he gave an address to the YMCA on 'A Quiet Life: Its Joy and Power'.[58] In his 1892 Lent letter to his clergy and laity he deplored 'the hurry of modern life' and urged them to find time to be silent and to meditate.[59] The life of a bishop was proving to be very different from that of an academic, but there was a sense in which his call for contemplation in the midst of busyness was now more authentic simply because he was now more caught up in 'the hurry of modern life' than he had ever been before.

One of the memorable things in his commendation of the Johannine type of spirituality is how frequently he draws on the biblical metaphor of 'waiting'. It is a word which occurs in his writings quite frequently. One notable example is in his book on the resurrection narratives, where he comments that the necessity of waiting is the lesson of the forty days which elapsed between the crucifixion and the gift of the Holy Spirit.[60]

It is surprising that this thread in his work has never been noticed before. It is a significant one, expressing a very firm conviction about the spiritual life, and as always with Westcott, is part of his own life and practice. In more recent times the biblical concept of waiting was explored in a sensitive and profound work by W. H. Vanstone, *The Stature of Waiting* (1982), which may owe something to Westcott's exploration of the theme.[61]

5 Theology and prayer

Michael Ramsey once pointed out that one of the marks of the Anglican tradition since the seventeenth century has been the close relationship between theology and prayer. He writes of 'the Anglican sensitivity to the significance of spirituality, the life of prayer, for theology'.[62]

This is certainly one of the characteristics of the Cambridge triumvirate. For them, there was no dichotomy between the life of learning and the life of prayer. It must be remembered that this was not the case with those of their contemporaries who identified themselves with the two main parties within the Church of England. Both Evangelicals and High Churchmen were suspicious of, and sometimes hostile to, the methods and conclusions of biblical and historical criticism. For them there had opened up a gap between theology and prayer which had not been a characteristic of the earlier Anglican tradition.

It was an important witness of the Cambridge school to hold together scholarship and spirituality at a time when many were 'putting them asunder'. Some turned to their example in this respect with profound relief. This is the context for the oft-quoted words of Scott Holland on hearing Westcott expounding John's Gospel at Peterborough: 'We had never before seen such an identification of study with prayer.'[63] Scott Holland was an Oxford man, and had been nurtured in a very different theological and spiritual atmosphere.

If we look at Westcott's teaching we find him frequently underlining the close link between study and prayer. In an early sermon of 1852 he speaks of the victory Christians may know over material and intellectual evils: 'There is nothing in Christianity which is hostile to the development of man – nothing which checks the influence of reason and understanding in the domain of human knowledge.' Then, a little later, he puts the question, rather oddly in a village congregation: 'Do we carry our faith into our studies?'[64]

In the debate which took place in the 1870s about the suitability of universities for the training of ordinands, Westcott believed that for all the changes which had taken place they were still appropriate places for such training. As we saw in the last chapter, he believed that the intellectual and the spiritual are intrinsically related: 'That which the candidate for holy orders ought to look for at the University is intellectual training. His pastoral training belongs to another sphere. But it is of the gravest moment for his spiritual work what his intellectual training is.'[65]

One of his reservations about St Francis was that he had discouraged his followers from becoming scholars. The questions and debates of the day, however, could not be ignored by his later followers:

> Francis had discouraged learning, but his scholars were forced to meet the keen questionings of men for whom life was a real battle. In such encounters they were disciplined in the search for knowledge and in the use of it . . . In such service they learnt to question nature patiently, and laid the foundation of inductive science. In thought and work the sense of a divine communion was their strength, and they kindled in innumerable homes that fire of piety which saved Europe in the age of the Renaissance.[66]

We recall that it was Duns Scotus, one of those Franciscan scholars, who had such a crucial influence on Westcott's theological outlook.[67]

He was emphatic that Scripture gave no warrant for the commonly expressed antagonism between faith and reason. The biblical antithesis was rather between faith and sight.[68] He alludes indirectly to the first commandment of Jesus, to love God with heart, soul, mind and strength (Mark 12.30), in an address in which he stresses the limitations of doctrine and doctrinal systems. The Christian nevertheless still has a duty to pursue knowledge and there are no boundaries in this:

> Those who are 'in Christ' are bound to serve God with their whole being, with their intellect no less than with their heart and their strength and their substance . . . For them all that falls within human observation is a potential parable of spiritual realities, through which a fresh vision may be gained of the glory of God. They will be keenest of men to watch for the dawn of new ideas. For them there can be no despondency and no indifference. They bring to the Lord the firstfruits of all that He has lent to them and commit their gains to His keeping.[69]

'They will be keenest of men to watch for . . . new ideas'. Here is a buoyancy, an optimism, a positive approach to the intellectual quest which is wholly characteristic of the Cambridge scholars, but is not to be found in the teaching of many of their contemporaries.

In his insistence on the essential unity of the intellectual and the spiritual quest Westcott is recognizably the heir of the seventeenth century Cambridge Platonists. As we saw in Chapter 3 he had a special admiration for one of the group, Benjamin Whichcote. All of them, however, believed that there could be no sharp division between the rational and the spiritual. In them, as in the whole Platonic tradition, there is that intellectual love of God, the conviction that union with God is the goal both of philosophy and of faith. Westcott stands firmly within that tradition.

6 *Solidarity in the body of Christ*

Westcott was sometimes critical of the Oxford Movement, as we have seen, but he shared its strong conviction about the corporate nature of Christian faith. His spirituality was fed and nurtured by his life within the Church of England, and he frequently spoke about the solidarity of Christians within the body of Christ.

The festival of Pentecost was not about the saving of individuals but rather about the building of a society. Christians are bound in fellowship in a common work, and the festival is the 'consecration of social existence . . . by an eternal and infinite Presence'.[70] Westcott regards the incident in John 20.22–3 where Jesus breathes his Spirit on the disciples as an alternative account of the giving of the Spirit to that in Acts 2, and makes it clear that there too the gift of the Spirit is made not to individuals but to the body of the disciples: 'it is through the Body that the mind of Christ finds natural expression: that the fulness of the Truth is reached: that the Christian character is effective in the world'.[71] The phrase 'the Kingdom of God', which is found so frequently in the teaching of Jesus, is also significant in this respect: 'The object of Redemption is set before us not simply as the deliverance of individual souls but as the establishment of a Divine Society.'[72]

Christian worship he sees as an expression of this solidarity within the Church. Common Prayer is for him a sign of the 'social character' of Christian faith, a 'sacrament of human fellowship' which lifts people above their personal isolation and gives them a sense that they are part of a larger whole. It is significant that prayers in public worship are always in the first person plural, and the first person singular occurs only in the Apostles' Creed.[73] He is quite frequently critical of those who think of religion as a personal, private matter; the spirit of individualism has dominated both civil and religious life, to the detriment of both.

Westcott's consistent advocacy that lay people should play a much fuller part in the life and counsels of the Church of England is related to this belief. He was convinced that the clergy were sometimes guilty of this individualism. There is an ordination address in which he urges the clergy to closer co-operation with their lay people, and criticizes their lack of trust in others and their proud independence. 'Nothing ... more weakens the force of Christian life than this isolation.' 'We have kept too much to ourselves the privilege of social service.'[74] He told his 1893 Diocesan Conference at Gateshead that there was no justification in the New Testament for many of the distinctions that had been drawn between the obligations of the clergy and those of the laity.[75] There is evidence that he envied the fuller involvement in the life of the Church of lay people within the nonconformist groups. In the 'Enquiry about Primitive Methodism in the Diocese of Durham, 1900' which he sent out to his clergy he included these questions:

How far are congregations left to the care of Local Preachers? Have the congregation any voice in their appointment? Why are Local Preachers welcomed more readily than other lay Evangelists? ... Do you find their laity more ready than our own to minister spiritually to one another in private?[76]

Where Westcott diverged most clearly from the high churchmen was in his suspicion of ritualism, and in his unhappiness with many of the new ceremonies which were being introduced into parishes all over the country. He could not enter into the minds of those who believed that more colour and symbolism in worship would make the Church more attractive to working people. He believed that the English instinctively disliked ornate worship, and that the simplicity of the Prayer Book should be the ideal pattern.[77] He would not allow his clergy to offer Prayers for the Dead in public worship, nor the offering of Holy Communion for an individual as in the Roman Catholic tradition.[78] The Reservation of the Sacrament, a key practice for many high churchmen, was an issue which exercised him greatly. He was very unhappy with it set aside in a chapel for private purposes, but drew up a special adaptation of it based on the practice of Justin Martyr in which the elements were taken during the service to sick absentees.[79]

What is significant is that the sacraments in general are much less central in his spirituality than they were for high churchmen. He believed that Christianity was a sacramental religion, affirming that there is 'a true correspondence between things seen and unseen . . . It enables us to recognise that the whole of human life . . . has a spiritual side: that the eternal lies beneath things temporal.' The two gospel sacraments, baptism and holy communion, express this truth, and the incarnation gives 'a new significance to forms so far as they are effective signs of spiritual realities'.[80] The truth is, however, that he seems to have given relatively little attention and thought to the meaning and significance of the two sacraments at a time when there was much controversy and debate about their interpretation. In his lengthy exposition of Westcott's theology Olofsson has barely more than half a page on his view of 'Sacramental life in the Body of Christ'. Westcott seems to have believed that the Eucharist was a subject like the atonement, about which speculation was somehow inappropriate. It is in this comparative lack of interest in the sacraments that he diverges from former pupils like Gore and Scott Holland, who were far more deeply influenced by the high church concentration upon the Eucharist and baptism. Even his colleague, Hort, who also had high church sympathies, seems to have been much more interested in these matters than he.[81]

It must be regarded as something of a surprise that one who gave so much attention and thought to the doctrine of the incarnation should show such little interest in sacramental theology, for the two are often linked and go together. W. M. Teape, a confessed disciple of Westcott, quotes the criticism made by Armitage Robinson of the three Cambridge scholars that 'the problems of the Eucharist were not among those to which their strenuous labours were devoted', and adds his own regret that the trio stopped short 'at the investigation of the history and meaning of liturgies'.[82]

These, then are some of the themes which emerge from a study of Westcott's practice and teaching of the spiritual life. He is a man of his time, his concerns closely related to his context in later Victorian England. And yet it is interesting to see how he anticipates some of the preoccupations which have dominated thinking about spirituality in more recent times.

Wide ranging and versatile as his scholarship was, there is clearly another dimension to his life and thought which must be recognized if he is to be properly understood. The search for holiness of life was for him inseparable from the quest for knowledge and truth, yet there was a sense in which it was the ultimate goal of the Christian life. There is a telling sentence in his *Gospel of St John* where he is commenting on the words of Jesus in John 17.17, 'Sanctify them through thy truth': 'The end of the Truth is not wisdom, which is partial, but holiness, which is universal.'[83] In a similar vein he tells a group of ordinands at Auckland in 1897 that it is 'not power or knowledge which will bring a fruitful ministry – these may exist in the worst men – but love'.[84] According to his son, the book of devotion which he continually studied was *On the Imitation of Christ* by Thomas à Kempis.[85]

It was fundamental to his whole understanding of the Christian life, however, that such holiness must be a 'worldly holiness', rooted and grounded in the world of class conflict and greed and commercial exploitation. He would have agreed with the maxim of John Wesley: 'There is no holiness but social holiness.' Prayer and contemplation which sought to detach themselves from such things were, for him, a betrayal of the authentic Christian spirit. Outside the chapel at Auckland he posted up daily themes for meditation for his students and ordinands, which reflect his conviction that 'the world' must be their concern:

Monday	Foreign Missions
Tuesday	Education
Wednesday	The Empire
Thursday	The Diocese
Friday	The Church Universal
Saturday	The Kingdom of God[86]

His prayers still appear regularly in anthologies of prayers; and one of them sums up well the distinctive flavour of his spirituality:

Behold, O God, our strivings after a truer and more abiding order. Grant us visions of the better things thou hast prepared for us. Scatter every excuse of frailty and unworthiness. Consecrate us all with a heavenly mission; open to us a clearer prospect of our work; and give us strength gladly to welcome and gratefully to fulfil it, in the power and for the sake of Jesus Christ our Saviour.[87]

EPILOGUE

The student of bridges, who knew all the bridges in his diocese when he became a bishop, spent much of his life trying to join together what people had 'put asunder'.

His early work centred on the study of the New Testament, in which he was always seeking to hold together the need for critical scholarship and a proper reverence for Scripture – attention to the minutest details of the text and a larger view which interpreted its teaching for his contemporaries.

In his study of the early history of the Church he tried to build bridges between the Alexandrian Fathers and the Church of his day, believing that the one had an important message for the other.

In his theological explorations he saw the incarnation as the supreme example of the reconciliation of seeming opposites, the seen and the unseen, the human and the divine. Theological controversy was damaging to the mission of the Church, opposing views closer than was commonly thought. Sympathy alone enabled one to enter into the thoughts and feelings of someone who held different views.

In his later years he devoted most of his energy to 'earthing' this theology in the fast-changing world of late Victorian England, bringing the faith 'into the market place' as he often put it. The brotherhood or solidarity created by the incarnation was the inspiration for his Christian Socialism, his mediation in the Miners' Strike, his interest in education, and his work for international peace and arbitration.

His special interest in India inspired him to work for closer links between the Church overseas and the Church at home, and to begin the long and difficult task of relating the Christian revelation to that of other great world faiths.

This coherence in his thought is mirrored in his life where there were no divisions between faith and reason, the life of the spirit and the life of the mind, between prayer and theology. His suggestion in 1870 that members of the New Testament Revision Company should share in a Holy Communion service before their first meeting is at one with his mediation in the 1892 Durham Miners' Strike. He has often been criticized for his unreasonable optimism about human nature, but it was in part this quality which helped to make him a born reconciler.

In an age of the polarization of theological and religious parties there were few more eirenical churchmen than he.

Moreover, the story of how this shy and meticulous scholar of European standing became 'The Miners' Bishop' is surely one of the more remarkable of the nineteenth-century Church.

A hundred years after his death he is another Victorian whose contribution to his own age and legacy to ours deserves to be more widely known.

NOTES

Introduction

1 J. Llewelyn Davies in J. Clayton, *Bishop Westcott*, in the series Leaders of the Church 1800–1900, G. W. E. Russell (ed.), Mowbray, 1906, p. 187.

2 WFH pp. 201–12.

3 A. Watson, *A Great Labour Leader: Being a Life of the Right Hon. Thomas Burt, MP*, Brown, Langham, 1908, p. 252. He was also called 'The Pitmen's Bishop': see John Wilson, *A History of the Durham Miners' Association 1870–1904*, Veitch, 1907, p. 313.

4 Dr Alan Cadwallader, an Australian scholar, is currently at work on a biography.

5 The title of a recent book about the Victorian crisis of faith by A. N. Wilson (John Murray, 1999).

6 ACER AUC 3 Box 13 file 30.

1 Life and Career

1 J. H. Moulton, *The Christian Religion in the Study and the Street*, Epworth, 1918, p. 97.

2 LL1 and 2 provide the basic outline of his life and career.

3 *The Elements of the Gospel Harmony* (1851). See below, p. 4.

4 It was enlarged, rewritten, and published as *An Introduction to the Study of the Gospels* (1860). See below, p. 18.

5 LL1 p. 214.

6 *Essays on Cathedrals*, John Murray, 1872.

7 S. Paget (ed.), *Henry Scott Holland: Memoir and Letters*, John Murray, 1921, p. 59.

8 A. C. Benson, *The Leaves of the Tree*, Smith, Elder, 1911, p22.

9 See below, Chapter 5.

10 A. Roberts, *Salisbury: Victorian Titan*, Weidenfeld and Nicolson, 1999, p. 679.

11 G. R. Eden, 'Bishop Westcott', in R. S. Forman (ed.), *Great Christians*, Nicolson and Watson, 1934, pp. 578–9.

12 ACER AUC 38.

2 The Study of the New Testament

1 C. H. Boutflower, *The Adoring Student: A Recollection of Brooke Foss Westcott*, Cambridge University Press, 1924, pp. 12–13.

2 F. W. Wickenden (ed.), *Salpisae: Memorial Sermon after the death of the Rt. Rev. James Prince Lee*, Macmillan, 1870, p. 12.

3 LL1 p. 214. See above, p. 6.

4 EGH pp. vii–viii.

5 ISG p. 372.

6 ISG p. vii.

7 O. Chadwick, *Hensley Henson: A Study in the Relations between Church and State*, Oxford University Press, 1983, p. 161.

8 S. Neill, *The Interpretation of the New Testament 1861–1961*, Oxford University Press, 1966, p. 96; J. M. Creed, 'The Study of the New Testament', *Journal of Theological Studies* 42, 1941, pp. 5–6.

9 LL1 p. 42.

10 A. F. Hort, *Life and Letters of Fenton John Anthony Hort*, Macmillan, 1896, Vol. I p. 211.

11 'The Theological Correspondence of F. J. A. Hort', CUL Add. MS 6597. Quotations are taken from here unless otherwise indicated. Dates of letters: 12–14 October 1853; April 1861; November 1864; 9 March 1865; 9 October 1865; June, July 1869.

12 LL1 p. 281.

13 A. F. Hort, *Life of Hort*, Vol. I, p. 455.

14 LL1 p. 399; from *The Times*, 29 July 1901.

15 LL1 p. 402.

16 W. Smith, *Dictionary of the Bible*, John Murray, 1863, Vol. II pp. 528–31.

17 S. Neill, *The Interpretation of the New Testament 1861–1961*, p. 72.

18 The articles were later published as *The Revision Revised*, John Murray, 1883.

19 J. L. North, 'The Oxford Debate on the Textual Criticism of the New Testament Held at New College on May 6, 1897: An End, Not a Beginning for the Textus Receptus' in D. G. K. Taylor (ed.), *Studies in the Early Text of the*

Gospels and Acts, University of Birmingham Press, 1999, pp. 3–25.

20 See D. B. Wallace, 'The Majority Text Theory: History, Methods and Critique' in B. D. Ehrmann and M. W. Holmes (eds), *The Text of the New Testament in Contemporary Research*, Eerdmans, 1995, pp. 297–315.

21 LL2 p. 84.

22 See O. Chadwick, *The Victorian Church Part II*, Black, 1970, pp. 43–4.

23 LL1 pp. 391–5.

24 W. F. Moulton, *William F. Moulton*, Isbister, 1899, p. 104.

25 LL1 pp. 396–7.

26 ACER AUC Box 11.

27 LFW pp. 148–9.

28 S. Hempson, *A History of the Revised Version of the New Testament*, Elliott Stock, 1906, pp. 49–53.

29 G. W. E. Russell, *Selected Essays on Literary Subjects*, Dent, ND, pp. 93–4. See also O. Chadwick, *The Victorian Church Part II*, p. 48.

30 'The Theological Correspondence of F. J. A. Hort', CUL Add. MS 6597, July 1880.

31 LFW pp. 146–7.

32 W. Sanday, *The Expositor*, April 1882, p. 112.

33 CUL Add. MS 8317 (letters 1, 5 December 1881)

34 LFW pp. 171–2.

35 SLRVNT pp. 19, 222.

36 R. Standish and C. Standish, *Modern Bible Versions Unmasked*, Hartland, 1993; G. A. Riplinger, *New Age Bible Versions*, AV Publications, 1993.

37 CUL Add. MS 8316/7 (letter 5 November 1901).

38 W. F. Howard, *The Romance of New Testament Scholarship*, Epworth, 1949, p. 57.

39 E. C. Hoskyns, *The Fourth Gospel*, ed. F. N. Davey, 2nd edn, Faber, 1947, p. 41.

40 EH p. ix.

41 H. T. Kuist, 'The Interpreter at Work XV. Brooke Foss Westcott (1825–1901)', in *Interpretation* 7, 1953, p. 447.

42 E. C. Hoskyns, *The Fourth Gospel*, pp. 42–3.

43 *Expository Times* 1, Oct 1889–Sept 1890, p. 118.

44 EH p. vi.

45 Quoted in *Expository Times* 1, p. 267.

46 *The Gospel According to St. John: The Authorized Version*, with introduction and notes by B. F. Westcott and a new introduction by Adam Fox, James Clarke, 1958, p. iic.

47 See below, pp. 107–10.

48 ISG p. 33.

49 'The Language of the New Testament' in W. Smith, *Dictionary of the Bible*, p. 533.

50 ISG p. 36.

51 CAL p. 191.

52 EJ p. v; EH p. vi.

53 LFW pp. 173–4.

54 C. K. Barrett, *Westcott as Commentator*, Cambridge University Press, 1959, p. 17.

55 EH pp. 63–7.

56 *Essays and Reviews*, Longman Green, 1861, p. 391.

57 S. Neill, *The Interpretation of the New Testament 1861–1961*, p. 93.

58 A. C. Benson, *The Leaves of the Tree*, p. 27.

59 GJ pp. 302–3.

60 W. Smith, *Dictionary of the Bible*, p. 533.

61 EH p. v; see also EJ p. vi.

62 E. C. Hoskyns, *The Fourth Gospel*, p. 34.

63 GJ p. 202; see below pp. 169, 179.

64 GJ p. 246.

65 EJ pp. 156–62.

66 EH pp. 105–9.

67 C. K. Barrett, *Westcott as Commentator*, pp. 20–3.

68 C. R. Gregory, 'Brooke Foss Westcott', *American Journal of Theology*, October 1904, p. 763.

69 LFW pp. 136–7.

70 See below, pp. 71–2. The Archbishop of Canterbury, Dr Rowan Williams, explored this reverence for Scripture in Westcott and in other liberal Anglicans in his unpublished Wescott Centenary Lecture, 'The Fate of Liberal Anglicanism' (2001).

71 See above p. 8.

72 C. K. Barrett, *Westcott as Commentator*, p. 24.

3 The History of the Church: The Alexandrian Tradition and Christian Platonism

1 B. J. Kidd (ed.), *Selected Letters of William Bright, D.D.*, Wells, Gardner, Darton, 1903, p. 347.

2 *Birmingham Daily Post*, 26 November 1908.

Notes

3 S. Neill, *The Interpretation of the New Testament 1861–1961*, p. 34.

4 WFH pp. 3–16; SAC pp. 101–34.

5 ICL p. 345.

6 H. Chadwick, *The Vindication of Christianity in Westcott's Thought*, Cambridge University Press, 1961, p. 17.

7 GSHCNT p. 14.

8 GSHCNT p. viii.

9 GSHCNT p. 166.

10 H. Chadwick, *Vindication*, p. 18.

11 H. Chadwick, *Vindication*, pp. 11, 18.

12 B. Metzger, *The Canon of the New Testament: Its Origin, Development, and Significance*, Clarendon, 1997, p. 287.

13 'Canonicity' in R. Brown, J. Fitzmyer, R. Murphy (eds), *The New Jerome Bible Commentary*, Chapman, 1989, p. 1054.

14 For a survey of these debates, see B. Metzger, *The Canon of the New Testament*, pp. 267–88, and the article on 'Canonicity' cited in note 13.

15 BC p. 296.

16 O. Chadwick, *The Mind of the Oxford Movement*, Black, 1960, p. 29.

17 J. H. Newman, *Apologia Pro Vita Sua*, Dent, 1912, pp. 48–9.

18 F. Maurice (ed.), *The Life of Frederick Denison Maurice*, Macmillan, 1884, Vol. II p. 57.

19 EHRTW p. 188. His lectures at Cambridge on the Church in the West were published as *The Two Empires* (1909).

20 W. Smith and H. Wace, *A Dictionary of Christian Biography*, John Murray, 1877, Vols I and IV; W. Smith, *Dictionary of the Bible*; article on Origen in *Contemporary Review* 1883, later published in EHRTW pp. 194–252.

21 Both quotations are from W. Smith and H. Wace, *A Dictionary of Christian Biography*, Vol. I p. 566.

22 C. J. Bigg, *The Christian Platonists of Alexandria*, Oxford University Press, 1913, p. 151.

23 W. Smith and H. Wace, *A Dictionary of Christian Biography*, Vol. IV pp. 139–40. The article is dated 1882 but Vol. IV of the *Dictionary* was not published until 1887.

24 W. Smith and H. Wace, *A Dictionary of Christian Biography*, Vol. IV pp. 133, 139.

25 EHRTW p. 238.

26 EHRTW p. 345: 'it claims to bring a perfect unity of humanity without destroying the personality of any one man'.

27 EHRTW pp. 238–9, 239, 242.

28 EHRTW p. 246.

29 EHRTW p. 247.

30 EHRTW pp. 249, 251, 251–2.

31 B. J. Kidd (ed.), *Selected Letters of William Bright*, p. 347.

32 See, for example, L. Durrell, *The Alexandria Quartet*, Faber, 1957–60; W. Dalrymple, *From the Holy Mountain: A Journey in the Shadow of Byzantium*, HarperCollins, 1997.

33 EHRTW p. 197.

34 W. R. Inge, *The Platonic Tradition in English Religious Thought*, Longmans Green, 1926, p. 33.

35 LL1 pp. 175–6.

36 LL1 pp. 47, 138.

37 W. G. O'Dea, *Westcott the Theologian*, unpublished M. Litt. thesis, Cambridge University, 1972, p. 58.

38 EHRTW pp. 47–8, 49, 50.

39 EHRTW pp. 94–5.

40 EHRTW pp. 139–140.

41 W. Smith, *Dictionary of the Bible*, pp. 852–3.

42 D. Newsome, *Bishop Westcott and the Platonic Tradition*, Cambridge University Press, 1969, pp. 11–12.

43 LL2 p. 85.

44 Newsome, *Platonic Tradition*, p. 16.

45 Newsome, *Platonic Tradition*, p. 32–3, 34.

46 ACER AUC3 Box 13.

47 EHRTW p. 367. Westcott refers to this dictum of Whichcote several times in his addresses and sermons.

48 EHRTW p. 368.

49 EHRTW p. 375.

50 EHRTW p. 379.

51 EHRTW pp. 380–4.

52 EHRTW p. 391.

53 EHRTW p. 392.

54 C. A. Patrides (ed.), *The Cambridge Platonists*, Arnold, 1969, p. 41.

55 LL1 p. 261.

56 D. Newsome, *The Victorian World Picture*, John Murray, 1997, p. 151.

57 LL2 p. 4.

58 EHRTW p. 253.

59 EHRTW pp. 253–4.

60 EHRTW p. 255.

61 EHRTW pp. 255–6. David Newsome points out that this is the passage from Browning quoted most frequently in Westcott's writing, and that he sometimes misquotes it (*Platonic Tradition*, p. 29).

62 EHRTW p. 257. The lines are from 'Rabbi Ben Ezra'.

63 EHRTW p. 263.

64 EHRTW p. 254.

65 EHRTW p. 275.

66 Quoted in the essay on 'The Relation of Christianity to Art' which follows the essay on Browning, EHRTW p. 330. See Newsome, *Platonic Tradition*, pp. 29–30.

67 EHRTW p. 274.

68 EHRTW p. 272.

69 Newsome, *Platonic Tradition*, p. 30.

70 EHRTW p. 323.

71 W. Whitla, *The Central Truth: The Incarnation in Robert Browning's Poetry*, University of Toronto Press, 1963, p. 10.

72 W. Temple, *Religious Experience*, ed. A. E. Baker, James Clarke, 1958, p. 51.

73 LL2 p. 34.

74 E. Le Roy Lawson, *Very Sure of God: Religious Language in the Poetry of Robert Browning*, Vanderbilt University Press, 1974, p. 87. Newsome makes a similar point in *Platonic Tradition*, pp. 31–2.

75 In a letter to Edmund Gosse (quoted in B. Litzinger, *Time's Revenge: Browning's Reputation as a Thinker*, University of Tennessee Press, 1964, p. 16).

76 EHRTW p. vi.

77 B. J. Kidd, *Selected Letters of William Bright*, pp. 347–8.

78 EHRTW p. 365.

79 LL2 p. 34.

4 Theology: Mystery, Incarnation, Fulfilment

1 H. Chadwick, *Vindication*, pp. 3–4.

2 G. W. E. Russell, *Dr Liddon*, Mowbray, 1905, p. 174.

3 A. R. Vidler, 'Westcott's Christian Socialism', *F. D. Maurice and Company*, SCM Press, 1966, p. 269.

4 O'Dea, *Westcott the Theologian*; F. Olofsson, *Christus Redemptor et Consummator: A Study in the Theology of B. F. Westcott*, Alonquist & Wikrell, 1979.

5 A. E. McGrath (ed.), *The S.P.C.K. Handbook of Anglican Theologians*, SPCK, 1998.

6 LL1 pp. 160–1.

7 CAL p. 193; see also LL1 p. 27.

8 LL2 p. 79.

9 CC p. 90.

10 GL p. xviii.

11 RRL p. 102.

12 CAL p. 30.

13 GR pp. viii, xiv.

14 LL2 p. 354.

15 Olofsson, *Christus Redemptor*.

16 LL1 p. 77. John Henry Newman may be one of the people he has in mind.

17 LL1 pp. 337–8.

18 GR p. vi.

19 CAL pp. 76–7.

20 LFW p. 85.

21 O'Dea, *Westcott the Theologian*, p. 120.

22 O'Dea also quotes from F. D. Maurice: 'A man will not really be intelligible to you, if instead of listening to him and sympathizing with him, you determine to classify him' (*The Religions of the World and their Relations to Christianity*, Parker, 1848, p. 98).

23 CAL p. 195.

24 LFW p. 85.

25 LFW p. 119.

26 LFW p. 117.

27 RRL p. 12.

28 O'Dea, *Westcott the Theologian*, pp. 40–3.

29 GL pp. xviii–xix.

30 GFM pp. 7–8.

31 VS p. 229.

32 LFW p. 79.

33 See above, p. 53.

34 CGM p. 60.

35 CC p. 90. For the full quotation, see above, p. 70.

36 LFW pp. 81, 82.

37 PS pp. 270–1.

38 LFW pp. 63–4, 67.

39 ICL pp. vii, 44; CC p. 158; LFW p. 290.

40 GL p. 271.

41 LFW p. 64.

42 GJ p. 11.

43 RF pp. 111–12.

44 GL p. 252.

45 GFM p. 53.

46 GL pp. 52–3.

47 HF pp. 234–6.

48 A. G. B. West, *Memories of Brooke Foss Westcott*, Cambridge University Press, 1936, pp. 41–2.

49 RF p. 133.

50 A. S. Farrar, 'On Bishop Westcott', *Durham University Journal* 14, 30 November 1901, p. 267.

51 EJ pp. 286–328.

52 EJ pp. 305, 306.

53 EJ p. 324.

54 CC p. 104.

55 CC pp. 109–10.

56 GL p. 253.

57 LL1 p. 433.

58 EJ p. 328.

59 CC pp. 11–12.

60 EH p. 66.

61 Olofsson, *Christus Redemptor*, pp. 185–6.

62 CC pp. 76, 77.

63 CC pp. 132–3.

64 CC p. 13.

65 G. Rowell, *Hell and the Victorians*, Clarendon, 1974, p. 213.

66 P. Teilhard de Chardin, *Let Me Explain*, Collins, 1974, p. 101.

67 VS pp. 82–3.

68 VS pp. 83, 84, 86–7.

69 VS p. 315.

70 HF pp. 66–7.

71 GL pp. 196, 197.

72 CC pp. 116–17.

73 HF p. 66.

74 LL2 p. 77.

75 GL p. 196.

76 CC p. 118.

77 LL1 p. 433. See above, p. 86.

78 LL2 p. 365.

79 H. Scott Holland, *Personal Studies*, Wells, Gardner, Darton, 1905, p. 137. Cf. note 77 where Holland is quoted as making sin 'the centre of his theology'.

80 A. S. Farrar, 'On Bishop Westcott', p. 268.

81 A. C. Benson, *The Leaves of the Tree*, p. 46.

82 Olofsson, *Christus Redemptor*, pp. 299, 302, 303.

83 F. Maurice, *The Life of F. D. Maurice*, Vol. II, p. 358.

84 G. Treloar, *Lightfoot the Historian*, Mohr Siebeck, 1998, p. 115.

85 A. M. Ramsey, *From Gore to Temple*, Longmans, 1960, pp. 23–4.

86 W. Moore Ede, 'What we owe to Frederick Denison Maurice and his disciples', *Modern Churchman* 9, December 1933, Vol. xxiii p. 530.

87 LL1 p. 231.

88 LL1 pp. 239–40.

89 VC p. 75.

90 CC p. 25.

91 VC pp. 76, 78, 79.

92 VC pp. 3–17.

93 VC pp. 21–35.

94 VC p. 22

95 CC p. 125.

96 VC pp. 69–70. See also VC pp. 82, 84.

97 J. Bennett, *Crux Christi: Being a Consideration of Some Aspects of the Doctrine of the Atonement*, J. F. Shaw, 1892, p. 167.

98 A. C. Benson, *The Life of Edward White Benson*, Macmillan, 1900, Vol. II p. 578.

99 LL1 p. 249.

100 LL1 p. 253.

101 ISG p. 47.

102 GR p. 246.

103 GR p. 250.

104 Olofsson, *Christus Redemptor*, p. 225.

105 GR p. 88.

106 GR p. 260.

107 RRL pp. xxxiii–iv.

108 A. M. Ramsey, *The Resurrection of Christ*, Collins, 1961, p. 118.

109 CLMO pp. 33, 34, 37.

110 GR p. 8.

111 GR pp. 5, 241.

112 GR p. 6.

113 RRL p. xxvii.

114 Olofsson, *Christus Redemptor*, pp. 226, 248

115 A. M. Ramsey, *From Gore to Temple*, p. 28.

116 D. Newsome, *The Victorian World Picture*, p. 229.

117 R. Williams, *On Christian Theology*, Blackwell, 2000, p. 228.

118 Olofsson, *Christus Redemptor*, p. 323. See J. Denney, *The Death of Christ*, 4th edn, New York, 1903, p. 325.

119 Clayton, *Bishop Westcott*, p. 135.

120 C. Gore, *The Pilot* III, 11 May 1901, p. 586, quoted in J. Carpenter, *Gore: A Study in Liberal Catholic Thought*, Faith Press, 1960, p. 184.

121 C. Gore, *The Reconstruction of Belief*, John Murray, 1930, p. 589.

122 H. H. Henson, *Retrospect of an Unimportant Life*, Vol. III 1936–46, Oxford University Press, 1950, p. 381.

123 Clayton, *Bishop Westcott*, p. 184.

124 W. Moore Ede, 'What we owe to F. D. Maurice', pp. 527–8.

125 A. R. Vidler, *F. D. Maurice and Company*, pp. 275–6.

126 Clayton, *Bishop Westcott*, p. 185.

127 A. F. Hort, *Life of Hort*, Vol. 1, pp. 222–3. The date was June 1852.

128 A. F. Hort, *Life of Hort*, Vol. 2, p. 143.

129 LL1 p. 369; F. Maurice, *Life of F. D. Maurice*, Vol. I, pp. 578, 598.

130 CUL Add. MS 7348/11/160.

131 In H. D. A. Major and F. L. Cross, *Principles and Precepts*, Blackwell, 1927, p. 170.

132 C. C. J. Webb, *A Study of Religious Thought in England from 1850*, Clarendon, 1933, p. 86.

133 R. Williams, 'The Fate of Liberal Anglicanism'.

134 The most thorough discussion of this issue is in Olofsson, *Christus Redemptor*, pp. 49–57.

135 E.g. W. Sanday, 'Dr Westcott as Theologian and Writer 2', *The Pilot*, 14 September 1901, p. 265; Scott Holland, *Personal Studies*, pp. 132–3.

136 GR p. 20.

137 *Guardian*, 8 August 1883, p. 1179.

138 VC pp. 85–6.

139 W. Sanday, 'Dr Westcott as Theologian and Writer 2', *The Pilot*, pp. 291–2.

140 ACER AUC Box 13 file 11. See also A. S. Farrer, 'On Bishop Westcott', pp. 266–7.

141 LL2 p. 24.

142 J. A. Robinson, 'Dr Westcott as a teacher', *The Pilot*, 10 August 1901,

p. 158. See also B. Pollock, *A Twentieth Century Bishop: Recollections and Reflections*, Skeffington, 1944, p. 26.

143 Boutflower, *The Adoring Student*, p. 11.

144 Olofsson, *Christus Redemptor*, p. 57.

5 Practical Theology

1 C. R. Gregory, 'Brooke Foss Westcott', *American Journal of Theology*, October 1904, p. 759.

2 A. R. Vidler, *F. D. Maurice and Company*, pp. 262–3.

3 ICL p. 36. See also CAL pp. 285–6.

4 LL2 p. 15; quoted in A. R. Vidler, *F. D. Maurice and Company*, p. 262.

5 *Birmingham Daily Post*, 26 November 1908.

6 CAL p. 189.

7 Newsome, *Platonic Tradition*, p. 33.

8 LL1 p. 136.

9 LL1 p. 157.

10 CAL p. 79. In his novel *Sybil* (1845) Disraeli had written of 'two nations between whom there is no intercourse and no sympathy'.

11 LL1 p. 161.

12 LL2 p. 109.

13 SAC p. xii.

14 CLMO pp. 11–12.

15 CLMO pp. 55, 60, 60–1.

16 GR p. 161.

17 GR p. xv.

18 A. R. Vidler, *F. D. Maurice and Company*, p. 266.

19 LL2 p. 10

20 LL2 p. 51. The Imperial Federation League (1884–93) was a group of statesmen and scholars who formed a kind of 'think tank' propagating imperialist ideas.

21 A. C. Benson, *The Life of Edward White Benson*, Vol. II p. 154.

22 A. C. Benson, *The Life of Edward White Benson*, Vol. II pp. 221, 223.

23 LL2 p. 10.

24 LL2 p. 21 (from an 1889 paper on 'A Christian Policy of Peace').

25 LL2 p. 23.

26 A. C. Benson, *The Life of Edward White Benson*, Vol. II pp. 131, 295.

27 LL2 p. 67.

28 CC p. 148.

29 SAC p. v.

30 SAC p. 3.

31 SAC p. 8.

32 SAC p. 15.

33 SAC p. 4.

34 SAC p. 21.

35 SAC p. 31.

36 SAC p. 42.

37 SAC pp. 72, 74, 75.

38 SAC p. 91.

39 LL2 p. 35.

40 ICL p. v.

41 ICL p. ix.

42 ICL p. 34.

43 ICL p. 349.

44 CC p. viii.

45 GL p. xxi.

46 ICL p. 55.

47 ICL pp. 56–7.

48 ICL pp. 24–5.

49 ICL pp. 303, 304.

50 CAL p. 298.

51 CAL p. 309.

52 ICL p. 57.

53 CAL pp. 8–9.

54 ICL p. 94.

55 ICL p. 103.

56 ICL p. 126.

57 ICL pp. 102–3.

58 ICL p. 130.

59 CAL pp. 106–7.

60 B. Chaturvedi and M. Sykes, *Charles Freer Andrews: A Narrative,* Allen and Unwin, 1949, p. 17 (quoted in A. R. Vidler, *F. D. Maurice and Company,* p. 271).

61 GR p. 228.

62 ICL pp. 5–6.

63 O. Chadwick, *The Victorian Church Part II,* p. 273.

64 Clayton, *Bishop Westcott,* p. 76.

65 ICL pp. 225–37.

66 ICL p. 225.

67 ICL p. 226.

68 ICL p. 227.

69 ICL p. 231.

70 ICL pp. 232–3.

71 ICL p. 233.

72 ICL pp. 233–4.

73 ICL p. 234.

74 ICL p. 236–7.

75 Clayton, *Bishop Westcott*, p. 164.

76 CAL pp. 231, 232.

77 CAL pp. 233–4.

78 CAL p. 240.

79 CAL p. 237.

80 Scott Holland, *Personal Studies*, p. 132.

81 A. Wilkinson, *Christian Socialism: Scott Holland to Tony Blair*, SCM Press, 1998, p. 54.

82 P. d'A. Jones, *The Christian Socialist Revival 1877–1914*, Princeton University Press, 1968, p. 223.

83 Quoted in P. d'A. Jones, *The Christian Socialist Revival 1877–1914*, p. 166.

84 P. d'A Jones, *The Christian Socialist Revival 1877–1914*, p. 455.

85 E. R. Norman, *The Victorian Christian Socialists*, Cambridge University Press, 1987, p. 162.

86 A. R. Vidler, *F. D. Maurice and Company*, p. 278.

87 J. H. Foster, *Henry Scott Holland 1847–1918*, pp. 189–90, unpublished Ph.D. thesis, University of Wales, 1970.

88 Wilkinson, *Christian Socialism*, p. 240.

89 Wilkinson, *Christian Socialism*, p. 55.

90 Wilkinson, *Christian Socialism*, p. 53.

91 ACER Earl Grey Papers 264/1.

92 ACER Earl Grey Papers 264/1.

93 LL2 p. 135.

94 ACER Earl Grey Papers 196/1.

95 LL2 pp. 195–6.

96 LL2 p. 275.

97 LL2 p. 273; WFH pp. 127–35.

98 ACER Earl Grey Papers 196/1.

99 ACER AUC4 Diocesan Visitation Returns.

100 ACER AUC4 Diocesan Visitation Returns.

101 CAL pp. 258–9.

102 CAL p. 262.

103 CAL p. 263.

104 CAL p. 278.

105 G. Best, *Bishop Westcott and the Miners*, Cambridge University Press, 1967, pp. 5–22.

106 Best, *Bishop Westcott and the Miners*, pp. 22–3, 28–9.

107 Best, *Bishop Westcott and the Miners*, p. 26.

108 Best, *Bishop Westcott and the Miners*, pp. 34–5.

109 H. H. Henson, *Retrospect of an Unimportant Life*, Vol. II 1920–39, Oxford University Press, 1943, p. 25.

110 ICL p. 233.

111 CAL p. 273.

112 *Guardian*, 4 December 1901, p. 1665.

113 A. M. Ramsey, *From Gore to Temple*, p. 1.

6 Empire, War, and the Mission of the Church

1 LL2 p. 231. Basil was his youngest son who died from cholera in August 1900 after serving for four years with the Cambridge Mission to Delhi.

2 J. Morris, *Pax Britannica*, Faber, 1998, p. 22.

3 J. Morris, *Pax Britannica*, p. 502.

4 LFW p. 370.

5 LFW p. 373.

6 LFW p. 227.

7 SAC p. 54.

8 SAC p. 60.

9 SAC p. 62.

10 SAC p. 61.

11 SAC p. 62.

12 VS p. 21.

13 LFW pp. 375–6.

14 LFW p. 381.

15 LL2 p. 246.

16 LFW pp. 412–22.

17 LFW pp. 414–15.

18 LFW p. 421.

19 LL2 p. 245.

20 LFW p. 419.

21 Clayton, *Bishop Westcott*, p. 85.

22 K. Cracknell, *Justice, Courtesy and Love: Theologians and Missionaries Encountering World Religions 1846–1914*, Epworth, 1995.

23 LL1 pp. 2–4.

24 CUL Add. MS 8316/3 (24 February 1889).

25 ROU p. 41. The sermon is discussed in detail on pp. 157–8.

26 ROU p. 42.

27 CUL Add. MS 8316/1.

28 CUL Add. MS 8316/1 (11 letters to his father); Add. MS 8316/3 (170 letters to his mother).

29 LFW pp. 403–11; LL2 pp. 198–201.

30 'Bishop Westcott as a Diocesan', *Guardian*, Vol. LVI Part II, July–December 1901, p. 1087.

31 ACER AUC 37 file 6.

32 ROU p. 31.

33 ROU p. 32.

34 ROU p. 33.

35 ROU pp. 34–5.

36 ROU p. 35.

37 ROU p. 36.

38 ROU p. 37.

39 ROU p. 38.

40 ROU pp. 38–9.

41 ROU p. 41. See above, p. 155.

42 CAL p. 144.

43 CAL p. 148.

44 CAL p. 149.

45 CAL p. 146.

46 WHF p. 122.

47 A reminiscence of C. F. Andrews, quoted in B. Chaturvedi and M. Sykes, *Charles Freer Andrews*, p. 18. See below, p. 164, for the full quotation.

48 Cracknell, *Justice*, p. 69.

49 CAL p. 151.

50 CAL p. 152.

51 CAL p. 165.

52 CAL pp. 170–1.

53 CAL pp. 175–6.

54 CAL p. 177.

55 CAL pp. 178–9.

56 See GL pp. 103, 105.

57 Cited in J. Moore (ed.), *Religion in Victorian Britain*, Vol. III: Sources, Manchester University Press, 1988, p. 510.

58 A. G. B. West, *Memories*, p. 8.

59 G. Treloar published the first major study of J. B. Lightfoot in 1998, and A. Cadwallader is working on a biography of Westcott.

60 D. O'Connor and others, *Three Centuries of Mission: The United Society for the Propagation of the Gospel 1701–2000*, Continuum, 2000, pp. 138–40.

61 O'Connor and others, *Three Centuries of Mission*, p. 187.

62 Unpublished reminiscences quoted in B. Chaturvedi and M. Sykes, *Charles Freer Andrews*, p. 18.

63 O'Connor and others, *Three Centuries of Mission*, pp. 104–7.

64 D. O'Connor (ed.), *The Testimony of C. F. Andrews*, CSL Madras, 1974, p. 47.

65 C. F. Andrews, *What I Owe to Christ*, Hodder & Stoughton, 1932, pp. 182–3.

66 A. Hastings, *A History of English Christianity 1920–1985*, Collins, 1987, p. 94.

67 Cracknell, *Justice*, pp. 1–34.

68 O. Chadwick, *The Victorian Church Part II*, pp. 38–9.

69 GJ p. 4.

70 GJ p. 4.

71 GJ p. 7.

72 GJ p. 7.

73 GJ p. 7.

74 GJ p. 202.

75 Cracknell, *Justice*, p. 61.

76 PS p. 43.

77 PS p. 56.

78 G. A. McCool (ed.), *A Rahner Reader*, Darton, Longman and Todd, 1975, pp. 211–15.

79 CC p. 104.

80 CC p. 118.

81 CC p. 106 (the italics are Westcott's own).

82 CC p. 111 (italics Westcott's).

83 Cracknell, *Justice*, p. 63.

84 Cracknell, *Justice*, p. 63.

85 GL p. 112.

86 GL p. 113.

87 GL p. 116.

88 Cracknell, *Justice*, p. 64.

89 GL p. 116.

90 GL p. 116.

91 GL p. 117.

92 GL p. 117.

93 GL p. 119.

94 GL pp. 141–2. The Christian gospel contains these ideas but they have not yet been fully expressed in Christianity as it exists.

95 GL p. 149.

96 GL p. 150.

97 GL p. 153.

98 GL p. 160.

99 GL p. 168.

100 GL p. 169.

101 GL p. 170.

102 GL p. 181.

103 GL p. 229.

104 GL p. 251.

105 GL pp. x, 122–3: the heading to the introduction to his chapter on the other world faiths.

106 *The Cambridge Companion to the Bible*, Cambridge University Press, 1893, pp. 53–5 ('Appendix on the Sacred Books of Prae-Christian Religions').

107 J. E. C. Welldon, *Recollections and Reflections*, Cassell, 1915, p. 221.

108 Cracknell, *Justice*, p. 192. These were questions 5 and 6 in a list of eleven questions.

109 Cracknell, *Justice*, p. 202.

110 Cracknell, *Justice*, pp. 202–5.

111 The others were A. M. Fairbairn, the Scottish theologian, and C. C. Hall, an American Presbyterian.

112 Cracknell, *Justice*, pp. 217–19.

113 Cracknell, *Justice*, pp. 219–27.

114 Cracknell, *Justice*, p. 227.

115 *Expository Times*, January 2002, Vol. 113 No. 4, p. 114.

116 *Expository Times*, January 2002, p. 117.

117 GJ p. 202; see above, p. 169.

118 LL1 p. 307.

119 PS pp. 301–12.

120 PS pp. 307–12.

121 PS p. 311.

122 PS pp. 315–16.

123 PS p. 322.

124 CAL p. 298.

125 CAL p. 299.

126 CAL p. 301.

127 CAL p. 304.

128 CAL p. 306.

129 CAL pp. 312–13.

130 CAL pp. 316–17.

131 CAL p. 319.

132 O. Chadwick, *The Victorian Church Part II*, p. 224.

133 A. Wilkinson, *The Church of England and the First World War*, SPCK, 1978, p. 11.

134 LL2 p. 287.

135 LL2 p. 288.

136 LL2 p. 287.

137 LFW p. 360.

138 LFW p. 362.

139 Clayton, *Bishop Westcott*, p. 111.

7 Education

1 LL1 pp. 385–6.

2 CAL p. 190.

3 CAL p. 191.

4 See above, p. 37.

5 CAL p. 192.

6 CAL pp. 193–4.

7 CAL pp. 194–5.

8 CAL p. 195.

9 EJ p. vi.

10 EH p. vi. See above, p. 34.

11 GL p. xviii. See above, p. 70.

12 GL p. xxv.

13 GR p. vii.

14 A. C. Benson, *The Leaves of the Tree*, p. 32.

15 D. Newsome, *Godliness and Good Learning*, John Murray, 1961, p. 25.

16 D. Newsome *Godliness and Good Learning*, pp. 228–37.

17 LL1 p. 50. The date was 1 January 1847.

18 ACER AUC Box 13; 12 March 1852.

19 LL1 p. 224.

20 O'Dea, *Westcott the Theologian*, Chapter 3.

21 CUL Add. MS 8316/7 (a letter from Sir William Ffolkes to Arthur Westcott, 7 November 1901).

22 ACER AUC Box 13; letters from Lightfoot to Westcott.

23 ACER AUC Box 13; 17 December 1868. The advice was repeated in two subsequent letters, 28 and 29 December. The italics represent Lightfoot's own underlining.

24 VS p. 73. See below, p. 220.

25 ICL pp. 175–91.

26 ICL p. 188.

27 CAL pp. 203–4.

28 CAL p. 205.

29 CAL p. 206.

30 CAL pp. 207–8.

31 CAL p. 208.

32 CAL p. 209.

33 CAL p. 211.

34 LL2 p. 160. The lectures were published as *Learning and Working* (1855).

35 A. G. B. West, *Memories*, p. 11.

36 CUL Add. MS 8316/7; letter 32.

37 R. R. Houghton, *Bungay Grammar School 1565–1965*, pp. 90–91. The preacher was Revd Thomas Herbert Bindley, Rector of Hedenham near Bungay, an Oxford graduate and a Durham D.D.

38 T. Copley, *Black Tom: Arnold of Rugby: The Myth and the Man*, Continuum, 2002, p. 255.

39 O. Chadwick, *Westcott and the University*, Cambridge University Press, 1963, p. 25.

40 LL1 pp. 378–9.

41 G. Treloar, *Lightfoot the Historian*, p. 187.

42 O. Chadwick, *University*, p. 14.

43 ROU pp. 122–3.

44 ROU p. 123.

45 ROU pp. 4–5.

46 ROU pp. 10–18.

47 O. Chadwick, *University*, pp. 16–17. Christopher Wordsworth, a nephew

of the poet, was a conservative high churchman who became Bishop of Lincoln in 1869.

48 ROU p. 51.

49 ROU p. 57.

50 ROU p. 59.

51 ROU p. 60.

52 ROU p. 63. See also GL pp. 2ff.

53 ROU pp. 65–6.

54 ROU pp. 68–9.

55 O. Chadwick, *University*, pp. 26–7.

56 O. Chadwick, *University*, p. 29.

57 ROU p. 81.

58 ROU pp. 85–6.

59 ROU p. 91.

60 ROU pp. 105, 108–9.

61 See above, p. 197.

62 O. Chadwick, *University*, pp. 30–1.

63 ROU p. 93.

64 ROU p. 131.

65 ROU pp. 131–2.

66 ROU pp. 136–7.

67 B. K. Cunningham, *The History of Westcott House*, 1932, pp. 2–3.

68 LL2 pp. 269–70.

69 O. Chadwick, *University*, p. 35.

70 See below, pp. 212–13.

8 Spirituality

1 G. S. Wakefield, 'Anglican Spirituality' in L. Dupre and D. Salders (eds), *Christian Spirituality: Post Reformation and Modern*, SPCK, 1990, p. 281.

2 S. Paget (ed.), *Henry Scott Holland: Memoir and Letters*, John Murray, 1921, p. 59. The words about John's Gospel follow these words and are quoted on p. 8 above.

3 LL1 p. 410. See also A. Fox, *Dean Inge*, John Murray, 1960, p. 30.

4 G. R. Eden, 'Bishop Westcott' in R. S. Forman (ed.), *Great Christians*, Nicolson and Watson, 1934, pp. 584, 587.

5 LL2 p. 25.

6 C. R. Gregory, 'Brooke Foss Westcott', *American Journal of Theology*, October 1904, p. 757.

7 A. W. Dale, *The Life of R. W. Dale of Birmingham*, Hodder, 1898, p. 683.

8 LL2 p. 398.

9 *Guardian*, Vol LVI Part II, July–December 1901, p. 1087; see also LL2 p. 410.

10 A. M. Allchin, 'Anglican Spirituality' in S. Sykes, J. Booty and J. Knight (eds), *The Study of Anglicanism*, SPCK, 1998, pp. 355–6.

11 G. Rowell, K. Stevenson, R. Williams (eds), *Love's Redeeming Work is Done: An Anthology of Anglican Spirituality*, Oxford University Press, 2001.

12 G. Mursell, *English Spirituality: From 1700 to the Present Day*, SPCK 2001, pp. 201–16.

13 G. S. Wakefield (ed.), *A Dictionary of Christian Spirituality*, SCM, 1983, p. 361.

14 VS p. 183.

15 LFW p. 107.

16 LL1 pp. ix, 351; LL2 pp. 131, 292, 396.

17 A. G. B. West, *Memories*, p. 27.

18 WFH p. 14. For the influence of this sermon see A. M. Allchin, *The Silent Rebellion: Anglican Religious Communities 1845–1900*, SCM Press, 1958.

19 WFH p. 42.

20 D. Newsome, 'The Assault on Mammon: Charles Gore and John Neville Figgis', *Journal of Ecclesiastical History* XVII No. 2 (1966), p. 239.

21 SAC pp. 113–14.

22 B. Pollock, *A Twentieth Century Bishop: Recollections and Reflections*, p. 27.

23 LL2 p. 131.

24 Scott Holland, *Personal Studies*, p. 136.

25 ICL p. 29.

26 ICL p. 134.

27 LFW p. 348.

28 LFW p. 279.

29 ACER AUC 38.

30 LL1 p. 317; LL2 p. 147.

31 A. G. B. West, *Memories*, p. 19.

32 Scott Holland, *Personal Studies*, p. 136.

33 A. G. B. West, *Memories*, p. 17. See also B. Pollock, *A Twentieth Century Bishop*, p. 26.

34 A. G. B. West, *Memories*, p. 16.

35 Clayton, *Bishop Westcott*, p. 187.

36 CAL pp. 375–6. He goes on to quote Coleridge's verse from 'The Ancient Mariner':

> He prayeth best who loveth best
> All things both great and small;
> For the dear God who loveth us,
> He made and loveth all.

37 GFM p. 46.

38 PS p. 294.

39 WFH pp. 148–9.

40 CC pp. 131–43.

41 CC p. 133.

42 CC p. 139.

43 G. Mursell, *English Spirituality*, pp. 206–7.

44 G. A. Patrick, *F. J. A. Hort: Eminent Victorian*, Almond, 1988, pp. 54–6.

45 SAC p. 115.

46 The title of a book by Matthew Fox (1983), which brought together its main concerns.

47 LL1 p. 353.

48 A. C. Benson, *The Leaves of the Tree*, p. 45.

49 Scott Holland, *Personal Studies*, p. 136.

50 VS pp. 68–73. See above, p. 192.

51 CLMO p. 6. Cf. ICL p. 396: 'Our common business is the staple of our life. This, and not anything added to it, is our appointed sacrifice.'

52 PS pp. 263–4.

53 PS p. 55.

54 RRL p. 144.

55 RRL p. 148.

56 RRL pp. 149–50.

57 LL2 p. 240.

58 ICL pp. 327–38.

59 ICL pp. 395–6.

60 RRL p. 119.

61 Vanstone wrote a master's thesis on Westcott's theology while studying at Union Seminary New York in 1950.

62 A. M. Ramsey, *From Gore to Temple*, p. 164.

63 Scott Holland, *Personal Studies*, p. 130. His words are quoted by C. H. Boutflower, *The Adoring Student*, p. 15.

64 VS pp. 180–1, 183.

65 ROU p. 126.

66 SAC p. 109.

67 See above, Chapter 4.

68 ICL p. 363; the sermon has the text, 'We walk by faith, not by sight', from 2 Corinthians 5.7.

69 CAL p. 32.

70 VS p. 271.

71 CAL p. 37.

72 SAC p. 86.

73 WFH pp. 169, 172–3.

74 GM pp. 33, 34.

75 CAL pp. 407–11.

76 ACER AUC3 Box 13 file 30.

77 LL2 p. 301; see also West, *Memories*, p. 24.

78 LL2 pp. 349–50.

79 LL2 pp. 274, 356; W. M. Teape, *Westcott's Fear by a Disciple*, Cambridge University Press, 1930.

80 CAL p. 41.

81 See G.A. Patrick, *F. J. A. Hort: Eminent Victorian*, pp. 38–9.

82 Teape, *Westcott's Fear*, pp. 115–16.

83 GJ p. 245.

84 CAL p. 362.

85 LL2 p. 285.

86 A. G. B. West, *Memories*, p. 6.

87 F. Colquhoun (ed.), *God of Our Fathers*, Hodder, 1990, p. 173.

SELECT BIBLIOGRAPHY

Primary Sources

Unpublished

Durham University Library, Palace Green, Durham:
Auckland Castle Episcopal Records
Earl Grey Papers

Dean and Chapter Library, Durham Cathedral:
Lightfoot Papers

Cambridge University Library:
Westcott Papers: Add. MSS 8316, 8317
Selections from the Theological Correspondence of F. J. A. Hort: Add. MS 6597

Published

Books
The publisher is Macmillan, unless indicated.

The Bible in the Church, 1864.
Characteristics of the Gospel Miracles, 1859.
Christian Aspects of Life, 1897.
The Christian Life, Manifold and One, 1869.
Christus Consummator, 1886.
The Elements of the Gospel Harmony, 1851.
The Epistle to the Hebrews, 1889.
The Epistles of St John, 1883.
Essays in the Religious Thought of the West, 1891.
A General Survey of the History of the Canon of the New Testament, 1855.
Gifts for Ministry, 1889.

The Gospel according to St John: the Authorized Version with introduction and notes, reprinted from *The Speaker's Commentary*, John Murray, 1882. Reissued with a new introduction by Adam Fox, 1958.

The Gospel according to St John. The Greek text with introduction and notes, 2 vols, 1908.

The Gospel of Life, 1892.

The Gospel of the Resurrection, 1866.

The Historic Faith, 1883.

The Incarnation and Common Life, 1893.

An Introduction to the Study of the Gospels, 1860.

Lessons from Work, 1901.

The New Testament in the Original Greek, Vol I: Text, Vol II: Introduction and Appendix; with F. J. A. Hort, 1881.

On Some Points in the Religious Office of the Universities, 1873.

Peterborough Sermons, 1904.

The Revelation of the Father, 1884.

The Revelation of the Risen Lord, 1881.

Saint Paul's Epistle to the Ephesians, 1906.

Social Aspects of Christianity, 1887.

Some Lessons of the Revised Version of the New Testament, 1897.

The Two Empires: The Church and the World, 1909.

The Victory of the Cross, 1888.

Village Sermons, 1906.

Words of Faith and Hope, 1902.

Articles and essays

'Aspects of Positivism in Relation to Christianity' in *The Contemporary Review* Vol VIII, pp. 371–86 (also published as Appendix I in *The Gospel of the Resurrection*, 4th edn).

'Cathedral Foundations in Relation to Religious Thought', Essay V in J. S. Howson (ed.), *Essays on Cathedrals*, John Murray, 1872.

'Comte on the Philosophy of the History of Christianity' in *The Contemporary Review* Vol. VI, pp. 399–421.

Articles on 'Alexandria', 'Philo', 'Monasticism', 'Canon', 'Herod', 'New Testament', 'Philosophy', 'Vulgate' in W. Smith, *Dictionary of the Bible*, Vols I, II, III, John Murray, 1863.

Articles on 'Ambrosius', 'Clement of Alexandria', 'Demetrius', 'Dionysius' (Vol. I) and 'Origenes' (Vol. IV) in W. Smith and H. Wace, *A Dictionary of Christian Biography*, John Murray, 1877, 1887.

Select Bibliography

Secondary Works

C. K. Barrett, *Westcott as Commentator*, Cambridge University Press, 1959.

J. Bennett, *Crux Christi: Being a Consideration of Some Aspects of the Doctrine of the Atonement*, J. F. Shaw, 1892.

A. C. Benson, *The Leaves of the Tree*, Smith, Elder, 1911.

A. C. Benson, *The Life of Edward White Benson*, 2 vols, Macmillan, 1900.

G. Best, *Bishop Westcott and the Miners*, Cambridge University Press, 1967.

C. H. Boutflower, *The Adoring Student: A Recollection of Brooke Foss Westcott*, Heffer, 1924.

J. Clayton, *Bishop Westcott*, Mowbray, 1906 (Leaders of the Church 1800–1900).

H. Chadwick, *The Vindication of Christianity in Westcott's Thought*, Cambridge University Press, 1961.

O. Chadwick, *The Victorian Church Part II*, Black, 1970.

O. Chadwick, *Westcott and the University*, Cambridge University Press, 1963.

K. Cracknell, *Justice, Courtesy and Love: Theologians and Missionaries Encountering World Religions 1846–1914*, Epworth, 1995.

G. R. Eden, 'Bishop Westcott' in R. S. Forman (ed.), *Great Christians*, Nicolson and Watson, 1934.

D. L. Edwards, *Leaders of the Church of England 1828–1944*, Oxford University Press, 1971.

A. S. Farrar, 'On Bishop Westcott', *Durham University Journal* 14, 30 November 1901.

J. H. Foster, *Henry Scott Holland 1847–1918*, unpublished Ph.D. thesis, University of Wales, 1970.

'Bishop Westcott as a Diocesan', *Guardian*, Vol. LVI Part II, July–December 1901.

S. Hempson, *A History of the Revised Version of the New Testament*, Elliott Stock, 1906.

H. Scott Holland, *Personal Studies*, Wells, Gardner, Darton, 1905.

A. F. Hort, *Life and Letters of Fenton John Anthony Hort*, 2 vols, Macmillan, 1896.

E. C. Hoskyns, *The Fourth Gospel*, ed. F. N. Davey, Faber, 1947.

W. R. Inge, *The Platonic Tradition in English Religious Thought*, Longmans Green, 1926.

P. d'A. Jones, *The Christian Socialist Revival 1877–1914*, Princeton University Press, 1968.

H. T. Kuist, 'The Interpreter at Work. XV. Brooke Foss Westcott (1825–1901)', in *Interpretation* 7, 1953.

F. Maurice, *The Life of Frederick Denison Maurice*, 2 vols, Macmillan, 1884.

S. Neill, *The Interpretation of the New Testament 1861–1961*, Oxford University Press, 1966.

D. Newsome, *Bishop Westcott and the Platonic Tradition*, Cambridge University Press, 1969.

D. Newsome, *Godliness and Good Learning*, John Murray, 1961.

D. Newsome, *Two Classes of Men: Platonism and English Romantic Thought*, John Murray, 1974.

E. R. Norman, *The Victorian Christian Socialists*, Cambridge University Press, 1987.

W. G. O'Dea, *Westcott the Theologian*, unpublished M. Litt. thesis, Cambridge University, 1972.

F. Olofsson, *Christus Redemptor et Consummator: A Study in the Theology of B. F. Westcott*, Almquist & Wiksell, 1979.

G. A. Patrick, '1881–1981: The Centenary of the Westcott and Hort Text', *Expository Times* Vol. 92, September 1981.

G. A. Patrick, *F. J. A. Hort: Eminent Victorian*, Almond, 1988.

A. M. Ramsey, *From Gore to Temple*, Longmans, 1960.

A. M. Ramsey, *The Resurrection of Christ*, Collins, 1961.

G. A. Riplinger, *New Age Bible Versions*, AV Publications, 1993.

J. A. Robinson, 'Dr Westcott as a Teacher: A Recollection', in *The Pilot*, 10 August 1901.

W. Sanday, 'Dr Westcott as Theologian and Writer I', in *The Pilot*, 7 September 1901.

W. Sanday, 'Dr Westcott as Theologian and Writer II', in *The Pilot*, 14 September 1901.

W. H. Simcox, 'Canon Westcott' in *The Expositor*, third series, Vol. V, 1887.

R. Standish and C. Standish, *Modern Bible Versions Unmasked*, Hartland, 1993.

V. H. Stanton, 'Brooke Foss Westcott' in *Dictionary of National Biography*, Second Supplement 1912, Vol. III.

W. M. Teape, *Westcott's Fear: by a Disciple*, Heffer, 1930.

G. Treloar, *Lightfoot the Historian*, Mohr Siebeck, 1998.

A. R. Vidler, 'Westcott's Christian Socialism' in *F. D. Maurice and Company*, SCM Press, 1966.

A. G. B. West, *Memories of Brooke Foss Westcott*, Heffer, 1936.

A. Westcott, *Life and Letters of Brooke Foss Westcott*, 2 vols, Macmillan, 1903.

A. Wilkinson, *Christian Socialism: Scott Holland to Tony Blair*, SCM Press, 1998.

R. Williams, 'The Fate of Liberal Anglicanism', 2001, unpublished.

INDEX OF NAMES

INDEX OF SUBJECTS